THE PHRASE
THAT LAUNCHED
1,000 SHIPS

All's fair in love and war—
and in the word game, as
Nigel Rees proves in this
delightfully entertaining and
informative volume. *Open
sesame!* and discover a
mother lode of catch phrases,
clichés, idioms, popular
sayings, and slogans that run
the gamut from media neo-
logisms to business buzz
words, political palaver, and
beyond. *Where's the beef?*
Right here—and it's *99 ⁴⁴/₁₀₀%
pure* pleasure, a feast for the
speechwriter and word-lover
alike!

WHERE DOES *THAT* COME FROM?

Public Enemy Number 1—John Dillinger (1903–1934) was the first—and only—person ever officially so designated, thanks to Illinois Attorney General Homer Cummings.

Age before beauty—In the famous story, Clare Boothe Luce said it to Dorothy Parker, ushering her ahead. Parker allegedly assented, saying, *"Pearls before swine."*

To cry all the way to the bank—to be in a position to ignore criticism, popularized if not actually invented by the flamboyant pianist Liberace (1919–1987).

From Mae West's infamous *Peel me a grape* to Errol's racy *In like Flynn,* here are the sublime and the ridiculous, a panoply of phrases from the redoubtable riches of the English tongue.

THE PHRASE
THAT LAUNCHED
1,000 SHIPS

Nigel Rees

A Laurel Book
Published by
Dell Publishing
a division of
Bantam Doubleday Dell Publishing Group, Inc.
666 Fifth Avenue
New York, New York 10103

Cover illustration by Tudor Banus
Cover design by Designed To Print
Interior illustrations by Michael Flint

ISBN: 0-440-20824-6

Printed in the United States of America

Published simultaneously in Canada

July 1991

10 9 8 7 6 5 4 3 2 1

OPM

CONTENTS

INTRODUCTION

Everyday speech is frequently rendered more pithy and colorful by our use of phrases taken from entertainment, advertising, and from a great backlog of folklore material. After a while we may find that we have forgotten what the phrases once alluded to.

The purpose of this book is to record, where possible, something of the circumstances in which popular phrases, including catch phrases, slogans, idioms, and more, originated and how they are used.

But why do I use the term "popular phrase"? Well, Eric Partridge called his great work *A Dictionary of Slang and Unconventional English,* but I always felt that was too apologetic a way of describing what is the liveliest, richest, and most frequently used area of the English language. Partridge also compiled *A Dictionary of Catch Phrases* and *A Dictionary of Clichés,* books with which this one is more directly comparable, but neither of these titles would completely describe what I have tried to produce.

The Phrase that Launched 1,000 Ships is a selective examination of nearly one thousand contemporary catch phrases, clichés, idioms, popular sayings, and slogans. The ones I have chosen to include are those about which there is something interesting to say regarding their origins and use. As a rule of thumb I have only written about those phrases that are in popular use now as we enter the 1990s or that are still remembered from a few decades back. I have also made a special effort to discuss phrases not tackled previously by myself or others.

As I sometimes categorize the phrases, a word of explanation is necessary—though I should emphasize that, for the most part, these categories are not exclusive. It is possible for a phrase to be a catch phrase *and* a slogan, an idiom *and* a cliché, and it isn't worth agonizing too hard over what the status is at a particular moment.

Let me briefly define what I mean by the various categories of popular phrases used in this dictionary:

Catch phrase: simply a phrase that has "caught on" with the public and is, or has been, in frequent use. It might have originated with a particular person—as in "Call me Madam"—or it might not be traceable to a particular source—as in "Back to the drawing board!"

Cliché: a worn or hackneyed phrase. There are some who would say that the clichés of journalism are used in such a way that they amount to a special language—journalese—which does not deserve to be condemned. I disagree.

Colloquialism: I have used this term to describe any form of familiar speech or writing that does not readily fit into any of the other categories.

Format phrase: a basic phrase or sentence structure capable of infinite variation by the insertion of new words—as in "One small step for _____, one giant leap for _____," where the sentence structure can be adapted to suit the speaker's purpose.

Idiom: a picturesque expression that is used to convey a metaphorical meaning different from its literal one—or, as *The Oxford Dictionary of Current Idiomatic English* puts it, that has a meaning "not deducible from those of the separate words." For example, if I say someone is a "square peg in a round hole," it is obvious he or she cannot literally be such a thing. My hearers will know exactly what I mean, although I have not told them directly.

Like the term "catch phrase," idiom could be applied to

most of the phrases in this book, but I have tried to restrict its use to those that conform to the above definition.

Nickname: a pithy, descriptive additional or substitute name.

Saying: This is what is sometimes called "a well-known phrase or saying" (as in, "rearrange these words into a well-known phrase or saying"). But unlike a formal quotation, it is probably not attributable to a precise source, be it speaker, book, or show. Proverbial expressions most commonly fall into this category.

Slogan: a phrase designed to promote a product, idea, or cause—or one that has this effect. However, at times I have employed this label rather loosely to cover any phrase that is used in advertising—in headlines, footnotes, but not necessarily in a selling line that names the product. "Body odor/B.O." could hardly be described as a slogan in itself, but as an advertising line it did help to promote a product.

Stock phrase: a regularly used phrase that can't be said to have "caught on" like a full-blooded catch phrase—for example, a celebrity's verbal mannerism ("Can we talk?") by which he or she is known but which can't be said to have caught on with the public as a proper catch phrase should. It also refers to phrases that get trotted out regularly but that, again, cannot be said to have passed into the language generally.

On the whole, I have chosen to define a phrase as an expression made up of more than one word, though a one-word catch phrase is a possibility. Popular single words tend to be adequately dealt with by the ever-growing number of word dictionaries, phrases less so.

Partridge was always "game" (as someone once felicitously put it) to try and pinpoint when a phrase came into use, though many of his stabs at dating were no more than guesses. Using the citations available in *The Oxford English Dictionary* (2nd edition), I have tried to be a little more precise in this area. When I say that a phrase was "Current in 1975," I mean that I simply have a record of its use then—*not* that I think it was first used in that year. It may also have been current long after that date. When I say that a phrase was "Quoted in 1981," I mean precisely that—not that it was originated in that year. It might have been coined long before.

Within each chapter the phrases are listed in letter by letter order—in other words, in alphabetical order of letters within the whole phrase and not just of the first word. The chapters are simply a convenient way of arranging the material according to use—politics, TV, show business— though, naturally, they may move between these areas. "Go ahead, make my day" started in the movies, moved into politics, and is now in general use.

I am most grateful to all those people mentioned in the text who have responded to my queries. In the preparation of this book I have also been assisted on specific points by: Roy Alexander; Nicholas Comfort; Donald Hickling; William Shawcross; the London Bureau of *The New York Times*; the British Library Newspaper Library, Colindale; and the BBC Radio Research Library, London. I am also much indebted to the authors and publishers of books quoted in the text and to the editors and journalists of the many newspapers and magazines who have unwittingly provided citations.

Portions of this book first appeared in *A Dictionary of Popular Phrases* from Bloomsbury Publishing, London, in 1990.

Nigel Rees

ABBREVIATIONS

Bartlett	*Bartlett's Familiar Quotations* (15th ed.), 1980
Bible	*The Authorized King James Version,* 1611 (except where stated otherwise)
Brewer	*Brewer's Dictionary of Phrase and Fable* (14th ed.), 1989
CODP	*The Concise Oxford Dictionary of Proverbs,* 1982
DOAS	*Dictionary of American Slang,* 1960 (1975 revision)
Flexner	Stuart Berg Flexner, *I Hear America Talking,* 1976
Mencken	*H. L. Mencken's Dictionary of Quotations,* 1942
Morris	William and Mary Morris, *Morris Dictionary of Word and Phrase Origins,* 1977
ODP	*The Oxford Dictionary of Proverbs* (3rd ed.), 1970
ODQ	*The Oxford Dictionary of Quotations* (3rd ed.), 1979

OED2	*The Oxford English Dictionary* (2nd ed.), 1989
Partridge/ *Catch Phrases*	Eric Partridge, *A Dictionary of Catch Phrases* (2nd ed., edited by Paul Beale), 1985
Partridge/*Slang*	Eric Partridge, *A Dictionary of Slang and Unconventional English* (8th ed., edited by Paul Beale), 1984
Polite Conversation	Jonathan Swift, *A Complete Collection of Genteel and Ingenious Conversation &c.*, 1738
Prayer Book	The Book of Common Prayer, 1662
Safire	William Safire, *Safire's Political Dictionary*, 1978
Shakespeare	*Shakespeare the Complete Works* (edited by G. B. Harrison)

1

ALL THE NEWS
THAT'S FIT
TO PRINT

Adolph S. Ochs devised the slogan "All the news that's fit to print" when he bought The New York Times, *and it has been used in every edition since—first on the editorial page on October 25, 1896, and from the following February on the front page near the masthead. It became the paper's war cry in the 1890s battle against formidable competition from the* World, *the* Herald, *and the* Journal. *It has been parodied by Howard Dietz as "all the news that fits we print"—and at worst sounds like a slogan for the suppression of news. However, no newspaper prints everything. These are the phrases that journalists have seen fit to print —sometimes a little more than they should:*

Believe it or not!   This exclamation was popularized by its use as the title of a long-running syndicated newspaper feature, and as a radio and TV series. Robert Leroy Ripley (1893–1949) created and illustrated a comic strip, "Ripley's Believe It or Not," from circa 1923 onward. The researcher on the strip until 1975 was Norbert Pearlroth (who died in 1983 at age eighty-nine). He spent seven days a week in the New York Public Library unearthing 62,192 amazing facts and anecdotes . . . believe it or not.

Down memory lane.   Accepting the GOP presidential nomination in Dallas, Texas, on August 23, 1984, Ronald Reagan said, "Our opponents began this campaign hoping that America has a poor memory. Well, let's take them on a little stroll down memory lane. Let's remind them of how a four-point-eight percent inflation in 1976 became . . ." Once a pleasant phrase, "down memory lane" now verges on the cliché. It seems to have developed from "Memory Lane," the title of a popular waltz of the 1920s and 1930s written by Buddy De Sylva, Larry Spier, and Con Conrad —not to be confused with "Down Forget-Me-Not Lane" by Horatio Nicholls, Charlie Chester, and Reg Morgan (1941). *Down Memory Lane* was the title of a compilation of Mack Sennett comedy shorts (1949).

Famous for being famous.   Daniel J. Boorstin in *The Image* (1962) defined a "celebrity" as "a person who is known for his well-knownness." Dating from the 1960s–70s, "famous for being famous" has been used to describe people who are celebrated by the media although it is difficult to work out exactly what it is they have done to deserve such attention. Today they appear as guests on TV game shows, participate in charity telethons, and show up on guest lists for first nights and film premieres. The London *Daily Mail* (March 4, 1989) reported on the premiere of the film *Scandal* (based on the Profumo Affair in British politics in which Christine Keeler had slept with both a cabinet minister and a Soviet military attaché): "With Christine Keeler in person . . . and with the attendant chorus of show biz froth and nonentities famous for being famous, the film's premiere brazenly upheld all the meretricious values."

Feeding frenzy. Furious media attention. The image here is of sharks swimming to retrieve bait, or any potential food, thrown to them by a fisherman. The phrase became popular in media circles in the late 1980s. As for its origin, an article by Professor Perry W. Gilbert in *Scientific American* (July 1962) has this: "As the blood and body juices of the marlin flow from the wound, the other sharks in the pack become more and more agitated and move in rapidly for their share of the meal. Frequently three or four sharks will attack the marlin simultaneously. A wild scene sometimes called a 'feeding frenzy' now ensues."

_____**gate.** In the wake of Watergate—a name derived, lest it be forgot, from an apartment complex in Washington, D.C., where a bungled burglary led to the scandal—it has become standard practice to apply the suffix "-gate" to any political scandal anywhere in the world: Koreagate, Lancegate, Billygate, Liffeygate, Westlandgate, Contragate, Irangate, Thatchergate, and so on. Debategate and Briefingate were applied to the flap in 1983 over how Ronald Reagan's campaign team got hold of President Carter's briefing books before a 1980 debate on TV. The use shows no sign of fading.

How the other half lives. How people who belong to different social groups live, especially the rich. *The Longman Dictionary of English Idioms* (1979) suggests that this phrase was launched through the title of a book (1890) by Jacob Riis (1849–1914), a newspaper reporter who described the conditions in which poor people lived in New York City. Indeed, the expression seems basically to have referred to the poor, but has since been used about any "other half."

That may have been the origin, but Riis alludes to the

core saying in these words: "Long ago it was said that 'one
half of the world does not know how the other half lives.' "
The *OED2* finds this proverb in 1607 in English, and in
French in *Pantagruel,* by Rabelais (1532).

If a man bites a dog . . .   Definition of what makes
news. In the form "When a dog bites a man, that is not
news, because it happens so often; but if a man bites a dog,
that is news" ascribed to John B. Bogart, city editor of the
New York *Sun,* 1873–90. To Charles A. Dana, the editor of
the same paper from 1868 to 1897, it is ascribed in the
form "If a dog bites a man, it's a story; if a man bites a dog,
it's a good story."

If in doubt, strike it out.   A piece of journalistic lore,
meaning if you're not sure of a fact or the wisdom of including an item of information or opinion, leave it out. It
may be that the advice was originally more specific. In
Pudd'nhead Wilson's Calendar (1894), Mark Twain says:
"As to the Adjective: when in doubt, strike it out." Another
author (Ernest Hemingway, I believe) recommended
striking out adverbs. Compare this with the advice Samuel
Johnson quoted from a college tutor (April 30, 1773):
"Read over your compositions, and wherever you meet
with a passage which you think is particularly fine, strike it
out." Which might be recommended to journalists also.
The precise phrase appears in the notorious "Green Book"
issued circa 1949 to guide BBC entertainment producers
as to which jokes were, or were not, permissible on the
radio in the UK: "Material about which a producer has any
doubts should, if it cannot be submitted to someone in
higher authority, be deleted, and an artist's assurance that
it has been previously broadcast is no justification for repeating it. 'When in doubt, take it out' is the wisest
maxim."
    Partridge/*Slang* has "when/if in doubt, toss it out" as,
curiously, a "pharmaceutical catch phrase, 20th century."

Joe Bob says check it out. "Joe Bob Briggs" was the pseudonym for the drive-in movie critic of the Dallas *Times Herald* from 1982–85. Written by John Bloom, the reviews represented the views of a self-declared redneck. They frequently caused offense, not least because they tended to rate movies according to the number of "garbonzas" (breasts) on display. Joe Bob had a battery of stock phrases, including "No way, José;" "If you know what I mean, and I think you do;" and the inevitable closing comment, "Joe Bob says check it out."

The column was eventually dropped when Joe Bob poked fun at efforts to raise money for starving Africans. The columns were published in book form as *Joe Bob Goes to the Drive-In* in 1989.

Long hot summer, a/the. This once-bright phrase rapidly turned into a journalist's cliché following the 1967 race riots in eighteen cities, notably Detroit and Newark. In June of that year the Rev. Dr. Martin Luther King, Jr., warned: "Everyone is worrying about the long hot summer with its threat of riots. We had a long cold winter when little was done about the conditions that create riots." *The Long Hot Summer* was the title of a 1958 film based on stories by William Faulkner (using a phrase formulated by him in 1928) and also a spin-off TV series (1965–66).

Mr. Big. As a name for the supposed mastermind behind substantial crimes, I once thought this phrase originated in Ian Fleming's second James Bond novel, *Live and Let Die* (1954). "Mr. Big," a gangster, lives in Harlem: "Because of the initial letters of his fanciful name, Buonaparte Ignace Gallia, and because of his huge height and bulk, he came to be called, even as a youth, 'Big Boy' or just 'Big.' Later this became 'The Big Man' or 'Mr. Big.'" *OED2*, however, finds "Mr. Big" not only in a Groucho Marx letter of 1940 but, more significantly, in Raymond Chandler's *The Long Goodbye* (1953). However, I am not sure that either of these uses is specifically criminal. Now the phrase is also used to denote any major criminal. From the London *Observer* (August 6, 1989): " 'MR. BIG' HELD. Customs officers have arrested a man they believe to be one of London's top criminals."

No comment. This phrase, useful when newsmakers are hounded by journalists, has not quite been condemned as a cliché. After all, why should people in such a position be required to find something original to say? Nevertheless, it has come to be used as a consciously inadequate form of evasion, often in an obviously jokey way (as with "we are just good friends"). The phrase must have arisen as a reaction to the ferreting of Hollywood gossip columnists in the 1920s and 30s, or simply as a general reaction to the rise of the popular press in the first half of the century. Winston Churchill appears not to have known it until 1946. After a meeting with President Truman, Churchill said, "I think 'no comment' is a splendid expression. I got it from Sumner Welles [the diplomat and presidential adviser]." Martha "The Mouth" Mitchell, who helped get the Watergate investigations under way and who was the talkative wife of President Nixon's disgraced attorney general, once declared: "I don't believe in that 'no comment' business. I always have a comment."

One small step for _____, one giant leap for _____. What Neil Armstrong claimed he said when stepping onto the moon's surface for the first time on July 20, 1969, was, "That's one small step for a man, one giant leap for mankind." The indefinite article before "man" was, however, completely inaudible, thus ruining the sense. Many reference books have been thrown into confusion since. Several follow the version "One small step for (. . .) man, one big step for mankind [*sic*]," which appeared in the magazine *Nature* in 1974. Either way, Armstrong launched an imperishable format. The correct version has even been set to music. I have heard the Great Mormon Tabernacle

Choir sing: "One small step for a man, one giant leap for mankind/It shows what a man can do, if he has the will."

Public enemy number 1.   John Dillinger (1903–1934) was the first officially designated "public enemy number 1." He robbed so many banks and killed so many people in Illinois, Indiana, and Ohio during 1933–34 that the attorney general, Homer Cummings, gave him this dubious honor. He was the only person ever so described. (The FBI's ten most-wanted men list did not give a ranking.) Dillinger's exploits and his escape from captivity aroused great public interest. He was eventually shot dead by FBI agents outside a movie theater in Chicago.

The coining of the term "public enemy" in this context has been attributed to Frank Loesch, president of the Chicago Crime Commission, who tried to deal with Al Capone's hold over the city in 1923. The idea was to try and dispel the romantic aura such gangsters had been invested with by the popular press. James Cagney starred in a gangster film called *The Public Enemy* in 1931.

The phrase soon passed into general usage. In June 1934, British writer P. G. Wodehouse, referring to difficulties with U.S. income-tax officials, said in a letter, "I got an offer from Paramount to go to Hollywood at $1,500 a week and had to refuse as I am public enemy number 1 in America, and can't go there." Since 1987 there has been a male rap duo with the name Public Enemy.

Rich and famous.   Designated a cliché by me because the words are *always* and *inevitably* put together. The first example I have noted was in the film *Breakfast at Tiffany's* (1961). The usage has become set in concrete since the film *Rich and Famous* (1981). A TV series called *Lifestyles of the Rich and Famous* was launched in 1986.

We are just good friends.   The standard way of telling reporters that your relationship with another is not romantic (even if it is). From *Vivien: The Life of Vivien Leigh* by

Alexander Walker (1987): "At Cherbourg, Jack [Merivale—Vivien's lover as her marriage to Laurence Olivier was ending in 1960] experienced for the first time the bruising intrusiveness of the British press, who boarded the ship *en masse* to interrogate Vivien's handsome traveling companion. In self-defense, he fell back on the old 'just good friends' cliché." Now used only as a consciously humorous evasion, especially when not true.

Wheel has come full circle, the.   This expression probably owes its fame to Shakespeare's *King Lear.* In Act V, scene iii, line 173, Edmund the bastard says, "The wheel is come full circle." He is referring to the wheel of fortune, since at that moment he is back down at the bottom as he was before it began to revolve.

_____ who came in from the cold, the.   John le Carré's 1963 novel *The Spy Who Came in from the Cold* popularized this expression. From then on, any person coming in from any kind of exposed position or returning to favor might find himself described as "coming in from the cold." Douglas Hurd, the British foreign secretary, said in Berlin on June 22, 1990, "We should not forget the reason for which Checkpoint Charlie stood here for so many years, but no one can be sorry that it is going. At long last, we are bringing 'Charlie' in from the cold."

Who he?   This editorial interjection at a little-known person's name shows some signs of catching on. The phrase is borrowed from Harold Ross (1892–1951), editor of *The New Yorker.* James Thurber, in *The Years with Ross* (1959), describes how Ross would customarily jot this query on a manuscript when finding a name he didn't know (sometimes betraying his ignorance). Ross said the only two names everyone knew were Houdini and Sherlock Holmes. A book with the title *Who He? Goodman's Dictionary of the Unknown Famous* was published in 1984. The phrase echoes the Duke of Wellington's peremptory

"Who? Who?" on hearing the names of ministers in Lord Derby's new British administration (1852).

_____ **will never be the same again.** Any change, however unremarkable, requires this journalistic phrase. "The Broadway musical would never be the same again"—TV promo, New York, 1983. "Life for George Bush will never be the same again"—Tim Ewart, ITN news, January 20, 1989 (the day of the President's inauguration).

2

AS THE
SAYING GOES . . .

Boniface, the landlord in George Farquhar's play The Beaux' Stratagem *(1707), has a curious verbal mannerism. After almost every phrase he utters he adds, "As the saying is . . ." Today we are more likely to use "as the saying goes." Either way, here are some real "sayings"—mostly modern and mostly hovering on the edge of proverbial status:*

Accident waiting to happen, this was an.   Frequently uttered in the wake of disasters, this is the survivors' and experts' way of pointing to what, to them, seems a foreseeable, inevitable result of lax safety standards, which should have been corrected in advance but will now probably be corrected only as a result of the tragedy. Used as the title of a book on the subject by Judith Cook (U.K., 1989).

All is fair in love, war, and _____.   The basic proverb is "All's fair in love and war," which *CODP* finds in the form "Love and war are all one" in 1620 and well-established by the nineteenth century. But nowadays the extended form —which would include almost anything that the speaker might wish—is more common.

All publicity is good publicity.   This near-proverb must be as old as the public-relations business. Alternative forms include: "There's no such thing as bad publicity," "There's no such thing as overexposure—only bad exposure," "Don't read it—measure it," and "I don't care what the papers say about me as long as they spell my name right." The latter saying has been attributed to the Tammany Hall leader "Big Tim" Sullivan.

  CODP includes it in the form "Any publicity is good publicity," but finds no example before 1974.

And this, too, shall pass away.   Chuck Berry "spoke" a song (1979) called "Pass Away," which began:

> Once in Persia reigned a king
> Who upon his royal ring
> Carved these words so true and wise . . .
> Solemn words, and these are they:
> "Even this shall pass away."

George Harrison named his first (mostly solo) album "All Things Must Pass" in 1970. These musicians, however, were by no means the first people to be drawn to this saying.

  As Abraham Lincoln explained in an address to the Wisconsin State Agricultural Society in 1859: "An Eastern monarch once charged his wise men to invent him a sentence to be ever in view, and which should be true and appropriate in all times and situations. They presented him with the words, 'And this, too, shall pass away.' How much it expresses! How chastening in the hour of pride! How consoling in the depths of affliction!"

The next year Nathaniel Hawthorne wrote in *The Marble Faun* of the "greatest mortal consolation, which we derive from the transitoriness of all things—from the right of saying, in every conjuncture, 'This, too, will pass away.'"

But who was the oriental monarch that Lincoln referred to? Benham (author of *Benham's Book of Quotations*) says that, according to an Oriental tale, the phrase was an inscription on a ring given by Solomon to a sultan who "desired that the words should be appropriate at all times."

Cheer up! the worst is yet to come. Partridge/*Catch Phrases* manages no more than "a U.S. catch phrase of ironic encouragement since c. 1918." The most usual attribution is to the American writer Philander Johnson (1866–1939), in his *Shooting Stars* (c. 1920). However, it did appear earlier in *The Love Letters of Mark Twain*, in a letter to his wife in 1893 or '94.

The similar expression, "Cheer up . . . you'll soon be dead!" appears in several British entertainments during the period 1909–18. The non-ironic line, "The worst is yet to come," occurs in Tennyson's *Sea Dreams* (1864). The worst pun on the phrase concerns the man who started eating a German meal and was encouraged to continue with the words, "Cheer up, the *würst* is yet to come!"

Che sera. In 1956 Doris Day had a hit with the song "Whatever Will Be, Will Be," which made use of this foreign phrase. She had sung it that same year somewhat painfully—but importantly for the plot—in the remake of Alfred Hitchcock's *The Man Who Knew Too Much*. Ten years later Geno Washington and the Ram Jam Band had a hit with a song entitled *"Qué Sera, Sera."* So where does the phrase come from? Is it *che* or *qué?* What language is it?

There is no such phrase as *che sera sera* in modern Spanish or Italian, though *che* is an Italian word and *sera* is Spanish. If you were to say *¿qué sera? sera?* in Spanish, that would translate as "what will be? will be?"—which is not quite right, or *lo qué sera, sera* (which makes sense but is not the wording of the song). However, in Christopher Marlowe's *Doctor Faustus* you will find in Faustus's first soliloquy:

> What doctrine call you this? Che sera, sera,
> What will be, shall be.

This is an old spelling of what would be put, in modern Italian, as *che sara, sara.* In Faustus, however, it is probably Old French. Are you following this?

The *idea* behind the proverbial saying is simpler to trace. "What must be, must be" can be found as far back as Chaucer's *The Knight's Tale* (c. 1390): "When a thyng is shapen, it shal be."

Cleanliness is next to godliness.   Although this phrase appears in Sermon 93, "On Dress" (1791), by John Wesley, the English preacher and founder of Methodism, it is within quotation marks and without attribution. Brewer claims that it is to be found in the writings of Phinehas ben Yair, an ancient rabbi. Thomas J. Barratt (1842–1914), one of the fathers of modern advertising, seized upon it to promote Pears soap. On a visit to the U.S. in the 1880s, he sought a testimonial from a man of distinction. President Grant was too high up for him, but he ensnared the eminent divine, Henry Ward Beecher. Beecher happily complied with Barratt's request and wrote a short text beginning, "If cleanliness is next to Godliness . . ." and received no more for his pains than Barratt's "hearty thanks."

Death is nature's way of telling you to slow down.   This joke was current by 1978. The same year a bumper sticker appeared featuring Garfield, the cat, with the slogan, "My car is God's way of telling you to slow down."

Dogs bark—but the caravan passes by, the.   Sir Peter Hall, while director of Britain's National Theater, was given to quoting this "Turkish proverb" during outbursts of public hostility in the mid-1970s. I'm not sure that it is a Turkish proverb, but who can say? The meaning is clear: Critics make a noise, but it does not last. It has been quoted as a favorite saying of Jan Smuts, the South African politician.

In *Within a Budding Grove*—the 1924 translation of Marcel Proust's *À l'Ombre des Jeunes Filles en Fleurs* (1918)—C. K. Scott Moncrieff has the "fine Arab proverb, 'The dogs may bark; the caravan goes on!' "

Eat, drink, and be merry—for tomorrow we die.   Derived from Isaiah 22:13: "Let us eat and drink, for tomorrow we shall die." Brewer comments: "A traditional saying of the Egyptians, who, at their banquets, exhibited a skeleton to the guests to remind them of the brevity of life."

However, Ecclesiastes 8:15 has the first part: "A man hath no better thing under the sun, than to eat, and to drink, and to be merry," as does Luke 12:19: "Take thine ease, eat, drink and be merry."

Elephant never forgets, an.   What one might say of one's self when complimented on remembering a piece of information forgotten by others, especially an unhappy memory. Based on the view that elephants are supposed to remember trainers and keepers, especially those who have shown hostility to them. A song with the title "The Elephant Never Forgets" was featured in the play *The Golden Toy* by Carl Zuckmayer (1934). *Stevenson's Book of Proverbs, Maxims and Familiar Phrases* (1949) says it derives from a Greek proverb, "The *camel* never forgets *an injury*" (my italics).

Every day and in every way I am getting better and better (sometimes **every day in every way** . . . or **day by day in every way** . . .) The French psychologist Emile Coué was the originator of a system of "Self-Mastery through Conscious Auto-Suggestion," which was in vogue briefly in the 1920s. His patients had to repeat this phrase over and over and it became a popular catch phrase of the time, though physical improvement did not necessarily follow. The French original was: *"Tous les jours, à tous les points de vue, je vais de mieux en mieux."* Couéism died with its inventor in 1926, though there have been attempted revivals. John Lennon alluded to the slogan in his song "Beautiful Boy" (1980).

Every man has his price. Mencken says this was ascribed to the British statesman Robert Walpole (c. 1740) in William Coxe's *Memoirs of the Life and Administration of Robert Walpole* (1798). Here the form was, "All those men have their price." But *CODP* finds W. Wyndham writing in *The Bee* (1734), saying, "It is an old Maxim, that every Man has his Price, if you can but come up to it."

Fifty million Frenchmen can't be wrong. As a slightly grudging expression, this appears to have originated with U.S. servicemen during World War I, justifying support for their French allies. The precise number of millions varied. A song with this title (by Rose, Raskin, and Fisher) was recorded by Sophie Tucker on April 15, 1927. Cole Porter's musical *Fifty Million Frenchmen* opened in New York on November 27, 1929.

Confusion crept in when Texas Guinan (1884–1933)—the New York nightclub hostess famous for greeting clients with the phrase "hello, sucker!"—was refused entry into France with her girls in 1931 and said, "It goes to show that fifty million Frenchmen *can* be wrong." She returned to the U.S. and renamed her show *Too Hot for Paris*.

George Bernard Shaw also held out against the phrase. He insisted, "Fifty million Frenchmen can't be right."

God protect me from my friends.   The ethics of Sicilian
banditry caused Gavin Maxwell to call his 1956 book about
Salvatore Giuliano *God Protect Me from My Friends*. In
full, the expression is, "I can look after my enemies, but
God protect me from my friends." In fact, a proverb along
these lines is common to many languages.

   Morris cites Maréchal Villiers leaving Louis XIV with,
"Defend me from my friends; I can defend myself from
my enemies."

Good man is hard to find, a.   *CODP* found the proverb
"Good men are scarce" in 1609, but in this form it was the
title of a song by Eddie Green (1919). Today it is most
frequently encountered in reverse. "A hard man is good to
find" was used as the slogan for Soloflex body-building
equipment in 1985. Ads showed a woman's hand touching
the bodies of well-known, brawny athletes. In this form the
saying is sometimes attributed to Mae West.

Go placidly amid the noise and haste . . .   There can
have been few bedroom walls during the great poster
craze of the late 1960s that did not bear a copy of the text
Desiderata ("desirable things, things desired"), reputedly
found in Old St. Paul's Church, Baltimore, dating from
1692. It began, "Go placidly amid the noise and haste, and
remember what peace there may be in silence. . . ."

   However, "Desiderata" had nothing to do with Old St.
Paul's. That was a fanciful idea incorporated in the first
edition of the poster. Nor did 1692 come into it. The words
were written by Max Ehrmann as a meditation in 1927,
and copyright was renewed in 1954 by Bertha K.
Ehrmann. Les Crane spoke the words on a hit record in
1972. In 1990 the poster was still on sale as "from 1692,"
but carrying the Ehrmann copyright lines.

Go west, young man!   This advice is an early example of a
misattribution that refuses to be corrected. Its originator
was John Babsone Lane Soule, who first wrote it in the

Terre Haute, Indiana, *Express* in 1851 when, indeed, the thing to do in the United States was to head westward, where gold and much else lay promised. However, Horace Greeley repeated it in his New York newspaper, the *Tribune,* and being more famous—a candidate for the presidency—it stuck with him. Greeley reprinted Soule's article to show where he had taken it from, but to no avail.

The original sentence was, "Go west, young man, and grow up with the country."

Go West, Young Man was a film vehicle for Mae West (rather than anything to do with *the* West) in 1936. *Go West, Young Lady* followed in 1940. There have been two films called *Go West,* notably the 1940 one often called *The Marx Brothers Go West.* (To "go west," meaning "to die," dates back to the sixteenth century and alludes to the setting of the sun.)

Greeks had a word for it, the.   An expression used, a trifle archly, when one wishes to express disapproval—as one might say, "there's a name for that sort of behavior." From the title of a play by Zoë Akins (1856–1958). Although she said the "phrase is original and grew out of the dialogue," it does not appear anywhere in the text. The "it" refers to a type of woman. One character thinks that "tart" is meant, but the other corrects this and says "free soul" is more to the point.

"Happy Birthday to You."   This is the most frequently sung song in English, according to *The Guinness Book of Records 1985* (which also lists "For He's a Jolly Good Fellow" and "Auld Lang Syne" among the top three songs of all time). It started out as "Good Morning to All," with words by Patty Smith Hill (1868–1946) and music by Mildred J. Hill (1859 –1916) in *Song Stories for the Kindergarten* (1893):

> Good morning to you;
> Good morning to you;

Good morning, dear children;
Good morning to you.

"Happy birthday to you" is the first line of the second
stanza, but it was not promoted to the title page until 1935.

The song has had a checkered legal history due to the
widely held belief that it is in the public domain. In fact,
following the American practice of renewing copyrights,
the song will be controlled until 2010. In 1988 the copyright of the song was put up for sale and was reckoned to
be worth some $1,275,000 a year. The figure represents
only a portion of what could be its revenue if all perfor-
mances were paid for. In recent times "Happy Birthday"
has been sung in the films *10, The Great Santini, Oh, God,*
and *Fame.* On March 8, 1969, it was sung by the Apollo IX
astronauts as they orbited the moon.

If anything can go wrong, it will.   Most commonly known
as "Murphy's Law" (and indistinguishable from "Sod's
Law" or "Spode's Law"), this saying dates back to the
1940s. *The Macquarie Dictionary* (Australia, 1981) suggests
that it was named after a character who always made mistakes in a series of educational cartoons published by the
U.S. Navy.

CODP suggests that it was invented in 1949 by George
Nichols, a project manager for Northrop Aircraft. He de-
veloped the idea from a remark by a colleague, Captain E.
Murphy of the Wright Field-Aircraft Laboratory.

The most notable demonstration of Murphy's Law is
that a piece of bread when dropped on the floor will always
fall with its buttered side facing down (otherwise known as
the Law of Universal Cussedness). This, however, predates
the promulgation of the Law. In 1867 A. D. Eichardson
wrote in *Beyond Mississippi: "His* bread never fell on the
buttered side." In 1884 James Payn composed the lines:

I never had a piece of toast
Particularly long and wide,

> But fell upon the sanded floor
> And always on the buttered side.

The corollary of this aspect of the Law is that bread always falls buttered side down *except* when demonstrating the Law!

Some have argued that the point of Murphy's Law is constructive rather than defeatist—that it was a prescription for avoiding mistakes in the design of a valve for an aircraft's hydraulic system. If the valve could be fitted in more than one way, then sooner or later someone would fit it the wrong way. The idea was to design it so that the valve could only be fitted the right way.

There have been movies with the titles *Murphy's Law* (1986) and *Murphy's War* (1971).

If it ain't broke(n), why fix it? Bert Lance, President Carter's Director of the Office of Management and Budget, used this modern proverb speaking on the subject of governmental reorganization in 1977, though it is of older origin. In Britain the saying suddenly caught on in the late 1980s. The *Independent* (November 12, 1988) had this about changes made in the musical *Chess* once it had opened: "Tim Rice [the writer] said, 'The notices were very good and people liked it, so we could have said, "If it ain't broken, don't fix it." But we felt that certain aspects weren't quite right.'"

I never promised you a rose garden. Used by Hannah Green/Joanne Greenberg as the title of a best-selling novel (1964, film 1977) and as a line in the song "Rose Garden" (1971), sung by Lynn Anderson. The saying means, "It wasn't going to be 'roses, roses all the way' between us" or "you can't expect life to be a bed of roses."

Fernando Collor de Mello, president of Brazil, said in a TV address (reported June 26, 1990) to his shaken countrymen: "I never promised you a rose garden . . . following

the example of developed countries, we are also cutting
state spending."

"Into each life some rain must fall."   "But too much is
falling in mine"—so goes the song by Allan Roberts and
Doris Fisher (1944). They took the idea from Longfellow's
"The Rainy Day" (1842): "Thy fate is the common fate of
all,/Into each life some rain must fall,/Some days must be
dark and dreary."

I say it's spinach.   A caption written by Elwyn Brooks
White (1899–1985) for a cartoon by Carl Rose has passed
into the language. It appeared in the November 8, 1928,
issue of *The New Yorker* and showed a mother at table
saying, "It's broccoli, dear." Her little child replies, "I say
it's spinach, and I say to hell with it."

Harold Ross, then editor of the magazine, remembered
that when White asked for his opinion of the caption White
was clearly uncertain that he had hit on the right idea. "I
looked at the drawing and the caption and said, 'Yeh, it
seems okay to me,' but neither of us cracked a smile."

The use of the word "spinach" to mean nonsense stems
from this, as in the title *Fashion Is Spinach* by Elizabeth
Dawes (1933).

It never rains but it pours.   John Arbuthnot, the English
pamphleteer, entitled a piece thus in 1726. Since then, the
phrase has gained proverbial status, meaning "misfortunes
never come singly." "When it rains, it pours" was a famous
advertising slogan used since 1911 by Morton Salt. The
logo showed a girl in the rain, sheltering the salt under her
umbrella, and capitalized on the fact that the Morton
grade ran freely from salt shakers even when it was humid.
The film *Cocktail* (1989), about a barman played by Tom
Cruise, was promoted with the line "When he pours, he
reigns."

I would walk over my grandmother (to achieve something). When Richard Nixon sought reelection in 1972 he surrounded himself with an unsavory crew including Charles W. Colson (b. 1931), a special counsel and White House hatchet man. "I would walk over my grandmother if necessary to get Nixon reelected!" said Colson.

Subsequently convicted of offenses connected with Watergate, he started walking on the water instead. As a born-again Christian, he described in his book *Born Again* (1977) how a memo to his staff containing the offensive boast had been leaked to the press: "My mother failed to see the humor in the whole affair, convinced that I was disparaging the memory of my father's mother. . . . Even though both of my grandmothers had been dead for more than twenty-five years (I was very fond of both), two press conferences were called during the campaign by 'Charles Colson's grandmother' to announce her support for McGovern, one by an elderly black woman in Milwaukee who managed to draw a large crowd of newsmen before the joke was discovered."

Such are the penalties of tangling with figures of speech —even an old one.

Know him is to love him, to. Blanche Hozier wrote about her daughter in 1908, "Clementine is engaged to be married to Winston Churchill. I do not know which of the two is more in love. I think that to know him is to like him."

Thus the format existed, but as "To Know Him Is to Love Him," the phrase became the title of a song written in 1958 by Phil Spector, which was his first hit. The words have a biblical ring to them, but Spector was probably not aware of their use in No. 3 in *C.S.S.M. Choruses*. Written by R. Hudson Pope, it goes:

> All glory be to Jesus
> The sinner's only Saviour,
> Whose precious blood for sin atones
> And blots it out forever.

> To know Him is to love Him,
> To trust Him is to prove Him,
> And those He saves He ne'er forsakes—
> No, never, never, never!

Robert Burns came very close to the phrase on a couple of occasions. In "Bonnie Lesley," "To see her is to love her / And love but her for ever," and in "Ae Fond Kiss," "But to see her was to love her, / Love but her, and love for ever."

In fact, it appears that Phil Spector actually acquired the lines from his father's gravestone. He was seventeen at the time of this first hit.

Laugh and the world laughs with you; / weep, and you weep alone. These lines are from a poem called "Solitude" (1883) by Ella Wheeler Wilcox (1855–1919) and, as *CODP* points out, are an altered form of the sentiment expressed by Horace in his *Ars Poetica:* "Men's faces laugh on those who laugh, and correspondingly weep on those who weep."

Another alteration is: ". . . weep, and you sleep alone." This form was current by June 6, 1945, when it was said to the architectural historian James Lees-Milne and recorded in his diary (published in *Prophesying Peace,* 1977).

Life begins at forty. In 1932 William B. Pitkin (1878–1953), Professor of Journalism at Columbia University, published a book called *Life Begins at Forty,* in which he dealt with "adult reorientation" at a time when the problems of extended life and leisure were beginning to be recognized. Based on lectures Pitkin had given, the book was a hearty bit of uplift: "Every day brings forth some new thing that adds to the joy of life after forty. Work becomes easy and brief. Play grows richer and longer. Leisure lengthens. Life's afternoon is brighter, warmer, fuller of song; and long before shadows stretch, every fruit grows ripe. . . . Life begins at forty. This is the revolutionary outcome of our new era . . . today it is half a truth. Tomorrow it will be an axiom." It is certainly a well-established catch phrase. Helping it along was a song with that title written by Jack Yellen and Ted Shapiro (recorded by Sophie Tucker in 1937).

Life is what happens to you while you're busy making other plans. Dr. Laurence Peter in *Quotations for Our Time* (1977) credits this saying to Thomas La Mance, who remains untraced. In Barbara Rowe's *The Book of Quotes* (1979), she ascribes the saying to Betty Talmadge, divorced wife of Senator Herman Talmadge of Georgia, in the form "Life is what happens to you when you're making other plans." Wherever the saying originated, it is quoted in the lyrics of John Lennon's song "Beautiful Boy" (included on the "Double Fantasy" album, 1980).

Love me, love my dog. Meaning if you are inclined to take my side in matters generally, you must put up with one or two things you don't like at the same time.

It was St. Bernard, of all people, who wrote in a sermon, *"Qui me amat, amat et canem meum"* (which is Latin for "Who loves me, also loves my dog"). Alas, to spoil a good story, this was a different St. Bernard than the one after whom the breed of Alpine dog is named. It was said (or quoted) by St. Bernard of Clairvaux (1090–1153) rather than St. Bernard of Menthon (923–1008).

Money makes the world go around. We may have to thank the writers of the musical *Cabaret* for either creating an instant saying or perhaps for introducing to the English language something that was long known in others. "Money makes the world go around," echoing the French song " 'Tis, 'tis love, that makes the world go round," is not recorded in either the *ODP* or the *CODP*.

It appears in the English language translation to the Flemish painting "The Proverbs" by David Teniers the Younger (1610–90). The painting shows an obviously wealthy man holding a globe. How odd that it should have taken a song in a 1960s musical to get this expression into English.

Muddling through, to keep on.   Supposedly what the British have a great talent for. Mencken says, "The English always manage to muddle through—author unidentified; first heard c. 1885." Ira Gershwin celebrated the trait in the song "Stiff Upper Lip" from *A Damsel in Distress* (1937). He remembered the phrase "Keep muddling through" from its frequent use during World War I. But Gershwin knew that it had first been noted in a speech by member of Parliament John Bright, in c. 1864, referring to the northern states in the American Civil War.

Never swap/change horses in midstream.   Mencken has "Never swap horses crossing a stream" as an "American proverb, traced to c. 1840." Bartlett cites Abraham Lincoln's reply to the National Union League (June 9, 1864) on the question of his continued presidency during the Civil War: "I do not allow myself to suppose that the convention or the League have concluded that I am either the greatest or best man in America, but rather they have concluded that it is not best to swap horses while crossing the river." On another occasion Lincoln attributed the remark that "it was best not to swap horses when crossing streams" to "an old Dutch farmer."

"Don't change barrels going over Niagara" was a slogan attributed (satirically) to the Republicans during the presidential campaign of 1932, and is clearly derived from the above.

Never work with children or animals.   This is a well-known piece of show-business lore, probably from vaudeville originally. Phyllis Hartnoll in *Plays and Players* (1985) has: "W. C. Fields is quoted as saying, 'Never act with animals or children.'" Although this line sounds like Fields, I suspect the attribution may result from confusion with "Any man who hates dogs and babies can't be all bad" (which he didn't say either: it was said by Leo Rosten *about* him at a dinner in 1939).

A similar feeling is contained in Noël Coward's remark about the child actress Bonnie Langford, who appeared along with a horse in a London West End musical version of *Gone With the Wind* in 1972. Inevitably there came the moment when the horse messed up the stage. Coward said, "If they'd stuffed the child's head up the horse's arse, they would have solved two problems at once."

Sarah Bernhardt, the great French actress, had a pronounced aversion to performing with animals. When she received an offer to appear in music hall in a scene from *L'Aiglon,* she replied, "Between monkeys, *non!*"

Nice guys finish last. During his time as manager of the Brooklyn Dodgers baseball team (1951–54), Leo Durocher (b. 1906) became known for this view—also stated as "Nice guys don't finish first" or ". . . don't play ball games." Partridge/*Catch Phrases* dates the popular use of the phrase from July 1946. Used as the title of a book by Paul Gardner in 1974, subtitled "Sport and American Life."

No good deed goes unpunished. This is a consciously ironic rewriting of the older expression "No *bad* deed goes unpunished" (surely proverbial but unlisted in *ODP* or *CODP*).

Joe Orton, the playwright, recorded it in his diary for June 13, 1967: "Very good line George [Greeves] came out with at dinner: 'No good deed ever goes unpunished.' " Before opening in Noël Coward's play *Waiting in the Wings* (1960), the actress Marie Lohr went to church and prayed for a good first night. On her way to the theater she slipped and broke her leg. "No good deed ever goes unpunished," was Coward's comment. It is also one of those remarks that has been ascribed to Oscar Wilde, and if it is one of his, it is a perfect example of the inversion technique used in so many of his witticisms.

Nothing venture, nothing win.   The first recorded use of the proverb in this form is in the English playwright Sir Charles Sedley's comedy *The Mulberry Garden* (1668). However, the variants "nothing venture, nothing gain" and "nothing venture, nothing have" go back further and may derive from a Latin original.

W. S. Gilbert used this form in the "proverb" song in Act II of *Iolanthe* (1882). Sir Edmund Hillary, the mountaineer, used it as the title of his autobiography in 1975.

Old as my tongue and a little older than my teeth, as. What British nannies (and other older folk) traditionally reply when asked how old they are by nosy young children. Swift has it in *Polite Conversation* (1738).

Old soldiers never die, they simply fade away.   A notable use of this was made by General Douglas MacArthur when, after his dismissal by President Truman, he addressed Congress on April 19, 1951. He ended his talk: "I still remember the refrain of one of the most popular barrack ballads of that day [turn of the century], which proclaimed, most proudly, that 'Old soldiers never die. They just fade away.' And like the old soldier of that ballad, I now close my military career and just fade away. . . ."

The origins of the ballad he quoted lie in a British army parody of the gospel hymn "Kind Words Can Never Die," which (never mind MacArthur's dating) came out of World War I. J. Foley copyrighted a version of the parody in 1920.

The format has appealed to many humorists over the years. From the early 1980s come these examples: "Old soldiers never die, just their privates"; "Old professors . . . just lose their faculties"; "Old golfers . . . just lose their balls"; "Old fishermen never die, they just smell that way."

Once a _____, always a _____.   This construction may be found in a series of proverbs dating back to the seventeenth or eighteenth centuries: "Once a knave/whore/

captain, always a _____." Partridge/*Slang* finds, more recently, "Once a teacher/policeman . . ." To which I would add "Once a marine, always a marine" (current in 1987) and the joke (which I first noted in 1967) "Once a knight, always a knight—and twice a night, you're doing all right!" Partridge/*Catch Phrases,* however, finishes the joke off: ". . . twice a night, dead at forty," and dates it c. 1950 "but probably from at least fifty years earlier."

Paris is for lovers. Spoken in Billy Wilder's film *Sabrina* (1954), this phrase has the ring of an official slogan, though this was long before the days of "I Love New York" (1977) and "Virginia is for Lovers" (1981). No song seems to have included the phrase or used it as a title, though Cole Porter's musical *Silk Stockings* (Broadway, 1955) has a song called "Paris Loves Lovers."

Picture is worth a thousand words, a. This famous saying is sometimes said to be a Chinese proverb. Bartlett lists it as such in the form, "One picture is worth more than ten thousand words," and compares what Turgenev says in *Fathers and Sons:* "A picture shows me at a glance what it takes dozens of pages of a book to expound."

But *CODP* points out that it originated in an American paper, *Printers' Ink* (December 8, 1921), in the form "One look is worth a thousand words" and was there ascribed by its actual author, Frederick R. Barnard, to a Chinese source (to give it instant proverbial status, I suppose).

More recently (1970s), the phrase "A picture paints a thousand words" occurs in the David Gates song "If."

Quick brown fox jumps over the lazy dog, the. Like "now is the time for all good men to come to the aid of the party," this is a typewriter exercise. Charles E. Weller, a court reporter, originated the second one in Milwaukee in 1867 to test the efficiency of the first practical typewriter, which his friend, Christopher L. Scholes, had made. Unfortunately, he did not do a very good job because the phrase contains only eighteen letters of the alphabet.

"The quick brown fox . . . ," on the other hand, has all twenty-six. This was once thought to be the shortest sentence in English containing all the letters of the alphabet, but it was superseded by "pack my box with five dozen liquor jugs" (which has three fewer letters overall).

Real men don't eat quiche.   This was the title of a book (1983) by Bruce Feirstein, following the title of an article by him in *Playboy* (1982). It was a joking yardstick of manliness in pop sociological discussions.

Rose is a rose is a rose, a.   The poem "Sacred Emily" by Gertrude Stein (1874–1946) is well-nigh impenetrable to most readers, but it has managed to give a format phrase to the language. If something is incapable of explanation, one says, for example, "a Republican is a Republican is a Republican."

What Stein wrote, however, is frequently misquoted and misunderstood. She did not say "a rose is a rose is a rose," as she might well have done, but "Rose is a rose is a rose is a rose" (i.e., upper case *R*, no indefinite article at the start, and three not two repetitions). The Rose in question was not a flower but an allusion to the English painter Sir Francis Rose, "whom she and I regarded," wrote Constantine Fitzgibbon, "as the peer of Matisse and Picasso, and whose paintings—or at least painting—hung in her Paris drawing room while a Gauguin was relegated to the lavatory" (letter to the London *Sunday Telegraph*, July 7, 1978).

Just to complicate matters, Stein also refers to a "Jack Rose" earlier in the poem.

(S)he done him/her wrong.   When Mae West's play *Diamond Lil* was transferred to the screen in 1933, it was renamed *She Done Him Wrong.* The title alludes to the refrain of the famous anonymous American ballad

"Frankie and Johnny," which Mencken dates c. 1875 and which is sung in the movie. There are numerous versions of the phrase (two-hundred is one estimate), and it may be of African-American origin. "Frankie and Johnny were lovers" (or husband and wife), but he (Johnny) does her wrong by going off with other women—"He was her man, but he done her wrong." So to equal the score Frankie shoots him, and has to be punished for it (in some versions in the electric chair):

> Frankie walked up to the scaffold, as calm as a girl
>   could be,
> She turned her eyes to Heaven and said "Good Lord,
>   I'm coming to Thee;
> He was my man, but I done him wrong."

Some like it hot. The film *Some Like It Hot* (1959) is a comedy about two unemployed musicians who are accidental witnesses to the St. Valentine's Day Massacre and flee to Miami disguised as members of an all-girl jazz band. So the "hotness" may come from the jazz or the position they find themselves in.

There had, however, been a completely different film with the same title in 1939 (starring Bob Hope). So where does the phrase come from? It is possible it grew out of the nursery rhyme "Pease porridge hot," which dates (in Britain) from about 1750. The second verse goes:

> Some like it hot
> Some like it cold
> Some like it in the pot
> Nine days old.

This is such nonsense that it is sometimes ended with a riddle, "Spell me that without a *P*" ("that" being quite easy to spell without a *P*).

Ring Lardner's story "Some Like Them Cold" (collected 1935) contains a song referring to women:

Some like them hot, some like them cold
Some like them fat, some like them lean

Talent will out. Meaning that if a person has talent, a way
of expressing it will be found. The only citation I have here
is from an advertisement for Lloyds Bank Young Theatre
Challenge in Britain (June 1988): "Talent will out, they say.
But only under the right conditions." The young Beatrix
Potter in her diary for June 5, 1891, mentions, "A theory I
have seen—that genius —like murder—will out—its bent
being simply a matter of circumstance." The proverb
"Murder will out" (i.e., will be found out, will reveal itself)
goes back at least to 1325, and "Truth will out" to 1439.

Thinking man's/person's/woman's _____, the. As long
ago as 1931, Pebeco toothpaste was being promoted as
"the toothpaste for thinking people." The format is still
going strong. In February 1989, *Spy* magazine drew up a
long list of examples of variations on the theme: *Hobbies*
magazine in 1977 described Descartes as "the thinking
man's philosopher"; *Boating* magazine (1984) described
the Mansfield TDC portable toilet as "the thinking man's
head"; *Horizon* (1965) called Lake Geneva "the thinking
man's lake"; and *Esquire* (1986) called actor William Hurt
"the thinking man's asshole."

Today is the first day of the rest of your life. A slogan
attributed to Charles Dederich, founder of antiheroin centers in c. 1969, this has also occurred in the form "Tomorrow is . . ." as a wall slogan, bumper sticker, etc.
   "Today Is the First Day of the Rest of My Life" was sung
in a late 1960s musical, *The Love Match*.

Toothpaste back in the tube, you can't put the. A modern
proverbial expression, attributed to President Richard
Nixon at the height of Watergate. His aide, John D. Ehrlichman, was also quoted, in 1975, as having said to John

Dean, "Once the toothpaste is out of the tube, it is awfully hard to get it back in again."

Touch the face of God, to.   In his TV broadcast (January 28, 1986) after the space shuttle *Challenger* disaster, President Reagan said, "We will never forget them nor the last time we saw them this morning as they prepared for their journey and waved good-bye, and slipped the surly bonds of earth to touch the face of God."

This immediately sent people the world over on fruitless journeys to their quotation books. The words sounded oddly familiar to some—not least because they had been used for years as a reading at late-night sign-off on a local Washington TV station. Reagan was quoting "High Flight," a sonnet written by John Gillespie Magee, an American-born pilot with the Royal Canadian Air Force in World War Two.

Magee died at the age of nineteen in 1941 during a mission from Britain. He is buried in Scopwick burial ground, near Lincoln. The poem "High Flight"—sometimes referred to as "the pilot's creed"—was published in 1943 in a volume called *More Poems from the Forces* (which was dedicated to the USSR).

In his lyrics for the musical *Les Misérables,* Herbert Kretzmer blended these words with something from Evelyn Waugh's *Brideshead Revisited* ("to know and love another human being is the root of all wisdom") to produce the line, "To love another person is to see the face of God."

The original words are curiously reminiscent of Oscar Wilde's lines prefixed to his *Poems,* Paris edition, 1903:

> Surely there was a time I might have trod
> The sunlit heights, and from life's dissonance
> Struck one clear chord to reach the ears of God.

Turn on, tune in, drop out.   Meaning turn on [drug] yourself; tune in to my values, reject those of your parents; deal with your problems and those of society by running away from them—this was the meaning of the hippie philosophy as encapsulated in a slogan by one of the movement's gurus, Dr. Timothy Leary (b. 1920). It was used as the title of a lecture by him in 1967, and the theme was explored further in his book *The Politics of Ecstasy*. More recently, Leary has taken to attributing the phrase to Marshall McLuhan, the Canadian media thinker.

A joke variant of what was also known as "the LSD motto" was: "Turn on, tune in, drop dead."

What a difference a day makes!   Almost proverbial, yet not listed in any of the proverb books. It expresses either surprise at someone's rapid recovery from a mood that had laid them low or the old thought that time is a great healer. The song "What a Difference a Day Made," written in 1934, was a hit for Esther Phillips in 1975.

When people are starving in India . . .   *The Complete Directory to Prime Time Network TV Shows* (1981) carries the information that when a proposed series called *B.A.D. Cats* crashed in 1980, Everett Chambers, its executive producer, said, "We bought forty-thousand dollars worth of cars to smash up, and we never got a chance to smash them up. I think that's kind of immoral, forty-thousand dollars worth of cars to smash up when people are starving in India."

Often used to nag children. Indeed, Sir Hugh Casson and Joyce Grenfell record it in *Nanny Says* (1972) in the form "Think of all the poor starving children who'd be grateful for that nice plain bread and butter."

Paul Beale in Partridge/*Catch Phrases*, commenting on another version—"Remember the starving Armenians"— notes: "The one used to exhort me as a child, late 1930s, to clear up my plate or to tackle something I found unpalatable was 'think of all the poor starving children in China!' "

With _____ like that, who needs _____?   The earliest example I have in the form "With friends like these . . .

who needs enemies?" is from the London *Daily Telegraph* (August 9, 1974). It was the headline over photographs of President Nixon's Watergate chums, John Mitchell, John Dean, James McCord, and E. Howard Hunt. But the phrase is of much older origin. Charlotte Brontë used it in a letter concerning the patronizing reviewer of one of her books. Partridge/*Slang* compares it to the proverb, "With a Hungarian for a friend, who needs an enemy?" George Canning, the nineteenth-century English politician, wrote a verse ending, "Save, save, oh, save me from the candid friend."

Would you buy a used car from this man?   Although attributed by some to Mort Sahl and by others to Lenny Bruce, and though the cartoonist Herblock denied that he was responsible (London *Guardian,* December 24, 1975), this is just a joke, and one is no more going to find an origin for it than for most jokes. The line accompanies a picture of a shifty-looking Richard Nixon and dates from 1952 at least (before any of the above-named humorists really got going). Hugh Brogan, writing in *New Society* (November 4, 1982), said, "Nixon is a double-barreled, treble-shotted twister, as my old history master would have remarked; and the fact has been a matter of universal knowledge since at least 1952, when, if I remember aright, the joke 'Would you buy a second-hand car from this man?' began to circulate."

It was a very effective slur, and by 1968—when Nixon was running (successfully) for president—a poster was in circulation bearing a picture of him with this line.

The phrase might now be used about anybody one has doubts about. *The Encyclopedia of Graffiti* (1974) even finds, "Governor Romney—would you buy a *new* car from this man?" In August 1984 John De Lorean said of himself —after being acquitted of drug-dealing—"I have aged six-hundred years and my life as a hard-working industrialist is in tatters. Would you buy a used car from me?"

You are what you eat.   This neat encapsulation of a sensible attitude toward diet was used as the title of an "alternative" film first shown in 1969. Of its content, *Films and Filming* (April 1969) noted: " 'You are what you eat,' says an old hermit in a fairy-tale-painted wood; a band of blissfully beautiful people hopefully munch flowers in the park." The British Film Institute's *Monthly Film Bulletin* described the film as "A disjointed psychedelic picture of America's hippy revolution. . . . The moralising note struck by the title is echoed nowhere else in the film." Very sixties, obviously.

   The idea behind the phrase has been around for many a year. Compare: Brillat-Savarin in *La Physiologie du Goût:* "Tell me what you eat and I will tell you what you are." And: L. A. Feuerbach in a review of Moleschott's *Lehre der Nahrungsmittel für das Volk* (1850): *"Der Mensch ist, was er iβt* (man is what he eats)." The German film *Heimat* (1984) included the version, *"Wie der Mensch iβt, so ist er"* ("As a man eats, so he is").

3

GREAT BALLS
OF FIRE

*To those who are familiar with this exclamation from the
Jerry Lee Lewis hit song of 1957 (written by Jack Hammer
and Otis Blackwell) or the biographical movie of 1989, it
should be pointed out that, of course, it didn't begin there.
In fact, it occurs several times in the script of* Gone With
the Wind *(1939). While the* OED2 *and other dictionaries
content themselves with the slang meaning of "ball of
fire" (glass of brandy; a person of great liveliness of spirit),*
Partridge/Slang *and American slang dictionaries seem to
avoid recording the phrase. I mean, goodness gra-
cious . . .*

Further exclamatory matter:

Age before beauty!   A phrase used (like "after you . . .")
when inviting another person to go through a door before
you. In one famous story Clare Boothe Luce said it to
Dorothy Parker, ushering her ahead. Parker assented, saying, "Pearls before swine." (Mrs. Luce, quoted in *You
Might as Well Live,* 1970, described this account as completely apocryphal to John Keats, Parker's biographer.)

A variant from a correspondent in New Zealand (1987)
was "Dirt before the broom," though Partridge/*Catch
Phrases* has this as the *response* to "Age before beauty"
(which it describes as a "mock courtesy").

And I don't mean maybe!   An intensifier, to show that you
have just issued a command, not expressed a wish.
Mencken lists it as an "American saying c. 1920." The
second line of the song "Yes, Sir, That's My Baby" (1922) is:
". . . No, sir, don't mean maybe."

And that ain't hay!   The title of a 1943 Abbott and Cos-
tello film that is said to have popularized this exclamation
was *It Ain't Hay.* But in the same year Mickey Rooney
exclaimed, "And that ain't hay!" as he went into the big "I
Got Rhythm" number in the film *Girl Crazy.* The scene is
set, appropriately, in an agricultural college.

The phrase means that's not to be sniffed at/not negligi-
ble, usually with reference to money. The *OED2* finds it—
also in 1943—in Raymond Chandler's *The Lady in the
Lake.*

Back to the drawing board!   Meaning we've got to start
again from scratch—usually said after the original plan has
failed. It is possible this originated in the caption to a Peter
Arno (1904–68) cartoon that appeared during the early
1940s in *The New Yorker.* An official, a rolled-up engineer-
ing plan under his arm, is walking away from a crashed
plane and saying, "Well, back to the old drawing board."
The *OED2* 's only citation for the phrase is also from *The*

New Yorker (November 6, 1965)—but not in a cartoon caption.

Can a duck swim! (sometimes **"does/will a fish swim!"**)
Meaning you bet!; of course what you say is to my liking.
ODP has "Will a duck swim?" in 1842. The earliest use I
have come across of the "can" version is by Winston Churchill, who claimed he said it to Stanley Baldwin when
Baldwin asked in 1924 if he would accept the post of chancellor of the exchequer. Lady Violet Bonham-Carter used
Churchill's own phrase *to* him when he asked her to serve
as a Governor of the BBC in 1941. Thence he proceeded to
refer to her as his "Bloody Duck" and she had to sign her
letters to him, "Your B.D."

Drop dead!   Said mostly by young people to someone
with whom they are in disagreement. Partridge/*Catch
Phrases* correctly notes that it is short for "Why don't you
drop dead!" and dates it from the late 1930s. The earliest
OED2 citation is from John O'Hara's novel *Appointment
in Samarra* (1934).
   Leo Rosten in *Hooray for Yiddish* (1982) draws attention
to the Yiddish equivalent, *Ver derharget!,* meaning "get
yourself killed." As he also suggests, this is a vigorous version of "Fuck you!" and the more useful because its component words are perfectly respectable. He points to the
enormous impact of the phrase in the Act Two curtain line
of Garson Kanin's play *Born Yesterday* (1946). Judy Holliday said, "Du-rop du-ead!"—and "the slow, sweet, studied rendition was stupendous. Waspish ladies have been
tossing 'Drop dead!' into their phones (to obscene callers)
and as retorts (to abusive cabbies) ever since."

_____, eat your heart out!   An unknown singer having
just finished a powerful ballad might exult defiantly,
"Frank Sinatra, eat your heart out!" Partridge/*Catch
Phrases* explains it as: "Doesn't *that* make you jealous,
fella!" As something said *to* another person, the expression

acquired popularity in the mid-twentieth century, largely
through its use by American show-biz personalities. Originally, "to eat one's (own) heart out" meaning "to pine,"
was current in English by the sixteenth century, and Leo
Rosten in *Hooray for Yiddish* (1982) finds it in the Yiddish
Es dir oys s'harts.

Expletive deleted!   On the release of transcripts of conversations between President Nixon and his aides—published as *The White House Transcripts* (1974)—"expletive
deleted" became known worldwide as a way of indicating
that an obscenity or blasphemous remark had been left out
of a printed document. The transcripts also used "expletive removed," "adjective omitted," and "characterization
omitted." For a while after Watergate people even exclaimed "Expletive deleted!" instead of swearing.
   I note this in a 1937 *Time* review of Hemingway's *To
Have and Have Not:* "No matter how a man alone ain't got
no bloody (obscenity deleted) chance."

F.T.A. (Fuck The Army)!   Especially as graffiti, much used
in the U.S. Army. *DOAS* adds: "Since c. 1960, as a counter
expression to disliked orders, rules, etc." *F.T.A.* was the
title of an anti-Vietnam war film made by Jane Fonda in
1972.

Geronimo!   It was during the North African campaign of
November 1942 that U.S. paratroopers are first said to
have shouted "Geronimo!" as they jumped out of planes. It
then became customary to do so and turned into a popular
exclamation akin to "Eureka!" A number of Native Americans in the paratroop units coined the expression, recalling
the Apache chief Geronimo who died in 1909.
   It is said that when Geronimo was being pursued by the
army over some steep hills near Fort Sill, Oklahoma, he
made a leap on horseback over a sheer cliff into water. As
the troops did not dare follow him, he cried "Geronimo!"
as he leapt. Some of the paratroopers who were trained at

Fort Bragg and Fort Campbell adopted this shout, not least because it reminded them to breathe deeply during a jump. In 1939 there had been a film entitled *Geronimo,* which may have reminded them.

Go for gold!   Meaning, literally, aim for a gold medal. As far as I can tell, this slogan was first used by the U.S. Olympic team at the Lake Placid Winter Olympics in 1980. *Going for Gold* became the title of an Emma Lathen thriller set in Lake Placid (1983), followed by a TV movie *Going for the Gold* in 1985. Other teams had taken it up by the time of the 1984 Olympics.

Just to show, as always, that there is nothing new under the sun: In 1832, there was a political slogan, "To Stop the Duke, Go for Gold"—which was somehow intended, through its alliterative force, to prevent the Duke of Wellington from forming a government in the run up to the Reform Bill. It was intended to cause a run on the Bank of England. The slogan was coined by a radical politician, Francis Place, for a poster, on May 12, 1832.

Go, man, go!   This was a phrase of encouragement originally shouted at jazz musicians in the 1940s. Then it took on wider use. At the beginning of the number "It's Too Darn Hot" in Cole Porter's *Kiss Me, Kate* (film version, 1953) a dancer cried, "Go, girl, go!"

TV newscaster Walter Cronkite gave it instant fame when he said, "Go, baby, go!" describing the launch of Apollo XI in 1969, and this became a fairly standard cry at rocket and missile launches thereafter. *Time* magazine reported it being shouted at a test firing of a Pershing missile (November 29, 1982). "Crazy, man, crazy!" Originated at about the same time as "Go, man, go!" but was, perhaps, better suited to rock 'n' roll usage than the earlier bop.

One wonders whether T. S. Eliot's "Go go go said the bird" ("Burnt Norton," *Four Quartets,* 1935) or Hamlet's "Come, bird, come" (the cry of a falconer recalling his hawk) relate to these cries in any way . . . ?

Great Scott!   One is dealing here with a watered-down expletive. "Great Scott!" clearly sounds like "Great God!" and yet is not blasphemous. Can one be precise about which particular Scott is having his name taken in vain?

Morris says the expression became popular in the mid-nineteenth century when General Winfield Scott (1786–1866) was the hero of the Mexican War (1847) and "probably our most admired general between Washington and Lee."

No rival candidate seems to have been proposed, and the origin of the phrase is almost certainly American. In 1902 Mark Twain was writing in *Harper's Weekly:* " 'Gerreat Scott!' ejaculated the Major. . . . The secretary said, wonderingly, 'Why, what are you Great-Scotting about, Major?' "

Have a nice day.   William Safire traced the origins of this pervasive American expression in his book *On Language* (1980). Beginning with an early flourish in Chaucer's *The Knight's Tale* ("Fare well, have good day"), it then jumped to 1956 and the Carson/Roberts advertising agency in Los Angeles. "Our phone was answered 'Good morning, Carson/Roberts. Have a happy day,' " recalled Ralph Carson. "We used the salutation on all letters, tie tacks, cuff buttons, beach towels, blazer crests, the works." Shortly after this, WCBS-TV weather-girl Carol Reed would wave goodbye with "Have a happy."

In the 1960s "Have a good day" was still going strong. Then the early 1970s saw "Have a nice day" push its insidious way in, although Kirk Douglas said it in the 1948 film *A Letter to Three Wives.* "Have a nice city" was a slogan in the 1970 Los Angeles mayoral election.

If you can't be good, be careful!   Mencken calls it an American proverb. Indeed, in 1907, there was an American song called "Be Good! If You Can't Be Good, Be Careful!"

It is a nudging good-bye, sometimes completed with

"And if you can't be careful, name it after me," and is similar to "Don't do anything I wouldn't do!"

Jesus wept!   John 11:35 is the shortest verse in the Bible. (the shortest sentence would be "Amen"). It occurs in the story of the raising of Lazarus. Jesus is moved by the plight of Mary and Martha, the sisters of Lazarus, who break down and weep when Lazarus dies. When Jesus sees the dead man he, too, weeps. Like it or not, the phrase has become an expletive to express exasperation.

Keep on truckin'!   This expression, meaning that you've got to persevere or "keep on keeping on," is described in Bartlett as the "slogan of a cartoon character" created by Robert Crumb (b. 1943). Crumb drew "dirty" cartoons for a number of underground periodicals like *Snatch* and created "Fritz the Cat," later the subject of a full-length cartoon film. By 1970 there were a number of records with the title, and there was certainly a vogue for the phrase in the 1960s and 70s.

There was a song in 1935 called simply "Truckin'" (words by Ted Koehler and music by Rube Bloom), and the *OED2* finds "the truck" or "trucking" was a jerky dance that came out of Harlem in the summer of 1934. Partridge/*Catch Phrases* plumps for a suggestion that the phrase, while of African-American dance origin, came out of the great dance marathons of the 1930s. (One of the book's contributors, however, hotly disputes this.)

Stuart Berg Flexner discussing "hoboes, tramps, and bums" on the American railroad in *Listening to America* (1982) probably gets nearest to the source. He defines "trucking it" as "riding or clinging to the trucking hardware between the wheels. This may have contributed to the jitterbug's use of *trucking* (also meaning to leave or move on in the 1930s) and to the 1960 students' phrase *keep on trucking,* keep moving, keep trying, keep 'doing one's (own) thing' with good cheer."

Nuts! Instead of "Balls!" (meaning testicles), this way of saying "Nonsense!" was used memorably in December 1944 when the Germans launched a counteroffensive in what came to be known as the Battle of the Bulge. General Anthony "Old Crock" McAuliffe (1898–1975) was acting commander of the 101st U. S. Airborne Division and was ordered to defend the strategic town of Bastogne in the Ardennes forest. This was important because Bastogne stood at a Belgian crossroads through which the advancing armies had to pass. When the Americans had been surrounded for seven days like "the hole in a doughnut," the Germans said they would accept a surrender. McAuliffe replied, "Nuts!"

The Germans at first interpreted this reply as meaning "Crazy" and took time to appreciate what they were being told. Encouraged by McAuliffe's spirit, his men managed to hold the line and defeat the last major enemy offensive of the war.

McAuliffe recounted the episode in January 1945: "When we got it [the surrender demand] we thought it was the funniest thing we ever heard. I just laughed and said, 'Nuts,' but the German major who brought it wanted a formal answer; so I decided—well, I'd just say 'Nuts,' so I had it written out: QUOTE, TO THE GERMAN COMMANDER: NUTS. SIGNED, THE AMERICAN COMMANDER, UN-QUOTE . . ."

When Agence France Presse sought a way of translating this, they resorted to, "*Vous n'êtes que de vieilles noix* [You are only old fogeys/fools]." When McAuliffe's obituary came to be written, *The New York Times* observed, "Unofficial versions strongly suggest that the actual language used by the feisty American general was considerably stronger and more profane than the comparatively mild 'Nuts,' but the official version will have to stand."

O.K.! The origin of this expression has occasioned more speculation and acrimonious debate than any other in the language. Some of the suggestions put forward:

1) President Andrew Jackson (1767–1845), while a court clerk in Tennessee, would mark "O.K." on legal documents as an abbreviation for the illiterate "Orl Korrect." However, there is no evidence to support this.

2) It was first used by President Martin Van Buren as an election slogan in 1840. The initials stood for "Old Kinderhook," his nickname, which derived from his birthplace in New York State.

3) The previous year (on March 23, 1839) had witnessed the first recorded use of the jocular "O.K." for "oll/orl korrect" ("all correct") in the Boston *Morning Post.*

4) Inspectors who weighed and graded bales of cotton as they were delivered to Mississippi River ports for shipment would write *aux quais* on any found faulty. This meant they had to be sent back to the jetty.

5) It comes from Aux Cayes, a port in Haiti famous for its rum.

6) It is an Anglicization of the word for "good" in Ewe or Wolof, the West African language spoken by many of the slaves brought to the southern U.S.

7) It derives from the Greek words *ola kala,* meaning "all is fine, everything is good."

8) In World War I, soldiers would report each night the number of deaths in their group. "O.K." stood for "0 killed."

9) A railroad freight agent, Obadiah Kelly, used his initials on bills of lading.

10) An Indian chief, Old Keokuk, used his initials on treaties.

11) It stood for "outer keel" when shipbuilders chalked it on timbers.

12) Teachers used it instead of *omnes korrectes* on perfect exam papers.

13) From boxes of Orrins-Kendall crackers, popular with Union troops during the Civil War.

14) From an English word "hoacky," meaning the last load of a harvest.

15) From a Finnish word *oikea,* meaning "correct."

16) From a Choctaw word *okeh* ("it is") or *hoke.*

I think one need go no further than explanations two and three, supported as they are by citations with firm dates. I feel sure the jocular initials started it, and Van Buren set the seal on the use of the formula.

Pop goes the weasel!   "Every night when I come home,/ The Monkey's on the table./I take a stick and knock him off/And pop goes the weasel!" Such is an American version of a peculiar song that originated in Britain, possibly in 1853, and may have been written by W. R. Mandale:

> Up and down the City Road,
> In and out of the Eagle,
> That's the way the money goes—
> Pop goes the weasel!

Mandale may have put these words to a tune or dance that already existed, but what did he mean by them? His song "Pop Goes the Weasel" is still the subject of debate. What is plain is that "the Eagle" refers to the Eagle Tavern, then a theater and pub in the City Road, London.

   Those who went "in and out" spent plenty of money and were forced to "pop," or pawn, something. But what was the "weasel" they pawned? That is the question. The word has been said to mean a kind of tool used by a carpenter or hatter, or a tailor's flat iron, but why anyone should wish to pawn a tool of the trade is a puzzle. Perhaps a "weasel" was no more than just an item of value.

Vernon Noble suggested to Partridge/*Catch Phrases* that a weasel was a flat iron in a domestic situation and therefore was an item that could easily be spared. No one seems to have suggested that the weasel might be from rhyming slang "weasel and stoat" to equal "coat." What could be more straightforward than having to pawn your coat if you ran out of money? As for "pop goes the weasel" meaning an orgasm, I feel this is probably a later play on an established phrase.

Other suggestions include: A weasel was the sewing machine used by Jewish tailors that they would pawn at the end of the week when their money ran out; or it was the fob on the end of a watch chain, named for the way it disappeared into the wearer's pocket.

Reach for the sky/stars!   (Sometimes just "reach for it!") This is what a character in a Western movie says when he wants someone to "put his hands up." However, Paul Brickhill's biography of Douglas Bader, the legless British flying ace (*Reach for the Sky,* 1954), was no doubt a blending of the phrase with an allusion to the Royal Air Force motto, *Per ardua ad astra* ("Through striving to the stars").

Speed the plow!   David Mamet's 1988 Broadway play *Speed-the-Plow,* about two Hollywood producers trying to get a project off the ground, takes its title from a very old phrase indeed. In the form "God speed the plough," it was what one would say to wish someone luck in a venture (not just an agricultural one). The wish was in use at least by 1500 and is also the title of a traditional English song and dance. *Speed the Plough* was the title of the novel (1798) by Thomas Morton that introduced the moralizing character "Mrs. Grundy."

Stop, look, listen! Said to have been devised in 1912 by Ralph R. Upton for use at railway crossings. Certainly, on December 27, 1915, a show (with music by Cole Porter) opened at the Globe Theater in New York, called *Stop! Look! Listen!* And by 1936 an advertisement for H. H. Sullivan Inc. "Technical merchandise" (Rochester, N.Y.) was playing on the phrase in "Stop, look and kiss 'em," which accompanied a picture of a leggy girl in cheesecake pose.

Watch the birdie! What photographers say to gain the attention of those they are photographing (especially children) and to make them look at the same point. Originally they probably held a toy bird near the camera lens. A song called "Watch the Birdie" appeared in the film *Hellzapoppin'* (1942).

To obtain the semblance of a smile, the photographer says, "Smile, please!" or "Say 'cheese!' " The late Sir Cecil Beaton, the British photographer and designer, is reported to have encouraged some of his subjects to, "Say 'lesbian!' "

We wuz robbed! A notable reaction to sporting defeat came from the lips of Joe Jacobs (1896–1940), manager of the boxer Max Schmeling. Believing his man to have been cheated of the heavyweight title in a fight against Jack Sharkey on June 21, 1932, Jacobs shouted his protest into a microphone: "We wuz robbed!"

On another occasion, in October 1935 Jacobs left his sickbed to attend the World Series, occurring in Detroit for the first and only time. Having bet on the losers, he opined, "I should of stood in bed."

Wish you were here! Although I have no citations for it in actual use, the cliché of holiday correspondence has been used as the title of songs that reached the charts in 1953 and 1984. In its full form "Having a wonderful time, wish you were here," Partridge/*Catch Phrases* suggests it dates to Edwardian times. But why not earlier, at any time since the introduction of the postcard? To be sure, cards on which you wrote your own message did not come on the scene until 1894, and the heyday of the picture postcard was in Edwardian times. In the early days perhaps the message was already printed on the card by the manufacturer. Today the phrase is used only in jest or ironically.

Having Wonderful Time, a play by Arthur Kober (1937) about a holiday hotel in the Catskills, became, in an exchange of phrases, the musical *Wish You Were Here* in 1952. *Wish You Were Here* was also used in 1975 as the title of a hit album by the rock group Pink Floyd and in 1987 as the title of a film about sexual awakening in a seaside resort.

Your money or your life!   The highwayman's/robber's challenge. In one of Jack Benny's most celebrated gags (playing on his legendary stinginess), when the robber says this, Benny pauses for a long time and then replies, "I'm thinking, I'm thinking!" This was on radio in the 1930s and 40s.

4

EVERYBODY HAS
ONE BOOK IN THEM

There is a saying to the effect that "everybody has one book in them"—meaning that every person has one story that he or she alone could tell, namely the story of his or her life. Or, as George Orwell noted in 1940: "It is commonly said that every human being has in him the material for one good book, which is true in the same sense as it is true that every block of stone contains a statue." This is a popular belief with which publishers might well disagree. How much better if the saying were, "Every book has at least one original phrase in it."

These were original once:

Across the River and into the Trees. The title of a novel (1950) by Ernest Hemingway alludes to the last words of

Stonewall Jackson, the Confederate general in the Civil War who was shot in error by his own troops in May 1863. He said, "Let us cross over the river, and rest under [the shade of] the trees." E. B. White's noted parody of Hemingway's style (collected 1954) was called "Across the Street and into the Grill."

All animals are equal, but some are more equal than others. A slogan from George Orwell's *Animal Farm* (1945), a commentary on the totalitarian excesses of communism. It had been anticipated: Hesketh Pearson recalled in his biography of the actor/manager Sir Herbert Beerbohm Tree that Tree wished to insert one of his own epigrams in a play by Stephen Phillips called *Nero*, produced in 1906. It was, "All men are equal—except myself."

The saying alludes, of course, to Thomas Jefferson's "All men are created equal," from the preamble to the Declaration of Independence.

All the President's Men. In 1974 Carl Bernstein and Bob Woodward entitled their first book on Watergate *All the President's Men* (filmed in 1976). This might seem to allude to the line, "All the king's horses and all the king's men,/ Couldn't put Humpty together again," from the nursery rhyme "Humpty Dumpty" (first recorded in 1803). There might be additional resonance for those who remember that the Robert Penn Warren novel and film (1949) based on the life of southern demagogue Huey "Kingfish" Long was called *All the King's Men.* More directly, though not spelled out by its authors, the Watergate book appears to have acquired its title from a saying of Henry Kissinger's at the time of the 1970 Cambodia invasion: "We are all the President's men and we must behave accordingly" (quoted in Kalb & Kalb, *Kissinger,* 1974).

All This and Heaven Too. The novel of this title by Rachel Field (1939, film 1940) acknowledges its source. She states that in *The Life of Philip Henry,* Matthew Henry

(1662–1714), the English Bible commentator, attributes the saying to his minister father. Compare the title of the 1976 film *All This and World War II*.

American Dream, The. This is the title of a play by Edward Albee (1961). *An American Dream* is the title of a novel by Norman Mailer (1965). Both titles derive from the expression used to describe the ideals of democracy and standards of living that inspired the founding of the United States, which was probably coined by J. T. Adams in *The Epic of America* (1931). Before that, in "America the Beautiful" (1893), Katharine Lee Bates had written of a "patriot dream that sees beyond the years."

Anatomy of _____, the. This journalist's cliché really dates back to *The Anatomy of Melancholy* (1621) by Robert Burton. That book used the word "anatomy" in an appropriate manner, its subject being a medical condition (*anatome* is the Greek word for dissection). The modern vogue for "anatomies" of this and that was typified by Anthony Sampson's *Anatomy of Britain,* first published in 1962 and revised a number of times since. The film *Anatomy of a Murder* had come out earlier, in 1959.

And they all lived happily ever after. The traditional ending to fairy tales is not used quite so frequently as ONCE UPON A TIME (this chapter), but it is (more or less) present in five of *The Classic Fairy Tales* (1974) gathered in their earliest known forms by Iona and Peter Opie. "Jack and the Giants" (c. 1760) ends: "He and his Lady lived the Residue of their Days in great Joy and Happiness." "Jack and the Bean-Stalk" (1807) ends: "His mother and he lived together a great many years, and continued always to be very happy."

A translation of "Snow White and the Seven Dwarfs" by the Brothers Grimm (1823) ends: "Snow-drop and the prince lived and reigned happily over that land many many years." From the same year, a translation of "The

Frog-Prince" ends: "They arrived safely, and lived happily a great many years."

A Scottish version of "Cinderella" (collected 1878) has: "They lived happily all their days."

Big Brother is watching you. A fictional slogan in George Orwell's novel *Nineteen Eighty-four* (1948). In a dictatorial state, every citizen is regimented and observed by a spying TV set in the home. Aspects of the "Ministry of Truth" in the novel were derived not only from Orwell's knowledge of the BBC (where he worked) but also from his first wife's work at the Ministry of Food, where she prepared "Kitchen Front" broadcasts during World War II, c. 1942–44. One campaign used the slogan "Potatoes are good for you" and was so successful that it had to be followed by "Potatoes are fattening." It is not hard to see where Orwell found the inspiration for his slogan.

Butler did it, the. This is the (often ironic) explanation suggested as the solution to a mystery, as in classic detective fiction of the 1920s and 30s. However, the earliest use of the phrase I can cite is in the film *My Man Godfrey* (1957 version—not the 1936 original), which is not even a whodunit: "The butler did it! He made every lady in the house, oh, so very happy!" The phrase also occurs in the film *Murder on the Orient Express* (1974), though not in Agatha Christie's original 1934 novel. However, a correspondent claims he heard it spoken by a member of the audience after the last episode of the film series *The Exploits of Elaine* at a London cinema in c. 1916.

So perhaps the well-known phrase was current by that date. But why did it enter common parlance? One of the conventions of whodunit writing of the period is that the butler or servants seldom, if ever, did "do it." Father Ronald Knox, compiling a list of rules for this kind of fiction in his introduction to *The Best Detective Stories of the Year, 1928,* noted, "The only person who is really scratch on morals is the aged butler. I cannot offhand recall any lapse of virtue on the part of a man who has been with the family for sixteen years. But I may be wrong; I have not read all the detective stories."

Alan Melville, the playwright, remembered (1983): "Years ago, a repertory actor up in Scotland ruined every available Agatha Christie or other crime drama by saying the line straight out to the audience when he was slightly drunk—'No need to wait to the end, the butler did it.' He was sacked, poor soul, but the sad thing is that the week he got his cards the play he was appearing in, however unsteadily, was one in which the butler really did do it."

The Georgette Heyer thriller *Why Shoot a Butler?* (1933) manages to avoid any mention of the phrase. It did, however, become the title of an instrumental number written (1958), and performed on drums, by Frank Butler —naturally.

Catch-22.   Few ideas have caught on from twentieth-century novels as extensively as "Catch-22" from Joseph Heller's book of the same name, published in 1955, about a group of American fliers in World War II. "It was a catch-22 situation," people will say, as if using a quasiproverbial expression like "Heads you win, tails I lose" or "Damned if you do, damned if you don't." Heller (b. 1923) appealed to the popular feeling that "there's always a catch"—some underlying law that defeats people by its brutal, ubiquitous logic. As it happens, the saying was prophetic—anticipating the paranoia over conspiracy theories in the 1960s and the way the U.S. painted itself into a corner over Vietnam.

In the book the idea is explored several times. Captain Yossarian, a U.S. Air Force bombardier, does not wish to fly any more missions. He goes to see the group's MO, Doc Daneeka, about getting grounded on the grounds that he is crazy. Daneeka: "There's a rule saying I have to ground anyone who's crazy." Yossarian: "Then why can't you ground me? I'm crazy." Daneeka: "Anyone who wants to get out of combat duty isn't really crazy."

This is the catch—Catch-22. (Oddly, when the first chapter of the book was published separately in 1955, the catch was numbered "Catch-18.")

Eagle Has Landed, The.   In an author's note at the beginning of his thriller of this title (1975, filmed in 1976), Jack Higgins suggests that Heinrich Himmler was informed on November 6, 1943 that "The Eagle has landed"—meaning that a small force of German paratroops had safely landed in England in order to kidnap Winston Churchill. Higgins then claims that "fifty percent of [this exploit] is documented historical fact. The reader must decide for himself how much of the rest is a matter of speculation, or fiction. . . ."

Well, yes, that may be. What I have always doubted is the wisdom of applying to a book "about" World War II a phrase that was well-known in a very different sphere. In July 1969, when the lunar module bearing Neil Armstrong touched down for the first-ever moon visit, Armstrong declared, "Tranquillity Base here—the Eagle has landed" ("Eagle" was the name of the craft, referring to the American national symbol).

Elementary, my dear Watson! The Sherlock Holmes phrase appears nowhere in the writings of Sir Arthur Conan Doyle (1859–1930), though the great detective does exclaim "Elementary" to Dr. Watson in *The Memoirs of Sherlock Holmes*, "The Crooked Man" (1894).

Conan Doyle brought out his last Holmes book in 1927. His son Adrian (in collaboration with John Dickson Carr) was one of those who used the phrase in follow-up stories—as have adapters of the stories in film and broadcast versions. In the 1929 film *The Return of Sherlock Holmes*—the first with sound—the final lines of dialogue are:

> *Watson:* Amazing, Holmes!
> *Holmes:* Elementary, my dear Watson, elementary.

Everything you always wanted to know about _____ but were afraid to ask.   *Everything You Always Wanted to Know about Sex but Were Afraid to Ask* was the self-explanatory title of a book published in 1970 by David Reuben M.D. (b. 1933). It gave to the language a format phrase, compounded by its use as a film title by Woody Allen in 1972—though, in fact, Allen simply bought the title of the book and none of its contents.

Subsequently, almost any subject you could think of has been inserted into the sentence. In 1984 I drew up this short list from the scores of books that bore similar titles: *Everything That Linguists Have Always Wanted to Know about Logic but Were Ashamed to Ask; Everything You Always Wanted to Know about Drinking Problems and Then a Few Things You Didn't Want to Know; Everything You Always Wanted to Know about Elementary Statistics but Were Afraid to Ask; Everything You Always Wanted to Know about Mergers, Acquisitions and Divestitures but Didn't Know Whom to Ask; Everything You Wanted to Know about Stars but Didn't Know Where to Ask; Everything You Wanted to Know about the Catholic Church but Were Too Pious to Ask; Everything You Wanted to Know about the Catholic Church but Were Too Weak to Ask. . . .*

Face that launched a thousand ships, the.   Referring to Helen of Troy, Christopher Marlowe's line, "Was this the face that launch'd a thousand ships" occurs in his play *Doctor Faustus*. Earlier, Marlowe had said something similar in *Tamburlaine the Great* (1587): "Helen, whose beauty . . . drew a thousand ships to Tenedos."

Shakespeare must have been alluding to Marlowe's "mighty line" when, in *Troilus and Cressida* (c. 1601), he said of Helen: "Why she is a pearl/Whose price hath launch'd above a thousand ships." He also alludes to it in *All's Well That Ends Well.*

The consistent feature of these mentions is the figure of a "thousand," which was a round number probably derived from the accounts of the Trojan War written by Ovid and Virgil. To Jack de Manio, the English broadcaster, is attributed a more recent version: sometime in the 1970s, he is alleged to have said of actress Glenda Jackson, "Her face could launch a thousand dredgers."

It was a dark and stormy night.   As a scene-setting, opening phrase, this appears to have been irresistible to more than one storyteller and has now become a joke. It was used in all seriousness by the English novelist Edward Bulwer-Lytton (1803–1873) at the start of *Paul Clifford* (1830): "It was a dark and stormy night, the rain falling in torrents—except at occasional intervals, when it was checked by a violent gust of wind which swept up the streets and then (for it is in London that our scene lies), rattling along the housetops, and fiercely agitating the scanty flames of the lamps that struggled against the darkness."

Stephen Leacock, the Canadian humorist (1869–1944), went for something similar to start his *Gertrude the Governess* (1911): "It was a wild and stormy night on the West Coast of Scotland. This, however, is immaterial to the present story as the scene is not laid in the West of Scotland."

At some stage the phrase became part of a children's game—"The tale without an end." Iona and Peter Opie in *The Lore and Language of Schoolchildren* (1959) describe the workings thus: "The tale usually begins: 'It was a dark and stormy night, and the Captain said to the Bo'sun, "Bo'sun, tell us a story," so the Bo'sun began . . .' Or it may be: 'It was a dark and stormy night, the rain came down in torrents, there were brigands on the mountains, and thieves, and the chief said unto Antonio: "Antonio, tell us a story." And Antonio, in fear and dread of the mighty chief, began his story: "It was a dark and stormy night, the rain came down in torrents, there were brigands on the mountains, and thieves . . ."' And such is any child's readiness to hear a good story that the tale may be told three times round before the listeners appreciate that they are being diddled."

The Opies noted that each of these variations was also current in the U. S., "except that in the first tale American children say: 'It was a dark and stormy night, some Indians were sitting around the campfire when their chief rose and said . . .'"

Presumably with knowledge of this game—if not of Bulwer-Lytton's mighty line—Charles M. Schulz (b. 1922), the creator of the "Peanuts" syndicated cartoon, gave the line to Snoopy in his doomed attempts to write the Great American Novel. Consequently, the dog is acclaimed as author of the world's greatest one-line novel. Paradoxically, Schulz's own book, *It Was a Dark and Stormy Night,* was a best seller.

The culmination of all this has been the Annual Bulwer-Lytton Fiction Contest, founded by Dr. Scott Rice, a professor of English literature at San Jose State University, California. Contestants are asked to compose truly atrocious opening sentences to hypothetical bad novels. Rice was quoted in *Time* (February 21, 1983) as saying, "We want the kind of writing that makes readers say, 'Don't go on.'" Some of the entries have now been published in book form—with the authors given every inducement not to keep on writing. . . .

Joy of _____, the. Cliché of book-titling. First on the scene were I. S. Rombauer and M. R. Becker, American cookery experts, with their classic *Joy of Cooking* (1931). *Joy of Living* was the title of a film (1938), which but for the Hollywood Production Code would have been called *Joy of Loving.* Then in 1972 along came Alex Comfort with the book *The Joy of Sex,* and then *More Joy of Sex.* At this point everyone joined in, so that we have had books about the joys of computers, chickens, cheesecake, breastfeeding, and geraniums, among many others. In 1984 I published *The Joy of Clichés*—which I thought would be seen as ironic.

Mean Streets. This phrase—as used for the title of a 1973 film about an Italian ghetto in New York—probably alludes to a noted sentence by Raymond Chandler (1888–1959) in "The Simple Art of Murder" (1950). "Down these mean streets a man must go who is not himself mean; who is neither tarnished nor afraid" refers to the heroic qualities a detective should have.

However, the phrase had been used long before this. In 1894 Arthur Morrison wrote *Tales of Mean Streets,* about impoverished life in the lowly, poor streets of the East End of London.

Once upon a time. "Never, in all my childhood, did anyone address to me the affecting preamble, 'Once upon a time!'" wrote Edmund Gosse in *Father and Son,* 1907. Poor deprived man. The traditional start to fairy stories has existed as a phrase for a very long time. George Peele has the line in his play *The Old Wives' Tale* (1595). The Old Woman begins a story she is telling with, "Once upon a time there was a King, or a Lord, or a Duke . . ."—which suggests that it was a "formula" phrase even then. No less than thirteen of the twenty-four *Classic Fairy Tales* (1974) collected in their earliest English versions by Iona and Peter Opie begin with the words. Mostly the versions are translations from the French of Charles Perrault's collected *Histories, or Tales of Past Times* (1697). The ready-made English phrase is used to translate his almost invariable *"Il estoit une fois."* "There was once upon a time a King and a Queen . . ."; "Once upon a time, and be sure 'twas a long time ago . . ."; "Once upon a time, and twice upon a time . . ."; "Once upon a time, and a very good time it was . . ."—all these variants hark back to a mythical past. The Opies comment that fairy stories "are the space fiction of the past. They describe events that took place when a different range of possibilities operated in the unidentified long ago; and this is part of their attraction. . . . The stories would, curiously, not be so believable if the period in which they took place was specified."

The Nelson *English Idioms* (c. 1912) calls it "a somewhat old-fashioned and pedantic phrase used to introduce an incident or story which took place at some indefinite time in the past."

Open sesame!   Meaning "open up (the door)!" As a mock password, this comes from the story of "Ali Baba and the Forty Thieves" in the ancient oriental tales of the *Arabian Nights.*
  Sesame seed is also famous for its other opening qualities —as a laxative.

Promises to Keep.   This phrase has been used as the title of both a memoir (1971) by Chester Knowles, an unrelated film (1985), and a novel (1988) by George Bernau. It comes from Robert Frost's poem "Stopping by Woods on a Snowy Evening" (1923): "The woods are lovely, dark and deep/ But I have promises to keep,/And miles to go before I sleep."

Small Is beautiful.   The title of the book published in 1973 by Professor E. F. Schumacher (1911–1977), it provided a catch phrase and a slogan for those who were opposed to the expansionist trend in business that was very apparent in the 1960s and 70s and who wanted "economics on a human scale." However, it appears that he very nearly didn't come up with the phrase. According to his daughter and a correspondent (London *Observer,* April 29, and June 6, 1984), the book was going to be called *The Homecomers.* His publisher, Anthony Blond, suggested "Small*ness* Is Beautiful," and then Desmond Briggs, the copublisher, came up with the eventual wording. Probably an echo of BLACK IS BEAUTIFUL (Chapter 15).

Sun Also Rises, The.   A mystifying title for a novel (1926, filmed in 1957) by Ernest Hemingway about American expatriates in Europe, unless you know that it comes from Ecclesiastes 1:5: "The sun also riseth, and the sun goeth down, and hasteth to his place where he arose." It gave rise to the Hollywood joke, "The son-in-law also rises," when Louis B. Mayer promoted his daughter's husband (David O. Selznick) in c. 1933. More recently there has been a book about the Japanese economy called *The Sun Also Sets* by Bill Emmott (1990).

War and Peace. The English title of Leo Tolstoy's epic novel (1865–1868). According to Henry Troyat's biography, Tolstoy did not decide on his title until very late. *"The Year 1805* would not do for a book that ended in 1812. He had chosen *All's Well That Ends Well,* thinking that would give the book the casual, romantic tone of a long English novel." Finally, the title was "borrowed from Proudhon" —*La Guerre et la Paix* (1862).

5

FAMOUS FOR FIFTEEN MINUTES

One of the most-quoted sayings of the century is to be found in a catalog for an exhibition of Andy Warhol's work in Stockholm (1968). He wrote: "In the future everyone will be world-famous for fifteen minutes." Now the phrase is often found to be used allusively—as in, "he's had his fifteen minutes," etc.

The following celebrities' phrases live on, even if their originators don't:

Are you four-square? Aimee Semple McPherson (1890–1944), the Canadian-born revivalist, had the Angelus Temple in Los Angeles as the center for her "Foursquare Gospel." This phrase was the greeting and slogan of her followers, and was used to mean "Are you solid, resolute?" "Being square," in this sense, dates from at least 1300 and suggests qualities of sound, regular construction, as in a building.

Compare Theodore Roosevelt's campaign promise in 1901: "We demand that big business give people a Square Deal. . . . If elected I shall see to it that every man has a Square Deal, no more and no less." This phrase, meaning "a fair deal," was current by 1876.

Because it is there.   As a flippant justification for doing anything, this makes use of a phrase chiefly associated with the British mountaineer George Leigh Mallory (1886–1924). He disappeared on his last attempt to scale Mount Everest. The previous year, during a lecture tour in the U.S., he had frequently been asked why he wanted to climb Everest. He replied, "Because it is there."

In 1911, apparently, at Cambridge University, England, A. C. Benson had urged Mallory to read Carlyle's life of John Stirling—a book that achieved high quality simply "by being *there.*" Perhaps that is how the construction entered Mallory's mind. On the other hand, Tom Holzel and Audrey Salkeld in *The Mystery of Mallory and Irvine* (1986) suggest that "the four most famous words in mountaineering" may have been invented for the climber by a reporter named Benson in *The New York Times* (March 18, 1923).

A report in the London *Observer* (November 2, 1986) stated that Howard Somervell, one of Mallory's climbing colleagues in the 1924 expedition, declared forty years later that the "much-quoted remark" had always given him a "shiver down the spine—it doesn't smell of George Mallory one bit." Mallory's niece, Mrs. B. M. Newton Dunn, claimed in a letter to the *Daily Telegraph* (November 11, 1986) that the mountaineer had once given the reply to his sister (Mrs. Newton Dunn's mother) "because a silly question deserves a silly answer."

The saying has become a catch phrase in situations where the speaker wishes to dismiss an impossible question about motives and also to express acceptance of a challenge that is in some way daunting or foolish.

There have been many variations (and misattributions).

Sir Edmund Hillary repeated it regarding his own successful attempt on Everest in 1953. Richard Ingrams of the
British satirical magazine, *Private Eye*, once invented a
reply for the Duke of Edinburgh to make to the question of
why he had married Queen Elizabeth II: "Because she was
there."

Bungalow Bill. This nickname was applied to a man
called Bill Wiggins who achieved a certain amount of media fame in 1987–88 simply for being an amour of Joan
Collins. "The Continuing Story of Bungalow Bill" (a joke
upon "Buffalo Bill," the sobriquet of William F. Cody, d.
1917) was the title of a Lennon and McCartney song
(1968). However, it was explained that Mr. Wiggins was so
called because he did not have much up top.

Call me madam.   Although this phrase cannot be said to
have "caught on" as a good catch phrase should, it has an
interesting story. Irving Berlin's musical *Call Me Madam*
was first performed on Broadway in 1950, starring Ethel
Merman as a woman ambassador appointed to represent
the U.S. in a tiny European state. It was inspired by the
case of Pearl Mesta, the society hostess whom Harry Truman had appointed as ambassador to Luxembourg.
   I suspect the title arose from a misquotation. When
Frances Perkins (1882–1965) was appointed Secretary of
Labor by President Roosevelt in 1933, she became the first
American woman to hold a cabinet post. It was held that
when she had been asked how she wished to be addressed
in cabinet, she had replied, "Call me Madam." She denied
that she had said this, however. Indeed, it was *after* her
first cabinet meeting that reporters asked how they should
address her. The Speaker-elect of the House of Representatives, Henry T. Rainey, answered for her: "When the
Secretary of Labor is a lady, she should be addressed with
the same general formalities as the Secretary of Labor who
is a gentleman. You call him 'Mr. Secretary.' You will call
her 'Madam Secretary.' You gentlemen know that when a

lady is presiding over a meeting, she is referred to as 'Madam Chairman' when you rise to address the chair" (quoted from George Martin, *Madam Secretary—Frances Perkins,* 1976).

Some of the reporters put this ruling into Perkins's own mouth, and that presumably is how the misquotation occurred. For years she had to put up with various other forms of address, of which "Madam Perkins" was the one she liked least. The misquotation occurs, for example, in *Ladies of Courage* by Eleanor Roosevelt and Lorena A. Hicock (1954): "Some fool reporter wanted to know what to call her. . . . 'Call me Madam,' she replied."

The phrase lives on. Xaviera Hollander—the "Happy Hooker" of the 1970s—was quoted as saying, "You can call me mercenary, or call me madam, but as I always tell my customers—just call me anytime!"

Can we talk? Stock phrase of Joan Rivers, especially around the time when she used to deputize for Johnny Carson on the *Tonight* show (1984).

Good evening, Mr. and Mrs. North America and all the ships at sea—let's go to press. Walter Winchell (1892–1972) was an ex-vaudevillian who became a top radio newscaster. This was how he introduced his zippy fifteen-minute broadcast on Sunday nights, starting in 1932. By 1948 it was the top-rated radio show in the U.S., with an average audience of twenty million people. A TV version ran from 1952 until 1955, in which Winchell entertained viewers by wearing his hat throughout. A variation of his greeting was "Mr. and Mrs. North *and South* America." Winchell also ran a syndicated newspaper gossip column and narrated the TV series *The Untouchables.* Many of his stories were pure fabrication.

Goodnight, Mrs. Calabash . . . wherever you are! Jimmy "Schnozzle" Durante (1893–1980), the big-nosed comedian, had a gaggle of phrases—including an exasperated "Everybody wants to get into the act!" and (after a successful joke) "I've got a million of 'em!" But he used to sign off his radio and TV shows in the 1940s and 1950s with the Calabash phrase. It was a pet name for his first wife, Maud, who died in 1943. The word comes from an American idiom for "empty head," taken from the calabash or gourd. For a long time Durante resisted explaining the phrase. His biographer, Gene Fowler, writing in 1952, could only note, "When he says that line, his manner changes to one of great seriousness, and his voice takes on a tender, emotional depth. . . . When asked to explain the Calabash farewells, Jim replied, 'That's my secret—I want it to rest where it is.' "

I am the greatest.   Muhammad Ali, formerly Cassius Clay (b. 1942), became world heavyweight boxing champion in 1964. He admitted that he copied his "I am the greatest . . . I am the prettiest" routine from a wrestler he once saw in Las Vegas called Gorgeous George: "I noticed they all paid to get in—and I said, this is a good idea!" In a moment of unusual modesty, Ali added, "I'm not really the greatest. I only say I'm the greatest because it sells tickets."

I dood it.   The catch phrase of "Junior, the Mean Widdle Kid"—as portrayed on radio by Red Skelton. This was how he owned up to mischief. Used as the title of a Red Skelton film in 1943. The character also appeared on TV's *The Red Skelton Show* (1951–71).

I never met a man I didn't like.   Will Rogers (1879–1935), the folksy "cowboy comedian" of the 1930s, used to proclaim this. If nothing else, the line gave rise to an amusing bumper sticker, seen in New York (1987) and ascribed to a disgruntled collaborator of the composer Marvin Hamlisch. It stated, "Will Rogers never met Marvin Hamlisch."

I think I go home.   At one time this phrase, spoken in a would-be Swedish accent, was as much part of the impressionist's view of the Swedish-born film actress Greta Garbo (1905–1990) as "I WANT TO BE ALONE." (this chapter). One version of how the line came to be spoken is told by Norman Zierold in *Moguls* (1969): "After such films as *The Torrent* and *Flesh and the Devil*, Garbo decided to exploit her box-office power and asked Louis B. Mayer for a raise—from three hundred and fifty to five thousand dollars a week. Mayer offered her twenty-five hundred. 'I tank I go home,' said Garbo. She went back to her hotel and stayed there for a full seven months until Mayer finally gave way."

In *Garbo* (1980), Alexander Walker remembers, however, what Sven-Hugo Borg, the actress's interpreter, said of the time in 1926 when Mauritz Stiller, who had come with Garbo from Sweden, was fired from directing *The Temptress:* "She was tired, terrified and lost. . . . As she returned to my side after a trying scene, she sank down beside me and said so low it was almost a whisper, 'Borg, I think I shall go home now. It isn't worth it, is it?' "

Walker comments: "That catch phrase, shortened into 'I think I go home,' soon passed into the repertoire of a legion of Garbo-imitators and helped publicize her strong-willed temperament."

A caricatured Garbo was shown hugging Mickey Mouse in a cartoon film in the 1930s. "Ah tahnk ah kees you now" and "ah tink ah go home," she said. (This cartoon was, incidentally, the last item to be shown on British television before the transmitters were closed down on the brink of war on September 1, 1939.)

I want to be alone.   Greta Garbo claimed that what she really said was "I want to be *let* alone"—she wanted privacy rather than solitude. Oddly, as Alexander Walker observed in *Sex in the Movies* (1968), "Nowhere in anything she said, either in the lengthy interviews she gave in her Hollywood days when she was perfectly approachable, or in the statements on-the-run from the publicity-shy fugitive she later became, has it been possible to find the famous phrase, 'I want to be alone.' What one can find, in abundance, later on, is 'Why don't you let me alone?' and 'I want to be left alone,' but neither is redolent of any more exotic order of being than a harassed celebrity. Yet the world prefers to believe the mythical and much more mysterious catch phrase utterance."

What complicates the issue is that Garbo herself *did* use the line several times on the screen. For example, in the 1929 silent film *The Single Standard* she gives the brush-off to a stranger, and the subtitle declares: "I am walking alone because I want to be alone." And as the aging ballerina who loses her nerve and flees back to her suite in *Grand Hotel* (1932), she actually *speaks* it. Walker calls this "an excellent example of art borrowing its effects from a myth that was reality for millions of people."

The phrase was obviously well-established by 1935 when Groucho Marx used it in *A Night at the Opera*. Garbo herself says, "Go to bed, little father. We want to be alone," in *Ninotchka* (1939). So it is not surprising that the myth has taken such firm hold, and particularly since Garbo became a virtual recluse for the second half of her life.

Say hey! The baseball player Willie Mays (b. 1931) was known during the early 1950s as "Say Hey Willie" or "the Say Hey Kid," from his frequent use of this exclamation.

Steel Magnolia, the. Nickname applied to Rosalynn Carter (b. 1927), wife of President Jimmy Carter. The First Lady's role apparently went further than holding hands with her husband in public. He consulted her on policy matters, and she seems to have had some influence over his decisions. Compare expressions like "an iron hand in a velvet glove." The magnolia is a flower particularly associated with southern U.S. areas.

In 1989 there was a film called *Steel Magnolias* based on Robert Harling's off-Broadway stage play, revolving around a beauty parlor and the friendship of six women who form the backbone of society in a small Louisiana town. Presumably the title was chosen to suggest the women's underlying strengths.

Thank you, music-lovers! The musician Spike Jones (1911–1964) specialized in comedy arrangements on radio, records, and films from the late 1930s onward. After massacring some well-known piece of music like "The Dance of the Hours," he would come forward and say this.

You cannot be serious! By 1980 John McEnroe, the tennis player and Wimbledon champion, had become celebrated for his "Superbrat" behavior toward umpires and linesmen—telling them "You cannot be serious," "You are the pits," and the like. "You cannot be serious!" was elevated to catch-phrase status through various show-biz takeoffs.

You dirty rat! Although impersonators of James Cagney (1899–1986) always have him saying "You dirty rat!", it may be that he never said it like that himself. In *Blonde Crazy* (1931), however, he calls someone a "dirty, double-crossing rat," which amounts to much the same thing.

In Joan Wyndham's wartime London diaries (*Love Lessons*, 1985), her entry for October 1, 1940, begins: "Double bill at the Forum with Rupert. *Elizabeth and Essex*, and a gangster film where somebody actually *did* say 'Stool on me would ya, ya doity rat!' " Note her surprise that the line was uttered at all. Although it was a strange double bill I think she must have been watching a revival of *Taxi* (1931), which is about cabbies fighting off a Mob-controlled fleet. Cagney's exact words in that film are "Come out and take it, you dirty yellow-bellied rat, or I'll give it to you through the door."

6

HOW TO SUCCEED
IN BUSINESS

How to Succeed in Business Without Really Trying *was the title of a business handbook published in 1953 by Shepherd Mead, but it is more widely known as the title of Frank Loesser's musical (1961, film 1967). In fact, the quickest way to succeed in business is to learn the language. How can a "game plan" be in a position to "go on all fours" if, to the businessman in charge, it's a "whole new ball game"? So, first things first. He or she must master these basic phrases, even with a "one-foot-in-the-water approach." It won't cost "an arm and a leg." You just have to "bite the bullet," even if you are "between a rock and a hard place." Just let those ideas "bubble up," and prevent the "whole ball of wax" from turning into a "can of worms."*

Then you will be able to stop any "rattlesnakes from crawling out of the woodwork." When you have most of the "players in place," the opposition's "snow job" won't have a "snowball's chance in hell" of "coming in from left field." If he thinks all this is a bit "iffy," he had better "orchestrate a scenario" of his own. But, frankly, we think it has the makings of a "womb-to-tomb deal."

Having mastered these phrases, the businessperson may now proceed to more complex constructions and say: "We must consider the political/optical/visual aspects of the situation"; "We must probe the gray areas for a concrete solution"; "We must have hands-on involvement in an arm's length situation"; "We must get both feet in the door and take a long-term view"; "When the rubber hits the road, cost comes walking in on two feet"; "Let's hit the ground running, when push comes to shove"; "When the shit really hits the fan, keep up to snuff, then have a gut feel"; "You've got to spend a buck to make a buck."

And now, a longer look at some of the most durable phrases from or about business:

Ace in the hole.　This expression was made familiar when it was used as the title of a Billy Wilder film in 1951. The film is literally about a hole. For his own sensation-seeking purposes, a journalist delays the rescue of a man stuck in a cave.

"Ace in the hole," meaning "hidden advantage" or "secret source of power," comes from stud poker. A "hole" card is one that is not revealed until the betting has taken place. If it's an ace, so much the better. *DOAS* dates the use of the expression in a poker context from the 1920s. *OED2* has it established by 1915.

Any color so long as it's black.　Now used to convey that there is no choice, this expression originated with Henry Ford (1863–1947). He is supposed to have said it about the Model T Ford that came out in 1909. In *Ford: Expansion and Challenge* (1957), Hill and Nevins have him saying,

"People can have it any color—so long as it's black." However, the company had to bow to the inevitable in 1925 and offer a choice of colors.

Beat a path to someone's door, to. "If a man write a better book, preach a better sermon, or make a better mousetrap than his neighbor, 'tho he build his house in the woods, the world will make a beaten path to his door." Sarah Yule claimed (1889) she heard Ralph Waldo Emerson say this in a lecture. Elbert Hubbard also claimed authorship. Either way, this is the remark alluded to when people talk of "beating a path to someone's door" or "building a better mousetrap." In his journal for February 1855, Emerson certainly entertained the thought: "If a man . . . can make better chairs or knives . . . than anybody else, you will find a broad hard-beaten road to his house, though it be in the woods."

Brownie points, to earn/win. This may have something to do with the junior branch of the Girl Scouts called Brownies and the points they might or might not gain for doing their "good deed for the day." Or it may have a scatological origin, not unconnected with brownnosing, brown-tonguing, ass-licking and other unsavory methods of sucking up to someone important.

Note also the term "Brownie," an award for doing something *wrong*. According to *DOAS*, "I got a pair of Brownies for that one" refers to a system of disciplinary demerits on the railroads (1942). The word was derived from the inventor of the system.

Cabbage Patch Kids. Millions of soft, ugly dolls with this name were sold in 1983–84. Created by Xavier Roberts, they became a craze around the world. People did not purchase them but "adopted" them. It is worth pointing out that whereas babies that are not delivered by stork are found in cabbage patches in the U. S., in Britain they are found "under a gooseberry bush." Compare the Kentucky children of *Mrs. Wiggs of the Cabbage Patch* (1901) by Alice Hegan Rice.

Cash/throw in one's chips, to. Originally meaning "to stop gambling." It later came to mean "to die," and as *DOAS* has it, "To terminate a business transaction, sell one's share of, or stock in, a business, or the like, in order to realize one's cash profits."

It may also mean "to make a final gesture." Tom Mangold wrote in the *Listener* (September 8, 1983), concerning the U.S. arms race in space: "Under malign command, a technological guarantee of invulnerability could induce the holder to cash his chips and go for a pre-emptive first strike."

Cool hundred/thousand/million. *OED2* says drily that the word "cool" "gives emphasis to the (large) amount." Is it because a large amount of money is rather chilling, lacking in warmth? Or is it because of the calm way in which the money is paid out? Perhaps the word "cool" in this context anticipates its more modern connection with jazz, as something thrilling, to be admired and approved of. In Henry Fielding's *Tom Jones* (1749) we read: "Watson rose from the table in some heat and declared he had lost a cool hundred . . ." In Charles Dickens's *Great Expectations* (1861): "She had wrote a little [codicil] . . . leaving a cool four thousand to Mr. Matthew Pocket." *A Cool Million* is the title of a Nathanael West satire (1934).

Cry all the way to the bank, to. Meaning to be in a position to ignore criticism. This expression was popularized, if not invented, by the flamboyant pianist Liberace (1919–1987). In his autobiography (1973), Liberace wrote, "When the reviews are bad I tell my staff that they can join me as I cry all the way to the bank."

Customer is always right, the. H. Gordon Selfridge (1856–1947) was an American who, after working for Marshall Field & Co., set off for England and introduced the idea of the monster department store. It appears that he was the first to say "the customer is always right" and many other phrases now associated with the business of selling through stores. He may also have invented the notion of "shopping days till Christmas." When he was still in Chicago he sent out an instruction to Marshall Field's heads of departments and their assistants: "The Christmas season has begun and but twenty-three more shopping days remain in which to make our holiday sales record."

Death of/by a thousand cuts. Meaning the cumulative effect of sniping, rather than one big blow. The earliest citation in the *OED2* seems to point to its being a Chinese proverbial expression. The English translation of Chairman Mao's "Little Red Book" (1966) quotes, "He who is not afraid of death by a thousand cuts dares to unhorse the emperor," and comments, "This is the indomitable spirit needed in our struggle to build socialism and communism."

Deep-six something, to. During Watergate—that rich source of colloquialisms (1973–74)—former presidential counsel John Dean told of a conversation he had had with another Nixon henchman, John Ehrlichman: "He told me to shred the documents and 'deep-six' the briefcase. I asked him what he meant by 'deep-six.' He leaned back in his chair and said, 'You drive across the river on your way home tonight, don't you? Well, when you cross over the bridge . . . just toss the briefcase into the river.'" (Ehrlichman, before going to prison, denied this conversation ever took place.)

As such, the word clearly means "to dispose of, with emphasis; to destroy or deliberately lose" (Safire). It comes from nautical speech used by men who took soundings. When they said "by the deep six," they meant six fathoms —which is thirty-six feet. In naval circles, "to deep-six" equally means "to jettison overboard."

DOAS notes an extension to this meaning in jive and jazz use since the 1940s: "the deep six" means "the grave."

Difficult we do immediately—the impossible takes a little longer, the. Bartlett attributes this motto, now widespread in business, to the U.S. Armed Service Forces and traces the idea behind it back to a nonbusinessman, Charles Alexandre De Calonne (1734–1802), who said, *"Madame, si c'est possible, c'est fait; impossible? cela se fera* [If it is possible, it is already done; if it is impossible, it will be done]."

Henry Kissinger once joked, "The illegal we do immediately, the unconstitutional takes a little longer" (quoted in William Shawcross, *Sideshow,* 1979).

Do not fold, spindle, or mutilate. When punched cards and computer cards began to accompany bills and statements in the 1950s, computerization was looked on as a harbinger of the Brave New World (though Bartlett dates the use of this somewhat bossy injunction to the 1930s). By the 1960s the words evoked a machine age that was taking over. By the 1980s the cards were no longer necessary.

A slogan of the 1960s student revolution was, "I am a human being—do not fold, spindle, or mutilate me." A graffito (1974) read: "I am a masochist—please spindle, fold, or mutilate." There was a film with this title in 1971.

Don't get mad—get even. When John F. Kennedy was elected president in 1960, attention was focused on several axioms said to have come from the Boston-Irish political jungle or, more precisely, from the President's father, Joseph P. Kennedy (1888–1969). At this distance it would be impossible to say for sure whether this wealthy, ambitious businessman/ambassador/politician originated these expressions, but he certainly instilled them in his sons:

If you want to make money, go where the money is.

We don't want any losers around here. In this family
we want winners. Don't come in second or third—that
doesn't count—but win. [Sometimes rendered as
"Kennedys always come first."]

We don't want any crying in this house. [Rendered by
his children as "Kennedys don't cry."]

Only winners come to dinner.

"Don't get mad—get even" was another one. It was used
as the title of a "manual for retaliation" by Alan Abel
(1983). (See also WHEN THE GOING GETS TOUGH . . . , this
chapter.)

Eleventh Commandment, the.   But what does it state?
Mencken has "Mind your own business" as "borrowed
from Cervantes, *Don Quixote*, 1605 . . . often called, in
the United States, the Eleventh Commandment." But he
also records "the Eleventh Commandment: Thou shalt not
be found out—George Whyte-Melville, *Holmby House*,
1860," and that is the much more usual meaning.

   OED2 adds from the *Pall Mall Gazette* of September 10,
1884, "The new and great commandment that nothing
succeeds like success," and from *Paston Carew* (1886), by
Mrs. Lynn Lynton, that the Eleventh Commandment was
"do not tell tales out of school."

   In 1850 Charles Kingsley suggested that it was "Buy
cheap, sell dear." So, all in all, one has to conclude that it
can be anything—slightly cynical—that one might wish it
to be.

   The 1981 remake of the film *The Postman Always Rings
Twice* was promoted with the slogan, "If there was an
Eleventh Commandment, they would have broken that
too."

Go for it!   This was a popular expression from the early
1980s. In June 1985 President Reagan's call for tax reform
was, "America, go for it!" Victor Kiam, a razor entrepre-

neur, entitled his 1986 memoirs *Going for It!* "Go for it,
America" was the slogan used by British Airways in the
same year to get more U.S. tourists to ignore the terrorist
threat and travel to Europe.

Lisa Birnbach in *The Official Preppy Handbook* (1981)
points to U.S. campuses as its possible place of origin, giving the phrase as an exhortation to act crazily. At about the
same time the phrase was being used in aerobics classes.
Jane Fonda, in her workout book (1981) and video (c.
1983), cried, "Go for it, go for the burn!" (The burn is a
sensation felt during strenuous exercise.) There was also
the slogan (current in 1981) for beer, "Go for it! Schlitz
makes it great."

Partridge/*Slang* has "to go for it" as Australian for being
"extremely eager for sexual intercourse" (c. 1925).

Horny-handed sons of toil.   The phrase for laborers bearing the marks of their trade is American in origin. Irish-
born Denis Kearney (1847–1907) used the expression in a
speech in San Francisco in c. 1878 when leading a "work-
ingman's protest movement against unemployment, un-
just taxes, unfair banking laws, and mainly against Chinese
labourers" (Flexner, *Listening to America*, 1982). Earlier,
J. R. Lowell (1819–1891) had written in "A Glance Behind
the Curtain" (1843), "And blessèd are the horny hands of
toil."

How to win friends and influence people.   More than the
title of a book. Dale Carnegie's courses incorporating this
principle had already been aimed at businesspeople for a
quarter of a century when, in 1936, an ad campaign
launched his book on self-improvement. One million copies were sold between December 1936 and November
1939.

If you have to ask the price you can't afford it.   John
Pierpoint Morgan, Jr. (1867–1943) was head of the Morgan
banking house. The story has it that a man was thinking of

buying a yacht similar to Morgan's and asked how much it
cost in annual upkeep. Replied Morgan: "If you have to
ask, you can't afford it." Compare the remark of John Paul
Getty (d. 1976): "If you can actually count your money, you
are not really rich."

In God we trust—all others pay cash.   After the Washington summit between Mikhail Gorbachev and Ronald Reagan in December 1987, Secretary of State George Schultz
commented on a Russian slogan that Reagan had made
much of: " 'Trust but verify' is really an ancient saying in
the United States, but in a different guise. Remember the
storekeeper who was a little leery of credit, and he had a
sign in his store that said, IN GOD WE TRUST—ALL OTHERS
PAY CASH? " Referring to the verification procedures over
arms reductions signed by the leaders in Washington,
Shultz said, "This is the cash."

In 1942 Mencken was listing "In God we trust; all others
must pay cash" as an "American saying." "In God we
trust" has been the official national motto of the United
States since 1956, when it superseded *"E pluribus unum,"*
but it had been known since 1864 when it was first put on a
two-cent coin.

A parallel saying is attributed to the striptease artist
Gypsy Rose Lee (1914–1970): "God is love, but get it in
writing."

let's _____ and see if _____.   Particularly in business and
advertising, this construction is much used to indicate how
an idea should be researched and tested or simply put to
the public to see what the reaction will be. Some of the
versions:

Let's . . .
   . . . run it up the flagpole and see if anyone salutes it.
   . . . put it on the porch and see if the cat will eat it.
   . . . put it on the train and see if it gets off at
Westchester.

. . . leave it in the water overnight and see if it springs any leaks.

Not to be forgotten: "Let me just pull something out of the hat here and see if it hops for us."

Streets paved with gold, to find the. When Hollywood was in its heyday many writers were reluctant to go there, fearing they would be treated badly. According to Arthur Marx in *Son of Groucho* (1973), his father tried very hard to persuade the dramatist George S. Kaufman to join him out on the West Coast.

"No, no," said Kaufman. "I don't care how much they pay me. I hate it out there."

"But, George," pleaded Groucho, "the streets out here are paved with gold."

There was a moment's pause and then Kaufman said, "You mean, you have to bend down and pick it up?"

But where did this near-cliché originate? In the story of Dick Whittington, he makes his way to London from Gloucestershire because he hears the streets are paved with gold and silver. The actual Dick Whittington was three times Lord Mayor of London in the late fourteenth and early fifteenth centuries. The popular legend does not appear to have been told before 1605.

The streets of heaven are also sometimes said to be paved with gold—though not in the Bible. There is, however, an African-American spiritual where the "streets in heaven am paved with gold."

Take the money and run, to. Meaning to settle for what you've got and not hang around. It might also be advice given to people worried about the worth of the job of work they're doing. The phrase was used as the title of Woody Allen's 1968 film *Take the Money and Run*.

That's the way the cookie crumbles. Meaning that's the way it is, there's no escaping it. Bartlett dates the basic phrase to the 1950s. It was, however, given a memorable twist in Billy Wilder's film *The Apartment* (1960). The main characters make much use of the suffix "-wise," as in "promotionwise" and "gracious-livingwise." When Miss Kubelik (Shirley MacLaine) says to C. C. Baxter (Jack Lemmon), "Why can't I ever fall in love with somebody nice like you?" Baxter replies, "Yeah, well, that's the way it crumbles, cookiewise."

A joke translation of the original phrase—*"Sic biscuitus disintegrat"*— occurred in an Iris Murdoch novel, written before 1978. A show-biz variant I heard in 1988 was "That's the way the mop flops."

There's gold in them thar hills. Meaning there are opportunities in the way indicated. Presumably this phrase was established in U.S. gold mining by the end of the nineteenth century. It seems to have had a resurgence in the 1930s and 40s, probably through use in Western films. Frank Marvin wrote and performed a song with the title in the 1930s. A Laurel and Hardy short called *Them Thar Hills* appeared in 1934. The melodrama *Gold in the Hills* by J. Frank Davis has been performed every season since 1936 by the Vicksburg Theater Guild in Mississippi. *OED2*'s earliest citation is from 1941.

The phrase is now applied jokingly to any enterprise that contains a hint of promise.

What a way to run a _____. A cartoon believed to have appeared in *Collier's* magazine (though *Ballyhoo* in 1932 has also been suggested) shows two trains about to collide. A signalman is looking out of his box and the caption is: "Tch-tch, what a way to run a railroad!"

The Boston & Maine railroad picked up this line when it sought "a statement which would explain some of the problems of the railroad in times of inclement weather." It took the "stock railroad phrase" derived from the cartoon and put it between each paragraph of the advertisement in the form, "That's A H**1 of a Way to Run a Railroad!"

Added at the foot of the ad was the line, "But the railroad always runs."

Thus the phrase came into the language as an exclamation concerning mismanagement or chaos of any kind, in the form, "What a way/hell of a way to run a railroad/railway."

When the going gets tough, the tough get going. Another of the axioms said to have come from President Kennedy's father. This one was subsequently used as a slogan for the film *The Jewel of the Nile* (1985), and a song with the title sung by Billy Ocean and the stars of the film was a hit in 1986. The slogan "When the going gets tough, the tough go shopping" had appeared on T-shirts by 1982.

World owes one a living, to believe the. I was first alerted to the obscure origin of this expression by its use in the epigraph to Graham Greene's novel *England Made Me* (1935):

> "All the world owes me a living."
> —Walt Disney—
> (*The Grasshopper and the Ants*)

Could Disney really claim credit for the phrase? Well, the cartoon in question—one of the first "Silly Symphonies"—was released in 1934. It is based on the Aesop fable "Of the Ant and the Grasshopper" (as it is called in Caxton's first English translation, 1484), which tells of a grasshopper asking an ant for corn to eat in winter. The ant asks, "What have you done all the summer past?" and the grasshopper can only answer, "I have sung." The moral is that you should provide yourself in the summer with what you need in winter.

Disney turns the grasshopper into a fiddler and gives him a song to sing. The song, written by Larry Morey to music by Leigh Harline, became quite well known and presumably helped John Llewellyn Rhys choose *The World Owes Me a Living* for his 1939 novel about a redundant air force hero who tries to make a living with a flying circus (filmed 1944).

It is odd rendered in this form, because on the whole it is not something people say about themselves. More often, another would say, pejoratively, "The trouble with you is you think the world owes you a living."

The phrase was used earlier in W. G. Sumner's book *Earth Hunger* (1896). He writes: "The men who start out with the notion that the world owes them a living generally find that the world pays its debt in the penitentiary or the poorhouse."

7

IT PAYS
TO ADVERTISE

*This has been the century of advertising slogans. They leap
out at us from countless billboards, TV screens, T-shirts,
bumper stickers, and buttons. There is a lot of meaningless
fluff. There is also much that is lively, arresting, and entertaining. However, only occasionally do slogans become
memorable or touch a popular chord. Strictly speaking,
the slogan comes at the end of an ad and encapsulates the
message. Some say that it should never use more than
seven words, but the days are long gone when a perfect
slogan had to name and define a product as well as promise some benefit. There are advertising lines regarded as
having the power of slogans because they are associated
with specific products—even if they don't name them.*

*"It pays to advertise" is a proverbial saying that almost
certainly originated in the U.S. Indeed, Mencken in 1942*

lists it as an "American proverb." Bartlett quotes the anonymous rhyme:

> The codfish lays ten thousand eggs,
> The homely hen lays one.
> The codfish never cackles
> To tell you what she's done.
>
> And so we scorn the codfish,
> While the humble hen we prize,
> Which only goes to show you
> That it pays to advertise.

I feel sure, though, that this rhyme came after the proverb or slogan was established. The origin of the phrase, in fact, dates from much earlier. There was a play cowritten in 1914 (and filmed in 1931) by Walter Hackett (1876–1944) that had the phrase for a title. Earlier still, Cole Porter titled one of his songs "It Pays to Advertise." The lyrics alluded to a number of advertising lines current when he was a student at Yale (c. 1912):

> I'd walk a mile for that schoolgirl complexion,
> Palmolive soap will do it every time . . .
> If you travel, travel, travel at all,
> You know, it pays to advertise.
>   (included in The Complete Lyrics of Cole
>   Porter, ed. Robert Kimball, 1983.)

The phrase was probably not yet much of a cliché by 1912. Ezra Pound wrote in a letter to his father in 1908 about the launch of his poems: "Sound trumpet. Let rip the drum and swatt the big bassoon. It pays to advertise."

The phrase probably originated in the 1870s to 1890s when advertising really took off in America. Indeed, Benham's Book of Quotations (1960 revision) lists an "American saying c. 1870—The man who on his trade relies must either bust or advertise," and notes that "Sir Thomas Lipton [d. 1931] is said to have derived inspiration and success through seeing this couplet in New York about 1875."

And now, phrases from advertising:

Ask the man who owns one.   This slogan for Packard Motors (1902) originated with James Ward Packard, the founder of the company, and appeared for many years in all Packard advertising and sales material. Someone had written asking for more information about his cars. Packard told his secretary, "Tell him that we have no literature —we aren't that big yet—but if he wants to know how good an automobile the Packard is, tell him to ask the man who owns one." A 1903 placard is the first printed evidence of the slogan's use. It lasted for more than thirty-five years.

At General Electric, progress is our most important product.   Not a slogan that trips lightly off the tongue, but memorable because of who said it. In 1955 Ronald Reagan became the host of the popular program *General Electric Theater* and ended every show with this closing line.

At sixty miles an hour, the loudest noise in this new Rolls-Royce comes from the electric clock.   The best-known promotional line ever for a car was devised not by a copywriter but by the technical editor of *The Motor,* who tested the 1958 Silver Cloud. David Ogilvy, who had the idea of using it in ad copy, presented it as a headline to a senior Rolls-Royce executive in New York, who shook his head sadly and said, "We really ought to do something about that damned clock."

Even the anonymous motoring journalist had not been entirely original. A 1907 review of the Silver Ghost in *The Autocar* read: "At whatever speed the car is driven, the auditory nerves when driving are troubled by no fuller sound than emanates from the eight-day clock."

Rolls-Royce originally promoted itself (and sometimes still does) as "the Best Car in the World" (current by 1929, and also, quoting a journalist, in a 1908 edition of *The Times* of London).

Avoid five o'clock shadow.   The expression "five o'clock shadow" for the stubbly growth that some dark-haired men acquire on their faces toward the end of the day would appear to have originated before 1939 in ads for Gem Razors and Blades. A 1937 ad added, "That unsightly beard growth which appears prematurely at about 5 p.m. looks bad."

The most famous sufferer was Richard Nixon, who may have lost the TV debates in his presidential race against John F. Kennedy in 1960 as a result. In his *Memoirs* (1978) he wrote: "Kennedy arrived . . . looking tanned, rested, and fit. My television adviser, Ted Rodgers, recommended that I use television makeup, but unwisely I refused, permitting only a little 'beard stick' on my perpetual five o'clock shadow."

Avon calling!   First used as a slogan in 1886. The first "Avon Lady," Mrs. P. F. A. Allre, was employed by the firm's founder, D. H. McConnell, to visit customers at home and sell them cosmetics.

Beanz meanz Heinz.   Slogan from 1967 for Heinz baked beans. It is the type of advertising line that drives teachers crazy because it appears to condone wrong spelling. Johnny Johnson wrote the music for the jingle that went:

> A million housewives every day
> Pick up a tin of beans and say
> Beanz meanz Heinz.

"I created the line at Young and Rubicam," copywriter Maurice Drake told me in 1981. "It was in fact written— although after much thinking—over two pints of bitter in the Victoria Pub in Mornington Crescent [London]."

Beer that made Milwaukee famous, the. The Joseph Schlitz Brewing Company started up in Milwaukee in 1849. By 1871, the year of the great Chicago fire, it was a thriving concern. The fire left Chicagoans thirsty. The city was desperately short of drinking water and its breweries had been virtually destroyed. So Joseph Schlitz floated a shipload of beer down Lake Michigan to refresh his parched neighbors. Long after the crisis, Milwaukee beer was still warmly remembered in Chicago. It is not known who coined the phrase, but this is the incident that led to it. The slogan was incorporated and registered in 1895.

Big one, the. This boast almost certainly dates back to 1907 when Ringling Brothers Circus bought up its rival, Barnum and Bailey. The two together were billed, understandably, as "The Big One." When the outfit closed in 1956, the *New York Post* had the headline, "THE BIG ONE IS NO MORE!"

DOAS points out that a "big one" is also a thousand-dollar bill (from gambling) and a nursery euphemism for a bowel movement. Partridge/*Slang* has "big one" or "big 'un" for "a notable person," and dates it to 1800–50.

Blow some my way. One of the immortals: for Chesterfield cigarettes, from 1926. It was used—some said suggestively—when a woman made her first appearance in cigarette advertising. "I'll tell the truth—they satisfy" was also current that year.

Body odor (or B.O.). The new, worrying concept was used to promote Lifebuoy soap and was current by 1933. In the 1930s this jingle was on the radio:

> Singing in the bathtub, singing for joy,
> Living a life of Lifebuoy—
> Can't help singing, 'cos I know
> That Lifebuoy really stops B.O.

The initials "B.O." were sung *basso profundo*, emphasizing the horror of the offense. In the U.K., TV ads showed pairs of male or female friends out on a spree, intending to attract partners. When one of the pair had a problem, the other whispered helpfully, "B.O."

Breakfast of champions.   Since at least 1950 this has been used to promote Wheaties breakfast cereal. A series of ads in the 1980s featured champion athletes, one of which was Jackie Robinson, "one of the greatest names in baseball. . . . This Dodgers star is a Wheaties man: 'A lot of us ball players go for milk, fruit and Wheaties,' says Jackie. . . . Had *your* Wheaties today?"

Kurt Vonnegut used the phrase as the title of a novel (1973).

Come alive—you're in the Pepsi Generation.   This slogan, dating back to 1964, has sometimes been difficult to translate. In German it became "Come alive out of the grave," and in Chinese, "Pepsi brings your ancestors back from the dead." "Twice as much for a nickel, too," a Pepsi ad line current in the 1930s, was written by Walter Mack and is considered the "first advertising jingle in history." (It was sung to the tune of "John Peel" an estimated six million times on radio.)

Diamond is forever, a.   In 1939 the South Africa-based De Beers Consolidated Mines launched a campaign to further promote the tradition of diamond engagement rings. Copywriter B. J. Kidd at the N. W. Ayer Agency in Chicago came up with this line, which passed easily into the language.

In 1925, Anita Loos expressed the same idea in *Gentlemen Prefer Blondes*: "Kissing your hand may make you feel very, very good but a diamond and sapphire bracelet lasts forever." A variation of the phrase was used as the title of Ian Fleming's 1956 James Bond novel *Diamonds Are Forever*.

(Technically speaking, however, they are not. It takes a very high temperature, but, being pure carbon, diamonds *will* burn.)

Does she . . . or doesn't she?   This suggestive phrase began life selling Clairol hair-coloring in 1955 and is the brainchild of Shirley Polykoff (whose advertising memoirs are entitled *Does She . . . or Doesn't She?*). The question first arose at a party when a girl with flaming red hair arrived. Polykoff involuntarily uttered the line to her husband, George. As she says, however, the words were planted in her mind twenty years earlier by her mother-in-law. George told Shirley of his mother's first reaction on meeting her: "She says you paint your hair. Well, do you?"

When Ms. Polykoff submitted the slogan to the Foote, Cone and Belding Agency in New York (along with two ideas she wished to have rejected), she suggested it be followed by the phrase "Only her mother knows for sure!" or "So natural, only her mother knows for sure." She felt she might have to change "mother" to "hairdresser" so as not to offend beauty salons, and, indeed, "only her hairdresser knows for sure" was eventually chosen.

However, the slogan's double meaning caused it to be rejected by *Life* magazine. When subsequent research at *Life* failed to turn up one female staff member who admitted detecting any innuendo, the phrases were locked into the form they kept for the next eighteen years.

The author "J" did find a double meaning, as shown by this comment from *The Sensuous Woman* (1969): "Our world has changed. It's no longer a question of 'Does she or doesn't she?' We all know she wants to, is about to, or does." A New York graffito from 1974 stated: "Only *his* hairdresser knows for sure."

Eventually/why not now?   Slogan for Gold Medal flour, from c. 1907. When Benjamin S. Bull, advertising manager of the Washburn Crosby Company, asked his employees to suggest catch phrases for the promotion of Gold Medal flour, nobody came up with anything worthwhile. Mr. Bull demanded, "When are you going to give me a decent slogan?" His employees staved him off by saying, "Eventually." "Eventually!" thundered Mr. Bull, "Why not now?"

Even your best friends won't tell you. A line from a Listerine mouthwash advertisement. Partridge/*Catch Phrases* has it in the form "your best friend(s) won't tell you" (i.e., "you stink!"). In the 1941 film *Dangerous Moonlight,* Anton Walbrook plays a character who says to a man putting on hair oil, "Even your best friend won't *smell* you."

Flavor of the month. Originally a phrase aimed at encouraging people to try new varieties of ice cream. Lately it has become an idiom for any fad, craze, or person that is quickly discarded after a period of great popularity and demand. "Young Dan Quisenberry, the Royals' bullpen flavor of the month in their shattered relief corps, got five final outs in a row for a save"—*Washington Post* (September 20, 1979).

Flick your Bic. Slogan for lighters, from 1975. Coined by copywriter Charlie Moss, the original line occurred in an ad that showed how smart, sophisticated people did not use lighters—they simply "flicked their Bics." The phrase caught on and was picked up by many comedians. During the energy crisis, Bob Hope said, "Things are getting so bad that the Statue of Liberty doesn't light up anymore. She just stands there and flicks her Bic."

Food shot from guns. Slogan for Quaker Puffed Wheat and Puffed Rice, current from the early 1900s. Claude C. Hopkins (1867–1932), one of the great American advertising gurus, wrote: "I watched the process where the grains were shot from guns. And I coined the phrase. The idea aroused ridicule. One of the greatest food advertisers in the country wrote an article about it. He said that of all the follies evolved in food advertising this certainly was the worst—the idea of appealing on 'Food shot from guns' was the theory of an imbecile. But the theory proved attractive. It was such a curiosity arouser that it proved itself the most successful campaign ever conducted in cereals."

For men of distinction.   This slogan for Lord Calvert custom-blended whiskey was current in 1945. "For years," the copy ran, "the most expensive whiskey blended in America, Lord Calvert is intended especially for those who can afford the finest." Marshall McLuhan wrote in *The Mechanical Bride* (1951): "Snob appeal might seem to be the most obvious feature of this type of ad, with its submerged syllogism that since all sorts of eminent men drink this whiskey they are eminent because they drink it. Or only this kind of whiskey is suited to the palate of distinguished men, therefore a taste for it confers, or at least displays an affinity for, distinction in those who have not yet achieved greatness."

Gets rid of film on teeth.   This slogan for Pepsodent, current in the early 1900s was another of Claude C. Hopkins's great coups—to claim something that every toothpaste could claim, and get away with it. He said, "People do not want to read of penalties. They want to be told of rewards. . . . People want to be told the ways to happiness and cheer. . . . I resolved to advertise this toothpaste as a creator of beauty."

Getting there is half the fun.   This expression popularizes Robert Louis Stevenson's views: "I travel not to go anywhere, but to go" and "To travel hopefully is a better thing than to arrive." It also reflects the idea that "the journey, not the arrival, matters" (used as the title of an autobiography by writer Leonard Woolf in 1969). The phrase was used to advertise Cunard steamships on both sides of the Atlantic in the 1920s and 30s. The Peter Sellers film *Being*

There (1980) had for its promotional line, "Getting there is half the fun. Being there is all of it."

Go now, pay later. Daniel Boorstin in *The Image* (1962) makes oblique reference to travel advertisements using the line "Go now, pay later." Was installment buying ever promoted with "Buy now, pay later" ? It seems likely. These lines seem to be the starting point for a construction much used and adapted since.

    Live Now, Pay Later was the title of Jack Trevor Story's 1962 screenplay based on the novel *All on the Never Never* by Jack Lindsay. The line was seen in a Los Angeles graffito (1970), according to *The Encyclopedia of Graffiti* (1974). The same book records a New York subway graffito on a funeral parlor ad that said, "Our layaway plan—die now, pay later."

Good to the last drop. This slogan for Maxwell House coffee dates from 1907. President Theodore Roosevelt was visiting Joel Cheek, perfector of the Maxwell House blend. After the President had had a cup, he said that it was "Good . . . to the last drop." It has been used as a slogan ever since, despite those who have wondered what was wrong with the last drop. Professors of English have been called in to consider the problem, and they've ruled that "to" can be inclusive and not just mean "up to but not including."

Greatest show on earth, the. This name/slogan was given by P. T. Barnum (1810–1891) to the circus formed by the merger with his rival, Bailey's, in 1881. It is still used by what is now Ringling Bros. and Barnum & Bailey Circus. It was the title of a Cecil B. De Mille circus film in 1952.

Happiness is _____. Samuel Johnson declared in 1766, "Happiness consists in the multiplicity of agreeable consciousness," but he wasn't the first to try to define happiness, nor the last. In 1942, along came E. Y. Harburg with the lyrics to his song "Happiness Is a Thing Called Joe." However, it was Charles M. Schulz, creator of the "Peanuts" comic strip, who really launched the "Happiness is _____ " format.

In c. 1957 Schulz had drawn a strip "centering around some kid hugging Snoopy and saying in the fourth panel that 'Happiness is a warm puppy.'" This became the title of a best-selling book in 1962 and let loose a stream of promotional phrases using the format, including: "Happiness is egg-shaped"; "Happiness is a cigar called Hamlet"; "Happiness is a warm earpiece" (U.K. ad slogans); "Happiness is being elected team captain—and getting a Bulova watch"; "Happiness is a $49 table"; "Happiness is seeing Lubbock, Texas, in the rearview mirror" (line from a country-western song); "Happiness Is a Warm Gun" (song title); "Happiness is wren-shaped"; and many, many more.

By which time one might conclude that "Happiness is . . . a worn cliché."

Heinz 57 Varieties.   This brand name has been used for Heinz canned foods since 1896. In that year Henry Heinz was traveling through New York City on the overhead railway. He saw a streetcar window advertising twenty-one styles of shoe; the idea appealed to him and, although he could list fifty-eight or fifty-nine Heinz products, he settled on fifty-seven because it sounded right. Heinz commented later, "I myself did not realize how successful a slogan it was going to be." In housey-housey or bingo, "all the beans" is now the cry for "fifty-seven."

Partridge/*Slang* has "Heinz" and "57 Varieties" as expressions for a "mongrel dog."

He who loves me, follows me.   Slogan for Jesus Jeans. In 1970, Italian clothing manufacturer Maglificio Calzificio Torinese launched an advertising campaign showing the rear view of a young girl in a tight-fitting pair of the company's new Jesus Jeans, cut very short. The slogan echoed

the New Testament, as did "thou shalt have no other jeans
before me."

Later, a spokesman for the company explained in the
International Herald Tribune (January 12, 1982): "We
were not looking for a scandal. It's just that it was the late
1960s and Jesus was emerging increasingly as a sort of cult
figure. There was the Jesus generation and *Jesus Christ
Superstar.* There was this enormous protest, in Italy and
around the world, and Jesus looked to a lot of people like
the biggest protester ever. . . . It's funny, we had no trouble in Mediterranean countries, but the biggest resistance
came in the Protestant countries, in North America and
northern Europe."

Jesus Jeans were eventually sold only in Italy, Greece,
and Spain. In Greece there was a threat of prosecution for
"insulting religion and offending the Christian conscience
of the public." In France complaints of blasphemy and
sacrilege flooded in when the slogan *"Qui m'aime me
suive,"* located on a girl's behind, was tried out in 1982.

He won't be happy till he gets it.   Slogan for Pears soap,
current 1888. Coupled with the picture of a baby stretch-
ing out of his bath to pick up a cake of Pears soap. Cartoon-
ists played with this idea—changing the baby into the Czar
or Kaiser and the soap into various disputed territories.

His Master's Voice.   A trademark and brand name that
carries the force of a slogan. In 1899 the English painter
Francis Barraud approached the Gramophone Company
in London to borrow one of their machines so that he could
paint his dog, Nipper, listening to it. Nipper was accus-
tomed, in fact, to hearing a phonograph, but his master
thought that the larger horn of the gramophone would
make a better picture. Subsequently, the Gramophone
Company bought the painting and adapted it as a trademark. In 1901 the Victor Talking Machine Company (slogan—"Loud enough for dancing") acquired the U.S.
rights. The company later became RCA Victor and took

Nipper with it. Today Britain's EMI owns the trademark in most countries, RCA owns it in North and South America, and JVC owns it in Japan.

Sometimes the phrase is used to describe a person who merely repeats the instructions or views of a superior.

I dreamed I _____ in my Maidenform bra.   Slogan for a classic advertisement from the days when bras were not for burning but for dreaming about. The series, devised by the Norman, Craig and Kummel agency, ran from 1949 to 1969. Maidenform offered prizes up to ten thousand dollars for dream situations that could be used in the advertising, in addition to: "I dreamed I . . . took the bull by the horns/went walking/stopped traffic/was a social butterfly/ rode in a gondola/was Cleopatra . . . in my Maidenform bra." "I dreamed I went to blazes . . ." was illustrated by a girl in bra, fireman's helmet, and boots, swinging from a fire engine.

I Love/♥ _____.   In June 1977 the New York State Department of Commerce launched a campaign to attract tourists. The first commercial showed people enjoying themselves in outdoor activities, each saying something like, "I'm from New Hampshire, but I love New York," or "I'm from Cape Cod, but I love New York"—and it ended with a man in a camping scene saying, "I'm from Brooklyn, but I loooove New York."

Since then "I Love New York" has become one of the best-known advertising slogans in the world. The use of the "I Love _____" formula has been copied the world over—particularly with the word "love" replaced by a heart shape.

Charlie Moss at the Wells, Rich, Green Agency is credited with having coined the phrase. He may have been inspired by the song "How About You?" (lyrics by Ralph Freed, music by Burton Lane) which was written for the Garland-Rooney film *Babes on Broadway* (1941) and includes the line "I like New York in June." Or the inspiration may have come from Cole Porter's tune "I Happen to Like New York" *(The New Yorkers,* 1930).

From *The New York Times,* April 22, 1981: "Connecticut came forth today with its official slogan, 'Better yet Connecticut'. . . . It was created by Joseph Roy, a 45-year-old graphics artist. . . . John J. Carson said the slogan would adorn T-shirts and be displayed in banks and on billboards and bumper stickers. Both state officials and Vacation Travel Council members voiced confidence that their slogan could vie in the marketplace with such tourism precursors as 'I love New York,' 'Make it in Massachusetts,' and 'Virginia is for lovers.' "

I'm _____, fly me.   As in "I'm Margie, fly me," referring to National Airlines stewardesses. The campaign current c. 1971 aroused the ire of feminist groups, as did the line, "I'm going to fly you like you've never been flown before." The group 10 cc had a hit with "I'm Mandy Fly Me" in 1976. That same year, Wall's Sausages in England parodied it with, "I'm meaty, fry me."

It beats as it sweeps as it cleans.   This line for Hoover carpet sweepers dates from 1919 and is still used in the 1990s. It was coined by Gerald Page-Wood of the Erwin Wasey Agency in Cleveland, Ohio. The exclusive feature of Hoovers was that they gently beat or tapped the carpet to loosen dirt and grit embedded in it. An agitator bar performed this function together with strong suction with revolving brushes—giving the Hoover the "triple action" enshrined in the slogan. The words "Hoover" and "to hoover" became generic terms for vacuum cleaners and for vacuuming.

It's fingerlickin' good!   Slogan for Kentucky Fried Chicken, current by 1958, from which several songs and instrumental numbers with the title "Fingerlickin' Good" have been derived. Lonnie Smith had a record album called "Fingerlickin' Good Soul Organ," and in 1966 "Fin-

ger Lickin' " was the title of an instrumental by Barbara
Clark. The phrase "licking good" was current in the 1890s.

Join the army/navy and see the world.   The army version
seems to have been used in the U.S. and Britain in the
1920s and 30s. Partridge/*Slang* dates the riposte ". . .
and see the next one" (meaning the next world) as c. 1948.
In the film *Duck Soup* (1933), Harpo Marx holds up a placard that says, "Join the Army and See the Navy." Irving
Berlin's song "We Saw the Sea" from *Follow the Fleet*
(1936) goes, "I joined the navy to see the world. And what
did I see? I saw the sea."

"I joined the navy to see the world" is quoted, ironically,
by a sailor in the film *In Which We Serve* (1942).

Keep that schoolgirl complexion.   This slogan used to
promote Palmolive soap since 1917 was coined by
Palmolive executive Charles S. Pearce. Beverley Nichols
wrote in *The Star-Spangled Manner* (1928) that in his "ri-
otous youth" he had been comforted through "numberless
orgies" only by the conviction that if he used a certain soap
he would retain his schoolboy complexion: "It did not matter how much I drank or smoked, how many nameless and
exquisite sins I enjoyed—they would all be washed out in
the morning by that magical soap. . . . I bought it merely
because years ago a bright young American sat down in an
office on the other side of the Atlantic and thought of a
slogan to sell soap. And he certainly sold it."

During World War II, Palmolive was still plugging the
old line in the U.K.: "Driving through blitzes won't spoil
that schoolgirl complexion."

Like mother makes/used to make, just.   This expression
which means "like home cooking," seems to have acquired
figurative quotation marks by the early 1900s. Of American origin, it was soon used by advertisers. (Compare the
pop song of World War II, "Ma, I Miss Your Apple Pie.")

Vance Packard in *The Hidden Persuaders* (1957) gives an

example of the effectiveness of this idea: "When the Mogen David wine people were seeking some way to add magic to their wine's sales appeal, they turned to motivation research via their agency. Psychiatrists and other probers listening to people talk at random about wine found that many related it to old family-centered or festive occasions. The campaign tied home and mother into the selling themes. One line was: 'the good old days—the home sweet home wine—the wine that grandma used to make.' As a result of these carefully 'motivated' slogans, the sales of Mogen David doubled within a year."

Which reminds me of the advertisement that proclaimed:

BUCKWHEAT CAKES
Like mother used to bake—$1.25
Like mother thought she made—$2.25.

LS/MFT.   Slogan for Lucky Strike cigarettes, current in the 1940s. The initials, used in radio ads, meant "Lucky Strike Means Fine Tobacco."

Makes you feel like a queen.   Slogan for the British product Summer County margarine, current in the 1960s. Barry Day, vice-chairman of McCann-Erickson Worldwide, pointed out that this slogan was originally used in the U.S. for Imperial margarine (like Summer County, a Unilever product): "The sudden magical appearance of the crown on the mother clever enough to use the brand made more sense. It was considered to be a successful brand property and used on several brands in other markets, irrespective of brand name. In none of the other cases was it markedly successful. The device seems to have been a piece of Americana that did not travel well."

The idea is not new. In November 1864 Tolstoy's wife Sonya wrote to him, "Without you, I am nothing. With you, I feel like a queen."

Man/woman who has everything, (the gift) for the. A slogan in use since the 1920s and 30s to promote a luxury item, inessential and overpriced —like a gold belly-button fluff remover. A salesman at the eponymous jewelry store in *Breakfast at Tiffany's* (film, 1961) produces something "for the lady and gentleman who have everything."

In January 1987 Alana Stewart was quoted as saying of her ex-husband Rod, the pop singer, "What do you give to the man who's had everyone?"

Milk from contented cows. Slogan for Carnation milk, from 1906. Elbridge A. Stuart launched Carnation evaporated milk in 1899. Seven years later he went to the Mahin Agency in Chicago to develop an advertising campaign. The copywriter was Helen Mar: 'Mr. Stuart gave me a description of the conditions under which Carnation was produced . . . the ever-verdant pastures of Washington and Oregon, where grazed the carefully kept Holstein herds that supplied the raw milk. He described in a manner worthy of Burton Holmes the picturesque background of these pastures from which danced and dashed the pure, sparkling waters to quench the thirst of the herds and render more tender the juicy grasses they fed on. He spoke of the shade of luxuriant trees under which the herds might rest. Remembering my lectures in medical college and recalling that milk produced in mental and physical ease is more readily digested—I involuntarily exclaimed, 'Ah! The milk of contented cows!' . . . 'That's our slogan' [said Mr. Stuart]."

And so it has remained—or almost, since the words on the can are usually *"From* contented cows."

Naughty but nice. The catch phrase in full is "It's naughty but it's nice." Partridge/*Slang* glosses it as "a reference to copulation since c. 1900; ex., a song that Minnie Schult sang and popularized in the U.S.A., 1890s." A 1939 film about a professor of classical music who accidentally wrote a popular song used "Naughty but Nice" as its title, as did various songs, notably one by Johnny Mercer and Harry Warren in *The Belle of New York* (film, 1952). Compare also "It's Foolish But It's Fun" (Gus Kahn and Robert Stolz) sung by Deanna Durbin in *Spring Parade* (1940).

Never underestimate the power of a woman.   Slogan for *Ladies' Home Journal,* from c. 1941. Gordon Page of N. W. Ayer and Son recalled: "It came off the back burner of a creative range where ideas simmer while the front burners are preoccupied with meeting closing dates. . . . It was just a more direct way of stating the case for the leading woman's magazine of the day. But always believing that you can do things with a twinkle that you can't do with a straight face, it was trotted to Leo Lionni. . . . It's largely *his* fault that you can't say 'never underestimate the power of *anything*' today without echoing the line." In fact, in 1981 the following ad appeared in *The New York Times:* "Ladies' Home Journalism—Never Underestimate Its Power."

Nine out of ten _____.   Favorite format phrase used by advertisers. "Nine out of ten screen stars use Lux Toilet Soap for their priceless smooth skins"—so ran a famous campaign that lasted for twenty years from 1927. Among the stars who were listed as Lux users were Fay Wray, Clara Bow, and Joan Crawford. Compare "four out of five people say Big John's Beans taste better" (ad, quoted 1977).

99 and 44/100 percent pure.   Slogan for Ivory Soap, from c. 1882. One of the most unwieldy but enduring slogans of all. In 1974 a gangster film with Richard Harris was entitled *99 and 44/100 Percent Dead.* For the benefit of non-Americans who would not understand the allusion, the film was later retitled *Call Harry Crown.* But *Variety* opined crisply that even the original version was "as clumsy as its title."

Now and forever. *Cats,* the longest-running musical in London's West End, has used this promotional line since at least 1987. Three films have been made with this title: 1934, with Gary Cooper; 1956, with Janette Scott; and 1983, with Cheryl Ladd. And there has been one hit song by Vera Lynn in 1954 (translated from the German). Indeed, the phrase enshrines an idea common to other languages. Basques demanding that Eta should stop its terror campaign (March 1989) bore a banner with the words, *"Paz ahora y para"* ("Peace now and forever").

Often a bridesmaid, but never a bride. This slogan for Listerine mouthwash, dating from c. 1923, and written by Milton Feasley is one of the best-known lines in advertising, written by Milton Feasley. There is, however, more than an echo of the British music-hall song "Why Am I Always a Bridesmaid?" made famous by Lily Morris (1917).

Priceless ingredient of every product is the honor and integrity of its maker, the. Slogan for Squibb drug products, from 1921. Before that year Squibb had never advertised to the public. The problem given to Raymond Rubicam, then a writer at N. W. Ayer and Son, was to produce a series of advertisements that would sell Squibb to the public and not offend the publicity-sensitive medical profession. David Ogilvy commented: "Raymond Rubicam's famous slogan . . . reminds me of my father's advice: When a company boasts about its integrity, or a woman about her virtue, avoid the former and cultivate the latter."

Put a tiger in your tank. The Esso Tiger had been around in the U.S. for a long time before 1964 when a cartoon version was introduced in the U.K. to promote Esso petroleum. It became a craze, with countless tiger tails adorning the gas caps of the nation's cars. Subsequently, with the slogan "Put a tiger in your tank," the idea spread even further afield. *"Mettez un tigre dans votre moteur"* appeared in France; in Germany, *"Pack den tiger in den tank."*

The slogan gave rise to numerous tiger derivatives: "If you feel like a tiger is in your throat, reach for Guardets lozenges." A hamburger stand advertised, "Put a tiger in your tummy." Tiger beer in the Japanese *Times* used the slogan, "Put a tiger in your tankard." Standard Rochester beer countered with, "Put a tankard in your tiger."

Perhaps the slogan owed something to the Muddy Waters song "(I Want to Put a) Tiger in Your Tank" (by W. Dixon), which he was performing by 1960 and which gave double meanings to a number of motoring phrases (not least in the title).

Reach for a Lucky instead of a sweet. Slogan for Lucky Strike cigarettes, current from the late 1920s. George Washington Hill of the American Tobacco Company was driving through New York City one day when he noticed a stout woman waiting to cross the street, eating a big piece of candy. A taxi pulled up alongside, in which a nice-looking woman was smoking a cigarette. The contrast inspired the slogan. Understandably, the confectionery industry wasn't very pleased, but this campaign apparently created more women smokers than any other promotion.

Real thing, it's the. There have been so many rivals to Coca-Cola that there has been a continuing necessity to maintain that Coke is the "real thing." This idea appeared in 1942 in the form, "The only thing like Coca-Cola is Coca-Cola itself." "It's the real thing" followed in 1970 and has proved one of the most enduring of the Coca-Cola slogans.

A 1982 Tom Stoppard play about love (as in "It's the real thing this time") was entitled *The Real Thing. OED2* has an example of this use—true love as distinct from infatuation—in 1857.

Some other Coke slogans include: "Thirst knows no season" (from 1922); "The pause that refreshes" (from 1929);

"It's the refreshing thing to do" (current 1937); "Things go better with Coke" (from 1963); "I'd like to buy the world a Coke" (from 1971—the jingle became a hit in its own right when retitled "I'd Like to Teach the World to Sing"); "Coke adds life" (from 1976); "Have a Coke and a smile" (current 1980).

When Coca-Cola started advertising in Peking, "Put a smile on your face" was translated as "Let your teeth rejoice." Odder still, the famous slogan "It's the real thing" came out as "The elephant bites the wax duck."

Say it with flowers. Henry Penn of Boston, Mass., was chairman of the National Publicity Committee of the Society of American Florists in 1917. He was discussing the need for a slogan with Major Patrick O'Keefe, head of an advertising agency. O'Keefe suggested, "Flowers are words that even a babe can understand"—a line he had found in a poetry book. Penn considered that too long. O'Keefe, agreeing, rejoined, "Why, you can say it with flowers in so many words." Mr. Penn's hand went *bang!* on the table. They had found their slogan. Later came several songs with the title.

See America first. Slogan for the Great Northern Railway Co., from c. 1914. This slogan was splashed all over the country and helped turn the tide of travel from the East to the West Coast. By 1916, it was the title of a show and a song by Cole Porter.

Snap! crackle! pop! Slogan for Kellogg's Rice Krispies, from c. 1928. A version earlier in the century had gone, "It pops! It snaps! It crackles!" The reference was to the little noises made by the crisped rice when milk was poured over it.

They laughed when I sat down at the piano, but when I started to play . . . ! Slogan for the U.S. School of Music piano tutor, from 1925. The copy underneath this headline was: "As the last notes of the 'Moonlight Sonata' died away, the room resounded with a sudden roar of applause. . . . Men shook my hand—wildly congratulated me—pounded me on the back in their enthusiasm! . . . And then I explained [how] I saw an interesting ad for the U.S. School of Music . . ."

This ad gave rise to various jokes: "They laughed when I sat down to play —someone had taken away the stool/how did I know the bathroom door was open/etc." John Caples, the copywriter, also came up with "They grinned when the waiter spoke to me in French—but their laughter changed to amazement at my reply" (presumably for another client).

Time to re-tire. Slogan for Fisk Rubber Co. tires, from 1907. Burr Griffin did the original sketch for this long-running pun of an ad, which showed a yawning youngster with candle, nightshirt—and tire. The original slogan was, "When it's time to re-tire, buy a Fisk."

Up, up and away . . . Originally from the comic strip "Superman," the phrase was used by Jim Webb as a song title in 1967 and, in the same year, was incorporated in the airline slogan "Up, up and away with TWA."

Superman was the brainchild of a teenage science-fiction addict, Jerry Siegel, in 1933. Five years later Superman appeared on the first cover (No. 1) of *Action Comics.* In 1940 he took to the radio airwaves on the Mutual Network, with Clayton "Bud" Collyer as the journalist Clark Kent who can turn into the Man of Steel whenever he is in a tight spot: "This looks like a job for . . . Superman! Now, off with these clothes! Up, up and awa-a-a-ay!" After appearing in film cartoons, Superman finally appeared as a live-action hero on the screen in a 1948 fifteen-episode serial. He was still on the big screen in the 1970s and 80s.

It was from the radio series, however, that the exciting phrases came:

Announcer: Kellogg's Pep . . . the super-delicious cereal . . . presents . . . *The Adventures of Superman!* Faster than a speeding bullet [*ricochet*]! More powerful than a locomotive [*locomotive roar*]! Able to leap tall buildings at a single bound [*rushing wind*]! Look! Up in the sky!

Voice 1: It's a bird!

Voice 2: It's a plane!

Voice 3: It's Superman!

Announcer: Yes, it's Superman—a strange visitor from another planet, who came to earth with powers and abilities far beyond those of mortal men. Superman!—who can change the course of mighty rivers, bend steel with his bare hands, and who—disguised as Clark Kent, mild-mannered reporter for a great metropolitan newspaper—fights a never-ending battle for truth, justice, and the American way.

We never sleep. Slogan for Pinkerton's national detective agency, which opened its first office in 1850 in Chicago (and which—through its open eye symbol—*may* have given us the term "private eye"). Was there an echo of this in the line chosen to promote Citibank's new twenty-four-hour service in 1977, "The Citi Never Sleeps"—apart, that is, from an allusion to the 1953 film title *The City That Never Sleeps*?

What becomes a legend most? This slogan for Blackglama mink (current in 1976) was the headline for a series of ads showing mink coats worn by "legendary" figures, including Margot Fonteyn, Martha Graham, Rudolf Nureyev (all three together in one ad), Shirley MacLaine, Ethel Merman, and Lillian Hellman.

When you got it, flaunt it. In c. 1969 Braniff airlines used this headline over ads featuring celebrities such as Sonny Liston, Andy Warhol, and Joe Namath. The line was proba-

bly picked up from the 1967 Mel Brooks movie *The Producers,* where it appears as, "That's it, baby! When you got
it, flaunt it."

Where's the beef?   A classic example of an advertising
slogan turning into a political catch phrase. In 1984, the
Wendy International hamburger chain promoted its wares
with TV commercials, one of which showed elderly
women eyeing a small hamburger on a huge bun—a
Wendy competitor's product. "It certainly is a big bun,"
asserted one. "It's a very big fluffy bun," the second
agreed. But the third asked, "Where's the beef?"
    The line widely caught on. Walter Mondale, running for
the Democratic presidential nomination, used it to question the substance of his rival Gary Hart's policies.

With a name like Smucker's it has to be good.   Slogan for
Smucker's preserves, from c. 1960. Lois Wyse of Wyse Advertising, New York, recalled (1981): "Slogans come and go
but [this one] has become a part of the language. I wrote it
for a company with an unusual name in answer to a challenge from Marc Wyse, who said he didn't feel our
Smucker advertising differed from the competition. The
real job, however, was not thinking up the slogan but selling it to Paul Smucker. The then-sales manager said, 'If you
run that line, Paul, we'll be out of business in six months!'
But it's still in use after twenty years."

You don't have to be Jewish . . .   "You don't have to be
Jewish to love Levy's Real Jewish Rye" was used in an ad
campaign current in 1967. Pictures of patently non-Jewish
people (Indians, Chinese, Eskimos) reinforced the words.
A show of Jewish humor titled *You Don't Have to Be Jewish*
ran on Broadway in 1965, which is probably where it all
started.
    Informal additions to the Levy bread posters were
many. They included: ". . . to be offended by this ad/to

be called one/to go to Columbia University, but it helps/to wear Levi's jeans/to be circumcised . . ."

You give us twenty minutes, we'll give you the world. Many all-news radio stations use this slogan. In 1982, CNN, the satellite TV-news channel, was declaring, "Give us *eighteen* minutes and we'll give you the world."

You know what comes between me and my Calvins? . . . Nothing. Brooke Shields, all of fifteen years of age, said this in a Calvin Klein jeans ad in 1980, and the line is remembered for its suggestiveness.

You'll wonder where the yellow went when you brush your teeth with Pepsodent. Slogan, current in the 1950s. An appeal to vanity rather than health, but curiously memorable.

You press the button, we do the rest. Slogan for Kodak cameras, current 1890. "It was literally edited out of a long piece of copy by George Eastman himself—one of the greatest advertising ideas" (Julian Lewis Watkins, *The 100 Greatest Advertisements*, 1959).

You, too, can have a body like mine. "Charles Atlas" was born Angelo Siciliano in Italy in 1894 and died in America in 1972. He won the title of "The World's Most Perfectly Developed Man" in a 1922 contest sponsored by Bernarr Macfadden and his *Physical Culture* magazine. Later he started giving mail-order body-building lessons. A famous promotional cartoon strip showed "How Joe's body brought him FAME instead of SHAME."

"Hey! Quit kicking sand in our faces," Joe says to a bully on the beach. Then he takes a Charles Atlas course and ends up with a girl by his side who says, "Oh, Joe! You are a real man after all!"

Like Joe, Atlas had himself been "a skinny, timid weakling of only ninety-eight pounds" (hence the expression I was a ninety-eight pound weakling). "I didn't know what real health and strength were. I was afraid to fight— ashamed to be seen in a bathing suit," said Atlas. But after watching a lion rippling its muscles at the zoo, he developed a method of pitting one muscle against another, which he called Dynamic Tension.

You've come a long way, baby (to get where you got to today). Slogan for Virginia Slims cigarettes (from 1968) that rode on the feminist mood of the times in selling to women smokers. Indeed, the phrase has also been used on woman's rights posters. One shows a woman giving a karate chop to a man's head. An article by Julie Baumgold with the title "You've Come a Long Way, Baby" appeared in *New York* magazine on June 9, 1969.

A song with the title followed in 1971. After the failure of the Equal Rights Amendment in 1982, a T-shirt appeared bearing the words, "I Haven't Come a Long Way."

8

THE LATE UNPLEASANTNESS

A euphemism for the previous war or recent hostilities, "the late unpleasantness" was introduced by David Ross in Ekkoes from Kentucky *(1868). As "Petroleum V. Nasby," he referred to the recently ended Civil War as "the late onpleasantniss," and the coinage spread. It still survives. "Here, for instance, is Dan Rather, America's father figure, on the hotline to Panama during the late unpleasantness [an invasion] . . ." (London* Independent, *January 20, 1990).*

Here are more military murmurings:

Abolish the draft. One of the antidraft slogans from the Vietnam War, c. 1968.

America, love it or leave it. One of the few memorable patriotic slogans from the era of the Vietnam War was "America, love it or leave it." This was probably inspired by the song "Love Me or Leave Me" (1928, hit version 1955), although the semiproverbial, semijocular farewell,

"I must love you and leave you," has existed since the nineteenth century. *Love 'Em and Leave 'Em* was the title of a 1927 Louise Brooks film.

Backs to the wall.   This phrase, meaning "up against it," dates back to 1535 according to the *OED2* and was most memorably used when, on March 21, 1918, the Germans launched their last great offensive of World War I. On April 12, Sir Douglas Haig (1861–1928), the British Commander-in-Chief on the western front, issued an order for his troops to stand firm: "Every position must be held to the last man: there must be no retirement. With our backs to the wall, and believing in the justice of our cause, each one of us must fight on to the end. The safety of our Homes and the Freedom of mankind alike depends on the conduct of each one of us at this critical moment."

A. J. P. Taylor in his *English History 1914–45* (1966) commented: "In England this sentence was ranked with Nelson's last message. At the front, the prospect of staff officers fighting with their backs to the walls of their luxurious châteaux had less effect."

Daddy, what did *you* do in the Great War?   This line was used on recruiting posters in World War I. The accompanying picture showed a distraught family man puzzling over a reply to the daughter on his knee. It became a catch phrase in the form, "What did you do in the Great War, Daddy?" and gave rise to such comebacks as "Shut up, you little bastard. Get the Bluebell and go and clean my medals" (Partridge/*Catch Phrases*). *What Did You Do in the War, Daddy?* was the title of a film (1966).

Eyeball to eyeball.   Meaning in close confrontation. Use of this expression is of comparatively recent origin. In the missile crisis of October 1962, the U.S. took a tough line when the Soviet Union placed missiles on Cuban soil. After a tense few days, the Soviets withdrew. Safire records that Secretary of State Dean Rusk (b. 1909) was speaking to an

ABC news correspondent, John Scali, on October 24, and said, "Remember when you report this, that, eyeball to eyeball, they blinked first." Columnists Charles Bartlett and Stewart Alsop then helped to popularize this as "We're eyeball to eyeball and the other fellow just blinked."

Before this, "eyeball to eyeball" was an African-American serviceman's idiom. Safire quotes a reply given by the all-Black 24th Infantry Regiment to an inquiry from General MacArthur's headquarters in Korea (November 1950): "Do you have contact with the enemy?" "We is eyeball to eyeball."

Firstest with the mostest. To describe anything as "the mostest" might seem exclusively American. However, the *OED2* finds English dialect use in the 1880s, and Partridge recognizes its use as a jocular superlative without restricting it to the U.S. As such, it is a consciously ungrammatical way of expressing extreme degree.

Whether this was consciously the case with the Confederate General Nathan B. Forrest (1821–1877) is doubtful. He could hardly read or write, but he managed to say that the way to win battles was to be "firstest with the mostest," or that you needed to "git thar fustest with the mostest." Bartlett gives this last as the usual rendering of the more formal "Get there first with the most men."

Irving Berlin's musical *Call Me Madam* (1950) has a song titled "The Hostess with the Mostes' on the Ball."

Hold the fort. "Hold the fort" can mean "Look after this place while I'm away," "Hang on, relief is at hand." The latter has its origin in the Civil War. General William T. Sherman signaled words to this effect to General John M. Corse at the Battle of Allatoona, Georgia, on October 5, 1864. What he actually semaphored from Keneshaw Mountain was: "Sherman says hold fast. We are coming" (Mencken) or "Hold out. Relief is coming" (Bartlett).

The phrase in its present form was popularized in the hymn/gospel song written by Philip Paul Bliss in c. 1870

("Ho, My Comrades, See the Signal!" in *The Charm*). This was introduced by the evangelists Moody and Sankey (but not written by them, as is sometimes supposed):

> "Hold the fort, for I am coming,"
>   Jesus signals still;
> Wave the answer back to heaven,
>   "By Thy grace we will."

Holocaust, the. Phrase for the mass murder of Jews and the attempted elimination of European Jewry by the German Nazis during the 1939–1945 war. A holocaust is an all-consuming conflagration and may not be the most accurate description of what happened to the estimated six million Jews under the Nazis, though many were burned as well as gassed.

The term seems to have arisen because "genocide" hardly sounded emotive enough. The popular use of "the Holocaust" for this purpose dates only from 1965, when A. Donat published a book on the subject entitled *The Holocaust Kingdom*. However, *OED2* has it in this sense in the *News Chronicle* by 1942, as well as in various other 1940s citations. As early as 1951 the Israeli Knesset had "The Holocaust and Ghetto Uprising Day"—translated from *Yom ha-Sho'ah*. The use was finally settled when a TV miniseries called *Holocaust* (1978) was shown and caused controversy in many countries.

Well before *that* happened, Eric Partridge was advising in his *Usage and Abusage* (1947): "Holocaust is 'destruction by fire': do not synonymize it with *disaster*. Moreover, it is properly an ecclesiastical technicality." In fact, the word derives from the Greek words *holos* and *kaustos,* meaning "wholly burnt," and was for many years used to describe a sacrifice or offering that was burnt. Some translations of the Bible use it to describe Abraham's preparations to slay his son Isaac.

The term has also been used to describe the mass slaughter of the people of Cambodia at the hands of the Khmer Rouge in the 1970s.

I shall return.   Forced to pull out of the Philippines by the Japanese, General Douglas MacArthur left Corregidor on March 11, 1942. He made his commitment to return at the railway station in Adelaide, South Australia. Carlos P. Romulo, the Filipino diplomat who later twice became his country's foreign minister, suggested the phrase to MacArthur. Romulo, who died at age 86 in 1984, had been a journalist before World War II and served as a brigadier general on MacArthur's staff.

I want *you* for the U.S. Army.   The most famous recruiting slogan of all was "Your country needs you." It accompanied a picture of Field Marshal Lord Kitchener with staring eyes and pointing finger and was used in Britain at the outbreak of World War I in 1914. The idea was widely imitated, and in the U.S. during World War I James Montgomery Flagg produced a poster of a pointing Uncle Sam with the legend, "I want *you* for the U.S. Army." There was also a version by Howard Chandler Christy featuring a woman with a mildly come-hither look saying, "I want you for the Navy."

I was only obeying orders.   The Charter of the International Military Tribunal at Nuremberg (1945–46) specifically excluded the traditional German defense of "superior order." Nevertheless, the plea was much advanced.

This giving-up of responsibility was summed up in the catch phrase "I was only obeying orders," often used grotesquely in parody of such buck-passing. Not that everyone seemed aware of this. From *The New York Times* (July 6, 1983): "Herbert Bechtold, a German-born officer in the [U.S.] counterintelligence who became [the "handler" of Klaus Barbie, the Nazi war criminal] was asked if he questioned the morality of hiring a man like Barbie by the

United States. 'I am not in a position to pass judgment on that,' Mr. Bechtold replied. 'I was just following orders.' "

The defense was also advanced during Watergate (1973–74) and Irangate (1987).

Killing fields, the.   Name for any place given over to mass executions, sometimes also referred to as "killing grounds." The phrase was popularized by the 1984 film titled *The Killing Fields* concerning the mass murders carried out by the communist Khmer Rouge, under Pol Pot, in Cambodia between 1975–78. An estimated three million were killed by the Khmer Rouge. The mass graves were discovered in April 1979.

In the film the phrase refers literally to paddy fields where prisoners were first forced to work and then callously shot. The film, based on the article "The Death and Life of Dith Pran" by Sydney Schanberg, published in *The New York Times Magazine* (January 20, 1980), tells of the journalist's quest for reunion with his former assistant. The phrase appears in the beginning of the article: "In July of 1975—two months after Pran and I had been forced apart on April 20—an American diplomat who had known Pran wrote me a consoling letter. The diplomat, who had served in Phnom Penh, knew the odds of anyone emerging safely from a country that was being transformed into a society of terror and purges and 'killing fields.' " So it appears that the coinage is due to the unnamed diplomat. Haing S. Ngor, who played Pran in the film, wrote a book called *Surviving the Killing Fields* (1988). William Shawcross, author of two books on Cambodia, says that he had never heard the phrase used in this or any other connection until the film was in preparation.

Never again!   A popular cry during and after World War I. Winston Churchill in his *The Second World War* (Vol. 1) says of the French, "With one passionate spasm [they cried] never again." Later, in the mid-1960s, it became the slogan of the militant Jewish Defense League —referring to the HOLOCAUST (this chapter). A stone monument erected near the birthplace of Adolf Hitler at Branau, Austria, in 1989 (the centennial of his birth) bore the lines "For Peace, Freedom and Democracy—Never Again Fascism [*Nie wieder Faschismus*]—Millions of Dead Are a Warning."

No more war. A recurring slogan of the twentieth century. At the UN in 1965, Pope Paul VI said, quoting President Kennedy, that "mankind must put an end to war, or war will put an end to mankind. . . . No more war, never again war." (He said this in Italian.)

Earlier (in 1928), Winston Churchill used the phrase at the end of a letter to Lord Beaverbrook (quoted in Martin Gilbert's biography of Churchill, Vol. 5). In *Goodbye to Berlin* (1939), Christopher Isherwood describes a Nazi book-burning. The books are from a "small liberal pacifist publisher." One of the Nazis holds up a book called *Nie Wieder Krieg* as though it were "a nasty kind of reptile. 'No More War!' a fat, well-dressed woman laughs scornfully and savagely. 'What an idea!' "

Spread alarm and despondency, to. To have the effect of destabilization, purposely or not. During World War II Lt. Col. Vladimir Peniakoff (1897–1951) ran a small raiding and reconnaissance force on the British side, which became known as "Popski's Private Army." In his book *Private Army* (1950) he wrote: "A message came on the wireless for me. It said 'SPREAD ALARM AND DESPONDENCY' . . . The date was, I think, May 18th, 1942." When a German invasion was thought to be imminent at the beginning of July 1940, Winston Churchill had issued an "admonition" to "His Majesty's servants in high places . . . to report, or if necessary remove, any officers or officials who are found to be consciously exercising a disturbing or depressing influence, and whose talk is calculated to spread alarm and despondency." Prosecutions for doing this did, indeed, follow. The phrase goes back to the Army Act of

1879: "Every person subject to military law who . . . spreads reports calculated to create unnecessary alarm or despondency . . . shall . . . be liable to suffer penal servitude."

This is/was war. This is very serious, and justifies the particular course adopted. Wilson Goode, mayor of Philadelphia, defended a police firebombing raid that went disastrously wrong, saying, "This was not child's play. This was war" (*Time*, May 15, 1985). After the Heysel football stadium disaster: "Said a Belgian Red Cross rescue worker: 'This is not sport. This is war' " (*Time*, June 10, 1985). Sign outside the Las Vegas Hilton promoting a big fight (February 1989): "THIS TIME IT'S WAR. TYSON VS. BRUNO."

Compare this earlier version from President Nixon on September 15, 1972: "We are all in it together. This is a war. We take a few shots and it will be over. . . . I wouldn't want to be on the other side right now. Would you?" (*The White House Transcripts*, 1974).

Tora! Tora! Tora! The title of a film (1970) about the Japanese raid on Pearl Harbor in 1941. *"Tora-tora-tora"* (*tora* meaning "tiger") was the signal given by pilot Mituso Fuchida (who was leading the Japanese attack) to confirm that the U.S. fleet was being taken by surprise.

Walls have ears, the. This was the neatest encapsulation of the security theme in World War II. Others were "Careless talk costs lives"; "Enemy ears are listening"; "Tittle tattle lost the battle"; and "Keep it under your hat/stetson."

The idea of inanimate objects being able to hear is a very old one—even before 1727 when Jonathan Swift wrote, "Walls have tongues, and hedges ears." In Vitzentzos Kornaros's epic poem *Erotokritos* (c. 1645) there is the following couplet (here translated from the Greek):

For the halls of our masters have ears and hear,
And the walls of the palace have eyes and watch.

9

PLAY IT AGAIN, SAM

In the beginning was the image; the word came second. The advent of movie sound in 1929 was a unique transformation in a medium of communication. By 1942 moviegoers were even hearing things that were not said.

As is widely known, neither Humphrey Bogart nor Ingrid Bergman actually used the phrase "Play it again, Sam" in the film Casablanca. *All one need say now is that the saying was well-established by the time Woody Allen thus titled his play (1969, filmed 1972) about a film critic who is abandoned by his wife and obtains the help of Bogart's "shade."*

More lines from the movies—most of which were actually said:

And so we say farewell . . .   The travelogues made by James A. Fitzpatrick were a supporting feature of films from 1925 onward. With the advent of sound, the commentaries to "Fitzpatrick Traveltalks" became noted for their closing words:

> And it's from this paradise of the Canadian Rockies that we reluctantly say farewell to beautiful Banff. . . .
>
> And as the midnight sun lingers on the skyline of the city, we most reluctantly say farewell to Stockholm, Venice of the North. . . .
>
> With its picturesque impressions indelibly fixed in our memory, it is time to conclude our visit and reluctantly say farewell to Hong Kong, the hub of the Orient. . . .

Ars gratia artis. This motto (hoping to carry the force of a slogan) has been used by the Metro-Goldwyn-Mayer film company since c. 1916. Howard Dietz (1896–1983), director of publicity and advertising with the original Goldwyn Pictures company, had left Columbia University not long before. When asked to design a trademark, he based it on the university's lion and added the Latin words, meaning "art for art's sake," underneath. It might be pushing it a bit for Hollywood, but there you are.

When Samuel Goldwyn retired to make way for the merger of Metropolitan with the interests of Louis B. Mayer, the trademark and motto were carried over in what has become known since as Metro-Goldwyn-Mayer. "Goldwyn Pictures Griddle the Earth" was a no-doubt apocryphal idea for a slogan said to have originated with Goldwyn himself.

Beulah, peel me a grape! This expression of dismissive unconcern was first said by Mae West to a maid in the film *I'm No Angel* (1933) after a male admirer had stormed out on her. It has had some wider currency since then but it's almost always used as a quotation.

Big Chill generation, the. In 1983 a film was released called *The Big Chill*—"the story of eight old friends searching for something they lost, and finding that all they needed was each other." Its slogan was "In a cold world you need your friends to keep you warm." *Halliwell's Film Guide* (1987) called it "a wry, satirical comedy, which seems to be nostalgic for the sixties," but added, "The movie was too American to become an international hit."

From the *Washington Post* (August 1, 1985): "A performance by the Temptations or the Four Tops is always a big thrill for the 'Big Chill' generation." From a report on Douglas Ginsburg's rejected nomination as a member of the U.S. Supreme Court, in *Time* (November 16, 1987): "Although Ginsburg's indiscretion may have been common among members of the Big Chill generation, his confessions fatally undermined his support among the Capitol Hill conservatives who had lobbied so hard for his nomination."

Blond bombshell.   Used to describe any blond woman of dynamic personality, usually a film star, show-business figure, or model. The original was Jean Harlow, who appeared in the 1933 film *Bombshell.* In Britain—presumably so as not to suggest that it was a war film—the title was changed to *Blonde Bombshell.*

Blue Velvet.   The title of David Lynch's disturbing film (1986) about drugs and menace alludes to both the song "Blue Velvet" (1951, Wayne and Morris), which is sung in the film by a nightclub singer, and to the name for "a mixture of paregoric, which contains opium, and . . . an antihistamine, to be injected" (as described in *DOAS)*

Close encounter of the ____ kind, a.   Format phrase following the title of the Steven Spielberg film *Close Encounters of the Third Kind* (1977), said to be taken from the categories used to denote UFOs. A "close encounter of the first kind" would be a simple UFO sighting; a "close encounter of the second kind" would be evidence of an alien landing; and a "close encounter of the third kind" would be actual contact with aliens. The categories were

devised by UFO researcher J. Allen Hyhek (source: Rick
Meyers, *The Great Science Fiction Films*).

Used allusively to describe intimacy: "For a close encounter of the fourth kind, ring . . ."; "Polanski's new
movie: Close Encounters with the Third Grade"—graffiti,
quoted 1982.

Come up and see me sometime.   Mae West (1892–1980)
had a notable stage hit on Broadway with her play *Diamond Lil* (first performed April 9, 1928). When she appeared in the 1933 film version entitled *She Done Him
Wrong,* she said to a very young Cary Grant (playing a coy
undercover policeman), "You know, I always did like a
man in uniform. And that one fits you grand. Why don't
you come up some time and see me? I'm home every
evening."

The words of the catch phrase have been rearranged to
make them easier to say. That is how W. C. Fields says
them to Mae West in the film *My Little Chickadee* (1939),
and she herself took to saying them in the rearranged
version.

Come with me to the Casbah.   A line associated with the
film *Algiers* (1938) and its star, Charles Boyer, who supposedly said it to Hedy Lamarr. Boyer impersonators used it;
the film was laughed at because of it; but nowhere is it said
in the film. It was simply a Hollywood legend that grew up.
Boyer himself denied he had ever said it and thought it
had been invented by a press agent.

Days of Wine and Roses.   The title of the film (1962)
about an alcoholic (though the phrase is often used to
evoke romance) comes from Ernest Dowson's poem *"Vi-
tae Summa Brevis"*: "They are not long, the days of wine
and roses."

Drive/go/ride/sail off into the sunset, to.   To end happily,
and probably romantically. Derived from the visual cliché

of the silent-film era when a united couple would often do just that at the end of a story. Inevitably, used when Ronald Reagan retired from the White House: "As Reagan rides off into the sunset we offer two opposing verdicts on his eight years in office. . . ." (London *Observer*, January 15, 1989). *OED2* 's first citation is from Harry Harrison's novel *Technicolor Time Machine* (1967): "He takes the girl with him and together they sail into the sunset to a new life."

Drop the gun, Looey!   Alistair Cooke, writing in *Six Men* (1977), remarked of Humphrey Bogart: "He gave currency to another phrase with which the small fry of the English-speaking world brought the neighborhood sneak to heel: 'Drop the gun, Looey!' " Quite how Bogart did this Cooke does not reveal. We have Bogart's word for it: "I never said, 'Drop the gun, Louie' " (quoted in Ezra Goodman, *Bogey: The Good-Bad Guy*).

It's just another of those lines that people would like to have heard spoken but that never were. At the end of *Casablanca* (1942), what Bogart says to Claude Rains (playing Captain Louis Renault) is, "Not so fast, Louis." Ironically, it is Rains who says, "Put that gun down."

End of civilization as we know it, the.   A Hollywood cliché, said when people are under threat by invaders from Mars, or wherever: "This could mean the end of civilization as we know it. . . ."

The deathless phrase is said in *Citizen Kane* (1941). Orson Welles as the newspaper magnate Kane is shown giving a prewar press conference: "I've talked with the responsible leaders of the Great Powers—England, France, Germany, and Italy. They're too intelligent to embark on a project which would mean the end of civilization as we now know it. You can take my word for it: there'll be no war!"

A film was announced in 1977 with the title *The End of*

Civilization As We Know It, but it does not seem to have been released. Could this be the end of . . . ?

5, 4, 3, 2, 1. A case of life imitating art. The backward countdown to a rocket launch is said to have been first thought of by the German film director Fritz Lang (1890–1976). He thought it would make things more suspenseful if the count was reversed—5, 4, 3, 2, 1—so, in his 1928 film *By Rocket to the Moon* (sometimes known by its German title, *Frau im Mond,* or "The Woman in the Moon"), he established the routine for future real-life space shots. The 1931 novel *By Rocket to the Moon* (by Otto Willi Gail) does not include the phrase, however.

Frankly, my dear, I don't give a damn. In the last scene of the film *Gone With the Wind* (1939), Scarlett O'Hara is finally abandoned by her husband, Rhett Butler. Although she believes she can get him back, her entreaty, "Where shall I go? What shall I do?" is met with "Frankly, my dear, I don't give a damn."

This was only allowed on the screen after months of negotiation with the Hays Office, which controlled film censorship. In those days the word "damn" was forbidden usage in Hollywood under Section V. (1) of the Hays Code, even if it was what Margaret Mitchell had written in her novel (though she hadn't included the "frankly").

Sidney Howard's original draft of the screenplay was accordingly changed to "Frankly, my dear, I don't care." The scene was shot with both versions of the line, and the producer, David Selznick, argued at great length with the censors over which was to be used. He did this not least because he thought he would look a fool if the famous line was excluded. He also wanted to show how faithful the film was to the novel.

Selznick argued that the *Oxford English Dictionary* described "damn" not as an oath but as a vulgarism, that many women's magazines used the word, and that preview audiences had expressed disappointment when the line was omitted. The censors suggested "darn" instead. Selznick finally won the day—but because he was technically in breach of the Hays Code he was fined five thousand dollars. The line still didn't sound quite right: Clark Gable, as Rhett, had to put the emphasis, unnaturally, on "give" rather than on "damn."

Go ahead, make my day.   In March 1985 President Ronald Reagan told the American Business Conference, "I have my veto pen drawn and ready for any tax increase that Congress might even think of sending up. And I have only one thing to say to the tax increasers: Go ahead— make my day."

For once he was not quoting from one of his own film roles, or from old Hollywood. The pithy line was originally said by Clint Eastwood, brandishing a .44 Magnum, to a gunman he was holding at bay in *Sudden Impact* (1983). At the end of the film he says to another villain, similarly armed, "Come on, make my day." In neither case does he add "punk," as is sometimes thought.

The phrase may have been picked up by Reagan's speechwriters after it appeared in a parody of the *New York Post* put together by editors—many of them anti-Reagan—in the autumn of 1984. Reagan was shown starting a nuclear war by throwing down this dare to the Kremlin (information from *Time,* March 25, 1985).

Gone With the Wind.   The title of the 1939 film, based on Margaret Mitchell's 1936 novel, is taken from Ernest Dowson's poem *"Non Sum Qualis Eram"* (1896): "I have forgot much, Cynara! Gone with the wind . . ." The title refers to the South before the Civil War, as is made clear by the on-screen prologue to the film: 'There was a land of Cavaliers and Cotton Fields called the Old South. Here in this patrician world the Age of Chivalry took its last bows. Here was the last ever seen of the Knights and their Ladies fair, of Master and Slave. Look for it only in books, for it is no

more than a dream remembered, a Civilization gone with
the wind . . ."

Hard Day's Night, A.   The title of the Beatles' first feature film (1964) was apparently decided toward the end of
filming when Ringo Starr used the phrase to describe a
"heavy" night they had had (Ray Coleman, *John Lennon*,
1984). In fact, what Ringo must have done was use the title
of the Lennon and McCartney song (presumably already
written if it was toward the end of filming) in a conversa-
tional way. Indeed, Hunter Davies in *The Beatles* (1968)
noted "Ringo Starr came out with the phrase, though John
had used it earlier in a poem." It certainly sounds like a
Lennonism.

It has had some general use subsequently as a catch
phrase meaning that one has had a very tiring time.

Heaven's Gate.   Michael Cimino's 1980 film with this title
is famous for having lost more money than any other film
to date, having cost some $34 million. In it, "Heaven's
Gate" is the name of a roller-skating rink used by settlers
and immigrants in Wyoming in 1891. Conceivably, the
name is meant to be taken as an ironic one for the rough
situation many of the characters find themselves in as they
arrive to start a new life.

The idea of a gate to heaven goes back to the Bible. For
example, Genesis 28:17 has: "This is none other but the
house of God, and this is the gate of heaven." Psalms 78:23
has: "He commanded the clouds from above, and opened
the doors of heaven." Shakespeare uses the phrase twice.
In *Cymbeline* (Act II, scene iii, line 20), there is the song,
"Hark, hark, the lark at heaven's gate sings," and Sonnet
29 has, "Like to the lark at break of day arising/ From
sullen earth sings hymns at heaven's gate."

Steven Bach cites more possible sources in his book
about the making of the film *(Final Cut,* 1985). William
Blake in *Jerusalem* (1820) wrote:

> I give you the end of a golden string,
> Only wind it into a ball:
> It will lead you in at Heaven's gate,
> Built in Jerusalem's wall.

Robert Browning uses the phrase, and there is a poem by Wallace Stevens with the title "The Worms at Heaven's Gate."

Here's another fine mess you've gotten me into!   The anguished cry of Oliver Hardy after another of Stan Laurel's blunders. It managed to instate itself as one of the few film catch phrases because there were a sufficient number of Laurel and Hardy features for it to register with audiences. One of their thirty-minute features (released in 1930) was actually called *Another Fine Mess*.

Here's looking at you, kid!   This line, said by Humphrey Bogart to Ingrid Bergman in the Paris flashback sequence of the film *Casablanca* (1942), becomes a symbol of the happier days in the relationship of Rick and Ilse. It had previously been a drinker's toast, like "Cheers!" or "Here's mud in your eye!," but has now been turned into a catch phrase by Humphrey Bogart impersonators.

I Cover the Waterfront   The title of a film (1933) about a newspaper reporter, it was based on a book (1932) by journalist Max Miller exposing corruption on the waterfront—hence "cover" in the journalistic sense. The song with this title (by John W. Green and Ed Heyman), sung by Billie Holiday, is unconnected with the film and sounds as if it might be about laying paving stones. "To cover the waterfront" has come to mean "to cover all aspects of a topic." In *The Wise Wound* (1978) by Penelope Shuttle and Peter Redgrove, "She's covering the waterfront" is listed among slang expressions for menstruation.

If you want anything, just whistle. This is derived from lines in the film *To Have and Have Not* (1944). What Lauren Bacall says to Humphrey Bogart (and not the other way around) is: "You know you don't have to act with me, Steve. You don't have to say anything, and you don't have to do anything. Not a thing. Oh, maybe just whistle. You know how to whistle, don't you, Steve? You just put your lips together and blow."

I'm going to make him an offer he can't refuse. In 1969 Mario Puzo (b. 1920) published his novel about the Mafia called *The Godfather*. It gave to the language a new expression that, as far as one can tell, was Puzo's invention. Johnny Fontane, a singer, desperately wants a part in a movie and goes to see his godfather, Don Corleone, for help. All the contracts have been signed and there is no chance of the studio chief changing his mind. Still, the godfather promises Fontane he will get him the part. As he says of the studio chief, "He's a businessman. I'll make him an offer he can't refuse."

In the 1971 film this was turned into the following dialogue:

"In a month from now this Hollywood big shot's going to give you what you want."

"Too late, they start shooting in a week."

"I'm going to make him an offer he can't refuse."

In 1973 Jimmy Helms had a hit with the song "Gonna Make You an Offer You Can't Refuse."

_____ is _____. Slogan format. The film *You Only Live Twice* (1967) was promoted with the slogan, "Sean Connery *is* James Bond"—surely debatable at the best of times and only likely to encourage a regrettable tendency, particularly among journalists, to confuse actors with their roles. Other examples: "Paul Hogan *is* Crocodile Dundee" (1987); "Phil Collins *is* Buster" (title of a video about the making of the film *Buster*, 1988); and "Domingo *is* Otello," ad in *Los Angeles Magazine*, March 1989.

It's absolutely vital to both the character and the integrity of the script. Actresses and actors invariably answer something like this to questions about nudity and appearing nude in a film or play. Actress Glenda Jackson suggested that the remark was usually made in reply to a reporter's question, "Is there any nudity in this film?"— "Yes, but it is absolutely vital to the character and the part." *The Naff Sex Guide* (1984) gave as one of the "naff things starlets say": "Yes, I would appear nude, as long as I trusted the director and the integrity of the script demanded it."

Alternative responses to the nudity question include, "I don't mind if it's *relevant* to the script" or ". . . if it's done in a meaningful way." Lord Delfont, the British impresario, is quoted by Hunter Davies in *The Grades* (1981) as saying, "I do allow four-letter words and nudity in my films, if they are in the right context, if it has integrity."

I've never believed in anything so much in all my life. Film scriptwriter's cliché, though perhaps not too painful as clichés go. An example occurs in *Dangerous Moonlight* (U.K., 1941). In Henry Fielding's novel *Tom Jones,* (1749) we find exactly the same format: "I will bear no jesting with this lady's character." "Jesting . . . d—n me if ever I was more earnest in my life."

I wasn't born yesterday. *OED2* has this as an established saying by 1757—meaning I'm no fool; I'm not as stupid as I may appear. Popularized by *Born Yesterday,* the title of a play (1946) memorably filmed (1951). In Garson Kanin's script, Judy Holliday plays an ignorant girl who wins out in the end.

Just when you thought it was safe to _____. The film *Jaws 2* (1978)—a sequel to the successful shark saga—was promoted with the line, "Just when you thought it was safe to go back in the water . . ." A graffito in 1979 was "Jaws 3 —just when you thought it was safe to go to the toilet."

Let's do the show (right here in the barn)! This is taken to be a staple line in the films featuring the young Mickey Rooney and Judy Garland from 1939 onward. It had several forms: "Hey! I've got it! Why don't we put on a show?" "Hey kids! We can put on the show in the backyard!" "Let's do the show right here in the barn!"

In *Babes in Arms* (1939) Rooney and Garland play the teenage children of retired vaudeville players who decide to put on a big show of their own. Alas, they do not actually say any of the above lines, though they do express their determination to "put on a show." In whatever form, the line became a film cliché, now used only with amused affection.

Let's get out of here! Hardly a mighty line but, according to the *Guinness Book of Film Facts and Feats* (1985), "a recent survey of 150 American features of the period 1938–74 showed that it was used at least once in 84 percent of Hollywood productions and more than once in 17 percent." Hence, it is nominated as "the most hackneyed line in movie scripts." One would guess that "Let's go!" is probably not far behind.

Let's go to a movie. This was a propaganda slogan for the motion picture industry in the 1940s when it was feeling the first hot breath of competition from TV.

Love means never having to say you're sorry. This phrase was used in the film, in the book, and as a promotional tag for the film, but it remains a curiously empty line. In the last moments of the film *Love Story* (1970), Ryan O'Neal says it to Ray Milland, who plays his father. He is quoting his student wife (Ali MacGraw) who has just died young in this three-handkerchief weepie. Eric Segal, who wrote the script, also produced a novelization of the story in which the line appears as the penultimate sentence, in the form "Love means *not ever* having to say you're sorry."

The insidious nature of the line is best demonstrated by

the parodies that followed: a graffito (quoted 1974) stated, "A vasectomy means never having to say you're sorry"; the film *The Abominable Dr. Phibes* (1971) was promoted with the slogan, "Love means never having to say you're ugly."

Man's gotta do what a man's gotta do, a.   Partridge/*Catch Phrases* dates this from c. 1945. A correspondent recalls hearing it in a wartime concert party in the U.K. and suggests it came out of some late 1930s Western (Hopalong Cassidy?) or an American cartoon strip.

In the Alan Ladd film *Shane* (1953), which was based on a novel by Jack Shaeffer, Ladd says, "A man has to be what he is, Joey." Another male character in the film says, "I couldn't do what I gotta do if . . ." And a woman notes, "Shane did what he had to do." In the novel we find only, "A man is what he is, Bob, and there's no breaking the mold."

John Steinbeck's novel *The Grapes of Wrath* (1939) has "A man got to do what he got to do." Other suggested residing places of the phrase include the films *High Noon, The Sheepman,* and *Stagecoach.* In the latter John Wayne gets to say something like, "There are some things a man just has to do." By the 1970s several songs had been recorded with the title.

Man you love to hate, the.   Coming across a 1979 film with this title, made as a tribute to the Hollywood director Erich Von Stroheim (1885–1957), I was curious to know where the phrase came from. In fact, it was a billing phrase applied to Von Stroheim himself when he appeared as an actor in the 1918 propaganda film *The Heart of Humanity.* In it he played an obnoxious German officer who not only attempted to violate the leading lady but nonchalantly tossed a baby out of the window. At the film's premiere in Los Angeles Von Stroheim was hooted and jeered at when he walked onstage. He had to explain that he was only an actor—and was himself an Austrian.

Martini—shaken not stirred, a.   This example of would-be sophistication became a running joke in the immensely popular James Bond films of the 1960s and 70s. The line was an invention of the screenwriters and does not occur as such in Ian Fleming's novels. However, the idea stems from the first book in the series, *Casino Royale* (1953), in which Bond orders a cocktail of his own design. It consists of one dry martini "in a deep champagne goblet," three measures of Gordon's gin, one of vodka—"made with grain instead of potatoes"—and half a measure of Kina Lillet. "Shake it very well until it's ice-cold." Bond justifies his fussiness a page or two later: "I take a ridiculous pleasure in what I eat and drink. It comes partly from being a bachelor, but mostly from a habit of taking a lot of trouble over details. It's very pernickety and old-maidish really, but when I'm working I generally have to eat all my meals alone and it makes them more interesting when one takes trouble."

This characteristic was aped by the writers of the first Bond story to be filmed, *Dr. No* (1962). A West Indian servant brings Bond a vodka and martini and says, "Martini like you said, sir, and not stirred." Dr. No also mentions the fad, though the words are not spoken by Bond. In the third film, *Goldfinger* (1964), Bond (played by Sean Connery) does get to say "a martini, shaken not stirred"—he needs a drink after just escaping a laser death-ray—and there are references to it in *You Only Live Twice* (1967) and *On Her Majesty's Secret Service* (1969), among others.

The phrase was taken up in all the numerous parodies of the Bond phenomenon on film, TV, and radio, though curiously enough it may be a piece of absolute nonsense. According to one expert, shaking a dry martini "turns it from something crystal-clear into a dreary frosted drink. It should be stirred quickly with ice in a jug."

May the Force be with you!   This benediction/valediction was a delicious piece of hokum from the film *Star Wars* (1977). In the movie, Alec Guinness explains what it means: "The Force is what gives the Jedi its power. It's an energy field created by all living things. It surrounds us, it penetrates us, it binds the galaxy together." The phrase echoes "The Lord be with you" in the Prayer Book.

President Reagan, promoting his "Star Wars" weapon system, later said, "It isn't about fear, it's about hope, and in that struggle, if you'll pardon my stealing a film line, 'The force is with us.' "

Mean! moody! magnificent!   Slogan from the most notorious of all film advertising campaigns—the campaign for the Howard Hughes production of *The Outlaw* in 1943. As if "The Two Great Reasons for Jane Russell's Rise to Stardom" (skillfully supported by the Hughes-designed cantilever bra) were not enough, there were various pictures of the skimpily clad new star. One version had her reclining with a long whip. It's a very tame film, but the campaign has to be an early example of promotional hype.

Meanwhile, back at the ranch . . .   One of the captions from the days of silent films that has endured. Another was "Comes the dawn . . ." In *A Fool There Was* (1914), Theda Bara "spoke" the subtitle "Kiss me, my fool," and this was taken up as a fad expression. Similarly, Jacqueline Logan "said" the line "Harness my zebras!" in Cecil B. De Mille's 1925 *King of Kings*. This became a fad expression for "Let's leave!" or a way of expressing amazement: "Well, harness my zebras!"

"Meanwhile, back at the ranch . . ." may also have been used in radio "horse operas" when recapping the story after a commercial break.

Me, Tarzan—you, Jane.   A 1932 box-office sensation was the first sound Tarzan film, *Tarzan the Ape Man*. It spawned a long-running series and starred Johnny Weissmuller, an ex-U.S. swimming champion, as Tarzan, and Maureen O'Sullivan as Jane. At one point the ape man whisks Jane away to his treetop abode and indulges in

some elementary conversation with her. Thumping his
chest, he says, "Tarzan!" Pointing at her, he says, "Jane!"
Interestingly, this great moment of movie dialogue appears to have been "written" by the British playwright and
actor Ivor Novello. In the original novel, *Tarzan of the
Apes* (1914) by Edgar Rice Burroughs, the line does not
occur—not least because, in the jungle, Tarzan and Jane
are able to communicate only by writing notes to each
other.

More stars than there are in heaven.   Howard Dietz (see
ARS GRATIA ARTIS, this chapter) devised this studio motto
for MGM, which was current in the 1930s.

Nice place you got here.   Dick Vosburgh and Trevor Lyt-
tleton included this film phrase in their delightful catalog
song "I Love a Film Cliché," which was included in the
Broadway hit, *A Day in Hollywood, A Night in the
Ukraine* (1980). In it they gave the longer version —the
one uttered by a gangster with a lump in his jacket: "Nice
place you got here, blue eyes. Be too bad if something was
to . . . happen to it!" At this point the heavy usually
knocks over an ornament, as a warning.

Often one hears the version "nice *little* place you've got
here"—used with equal amounts of irony about a dump or
somewhere impressively grand. However, in the film
Breakfast at Tiffany's (1961), it is said almost straight. Par-
tridge/*Catch Phrases* seems to think it all started in Britain
in the 1940s, but I feel sure the film use must have started
in U.S. gangster films of the 1930s.

From the London *Independent* (May 13, 1989): "To this
day [Stevie] Wonder habitually talks about 'seeing' and
catches out sighted friends by walking into unfamiliar
rooms, taking a 'look' around and saying: 'Hey, nice place
you've got here.' "

Number one son.   This nickname for an eldest son, in
imitation of Chinese speech, was popularized in the

"Charlie Chan" films of the 1930s, which featured an oriental detective (with a large family) created by Earl Derr Biggers. In his U.S. radio incarnation, Chan was also given to saying that he was "not very good detective, just lucky old Chinaman."

Son of _____.   Mostly used as the title of sequels. The *OED2* cites the first such book as *Son of Tarzan* by Edgar Rice Burroughs; the first such film was probably *Son of the Sheik* (1926) with Rudolph Valentino, following *The Sheik* (1921). Then *Son of Kong* (1933) followed *King Kong*. Others have been *Son of: Ali Baba, Captain Blood, Dr. Jekyll, Dracula, Frankenstein, Geronimo, Lassie, Monte Cristo, Paleface, Robin Hood, the Sheik, Zorro*.

Alternatively, you could stage a return: *The Return of: Dracula, the Scarlet Pimpernel, a Man Called Horse*. Or merely add a number. Following the example of *The Godfather, Part II* (1974), we have had not only *Rocky II–V* but also *Jaws II, French Connection II, Death Wish II, Damien: Omen II, Friday the Thirteenth, Part II, Crocodile Dundee 2*, and so on.

There were exceptions, of course. The sequel to *American Graffiti* was *More American Graffiti*. Forswearing "Pink Panther 2 etc.," Blake Edwards gave us *The Pink Panther Strikes Again, The Revenge of the Pink Panther,* and *The Return of the Pink Panther*. The *Airport* sequels followed their own peculiar sequence of titles —from *Airport 1975* to *Airport '77* and then *Airport '80—The Concorde*.

That's all, folks!   The concluding line—not usually spoken, but written on the screen—of *Merry Melodies,* the Warner Bros. cartoon series from 1930. When Mel Blanc (1908–1989), the voice behind so many cartoon characters, was asked for an epitaph, he decided on the following "in joined-up handwriting": "That's All, Folks!"

_____ : **the Movie.** I think the first film to be so labeled was *Abba: The Movie* in 1977. In these days of "concepts" and "merchandising" in pop music, the idea was probably to distinguish this product from "the tour," "the TV series," "the book," and "the album" (in 1978 "Abba: The Album" did indeed appear). The format has subsequently been used to poke fun at exploitation, self-promotion, and self-aggrandizement in certain quarters. In 1985 Michael Rogin, a professor of political science at Berkeley, California, entitled his exploration of President Reagan's (sometimes) unattributed use of film quotes, "Ronald Reagan: The Movie."

Along the same lines, in 1990 a novel by the film critic Iain Johnstone was published with the title *Cannes: the Novel,* and a short-lived London West End musical about Martin Luther King was dubbed *King—The Musical.*

They Might Be Giants   The title of a quirky film (1972) from a play by James Goldman about a man who thinks he is Sherlock Holmes. He recruits a female Dr. Watson who says, "You're just like Don Quixote, you think that everything is always something else." He replies, "He had a point—of course. He carried it a bit too far, that's all. He thought that every windmill was a giant. . . . If we never looked at things and thought what they *might* be we'd still all be in the tall grass with the apes."

A band took the name They Might Be Giants in c. 1989.

This thing is bigger than both of us.   ("This thing" meaning "our love.") A whopping film cliché that has more often been used ironically. Milton Berle popularized it, satirically, in his radio and TV shows of the 1940s and 50s. In the 1976 remake of *King Kong,* with the giant ape brushing against the side of the house they are in, Jeff Bridges as "Jack Prescott" says to Jessica Lange's "Dwan," "He's bigger than both of us, know what I mean?"

Tomorrow is another day. The last words of the film *Gone With the Wind* (1939), spoken by Vivien Leigh as Scarlett O'Hara, are, "Tara! Home! I'll go home, and I'll think of some way to get him back. After all, tomorrow is another day!" The last sentence is as it appears in Margaret Mitchell's novel, but the idea behind it is proverbial. Rastell's *Calisto & Melebea* (c. 1527) has the line, "Well mother to morrow is a new day."

View to a Kill, A. This was the title of a James Bond film (1985). The original title of the short story by Ian Fleming (published in 1960 with *For Your Eyes Only*) was "*From* a View to a Kill." As such it is very close to the title of Anthony Powell's 1933 novel *From a View to a Death*, which is a direct quotation from the song "D'ye ken John Peel," written in 1832 by John Woodcock Graves: "Yes, I ken John Peel, and Ruby too,/Ranter and Ringwood, Bellman and True,/From a find to a check, from a check to a view,/From a view to a death in the morning." In foxhunting terminology, a "check" is a loss of scent, a "view (halloo)" is the huntsman's shout when a fox breaks cover, and a "kill" or a "death" is what it says.

Watch the skies. The last words of the sci-fi film *The Thing* (1951) were, "Watch everywhere, keep looking, watch the skies!" This phrase was subsequently used to promote the film *Close Encounters of the Third Kind* (1977) and, indeed, was its original title. Another slogan for the film was "We are not alone."

We have ways of making you talk. The threat by evil inquisitor to victim appears to have come originally from 1930s Hollywood villains and was then handed down to Nazi characters from the 1940s onward.

Halliwell's Filmgoer's Book of Quotes (1978) found Douglas Dumbrille, as the evil Mohammed Khan, saying, "We have ways of making *men* talk," in *Lives of a Bengal Lancer* (1935)—by forcing slivers of wood under the fingernails and setting fire to them. A typical "film Nazi" use can be found in *Odette* (1950), in which the French Resistance worker (Anna Neagle) is threatened by one of her captors: "We have ways and means of making you talk." Then, after a little stoking of the fire with a poker, he urges her on with, "We have ways and means of making a woman talk."

Later, used in caricature, the phrase saw further action in TV programs like *Laugh-In* (c. 1968)—invariably pronounced with a German accent.

What's up, doc? The characteristic inquiry of Bugs Bunny, in the film series that ran from 1937–63, to Elmer Fudd, the doctor who devoted his life to attempting to destroy the rabbit. Bugs made his official debut in 1940. In full, the phrase was "Er, what's up, Doc?"—followed by a carrot crunch. Its origins may lie in an old Texan expression, introduced to the films by one of the animators, Tex Avery.

The voices of both Bugs and Elmer were done by Mel Blanc (1908–1989), who, upon emerging from a coma in 1983, inevitably put the question to his physician. The phrase was used as the title of a film starring Barbra Streisand and Ryan O'Neal (1972).

What we've got here is a failure to communicate. In the 1967 film *Cool Hand Luke*, Strother Martin (as a prison officer) says to Paul Newman (as a rebellious prisoner), "What we've got here is a failure to communicate. Some men you just can't reach." The line was also used to promote the film.

You're going out a youngster—but you've gotta come back a star! Not a cliché when new-minted in the film *42nd Street* (1933). Warren Baxter as a theatrical producer says the line to Ruby Keeler as the chorus girl who takes over on short notice for an indisposed star.

10

THE MOST FUN
I'VE HAD WITHOUT
LAUGHING

This is how the Woody Allen character compliments the Diane Keaton character in the film Annie Hall (1977). As a description of sex it is clearly derived from the old expression, "The most fun you can have with your clothes on." However, Mencken was recording "Love [he probably meant sex] is the most fun you can have without laughing" in 1942. And I have seen "Nothing beats making love—it's the most fun you can have without laughing" attributed to Humphrey Bogart.

Are there any more at home like you? Partridge/*Catch Phrases* traces this pickup line to the musical comedy

Floradora (1900), which contains the line, "Tell me, pretty maiden, are there any more at home like you?" (written by Leslie Stuart). Partridge adds that the line was "obsolete by 1970—except among those with long memories." Well, not quite. Tom Jones can be heard saying it to a member of the audience on the album *Tom Jones Live at Caesar's Palace Las Vegas* (1971).

Did the earth move for you?   Jokingly addressed to one's partner after sexual intercourse, this appears to have originated as "Did thee feel the earth move?" in Ernest Hemingway's *For Whom the Bell Tolls* (1940). I have not been able to find it in the 1943 film version, however.

Droit de seigneur.   This phrase suggests that a man is exercising some imagined right in forcing a woman to have sex with him, as a boss might do with his secretary. The belief in this "right" dates from the days when medieval barons would claim first go at the newly wedded daughters of their vassals—the so-called *ius primae noctis* (law of the first night). In the play *Le Mariage de Figaro* (1784) by Beaumarchais, the Count has just renounced his right and is beginning to regret it.

In March 1988 Dr. Wilhelm Schmidt-Bleibtreu of Bonn, who looked into the matter very thoroughly, discovered there was never any such legal right and that reliable records of it ever happening were rare. He concluded that the whole thing was really a male fantasy—and it was exclusively men who had used the phrase—though he didn't rule out that sex of this kind *had* taken place between lords and brides in one or two cases, legally or otherwise.

If I said you had a beautiful body, would you hold it against me?   This punning question became the title of a hit song by the Bellamy Brothers in 1979 (though they sang "have" instead of "had"). *The Naff Sex Guide* (1984) listed the saying among "Naff Pick-Up Lines."

The British comedian Max Miller ("The Cheeky Chappie") (1895–1963), characteristically, had got there first. In a selection of his jokes once published by the *Sunday Dispatch* (and reprinted in *The Last Empires,* ed. Benny Green, 1986), we find: "I saw a girl who was proud of her figure. Just to make conversation I asked her, 'What would you do if a chap criticised your figure?' 'Well,' she said, 'I wouldn't hold it against him.' "

In like Flynn. Alluding to the legendary bedroom prowess of Errol Flynn (1909–1959), the Australian-born film actor, the phrase describes a person who seizes an offered opportunity (of any kind, though in Australia, it means specifically, someone who is a quick seducer).

According to *The Intimate Sex Lives of Famous People* (Irving Wallace et al., 1981), Flynn frowned on the expression when it became popular, especially among servicemen in World War II. It "implied he was a fun-loving rapist," though "in fact, Flynn's reputation stemmed partly from his having been charged with statutory rape." After a celebrated trial he was acquitted. Nevertheless, he "boasted that he had spent between 12,000 and 14,000 nights making love."

A 1967 film was entitled *In Like Flint.* Partridge/*Catch Phrases* turns up an American version that refers to Ed Flynn, a Democratic-machine politician in the Bronx, New York, in the 1940s. Here the meaning is simply to be in automatically—as Flynn's candidates would have been.

Is she a friend of Dorothy? Meaning "Is he [*sic*] a homosexual?" Current among homosexuals by 1984. "Dorothy" was the put-upon heroine of *The Wizard of Oz* and was played in the film by Judy Garland, a woman much revered in male homosexual circles.

Lie down, I think I love you. A pickup line that is probably not often used in real life. A song titled "Sit Down, I Think I Love You" (written by Stephen Stills) was performed by The Mojo Men in 1967, and Malcolm Muggeridge recorded the graffito "Lie down! I think I love you" in Santa Monica before 1966. And then again, there was the Marx Brothers' line from *The Cocoanuts* (1929), "Ah, Mrs. Rittenhouse, won't you . . . lie down?"

As always, there is nothing new under the sun. Horace Walpole, in a letter to H. S. Conway on October 23, 1778, wrote: "This sublime age reduces everything to its quintessence; all periphrases and expletives are so much in disuse, that I suppose soon the only way to making love will be to say 'Lie down.'"

Most fun you can have with your clothes on, the. Said of something other than sex (naturally). This probably predates THE MOST FUN I'VE HAD WITHOUT LAUGHING (this chapter), though the earliest example I have is from Jerry Della Femina in *From Those Wonderful Folks Who Gave You Pearl Harbor* (1970): "Advertising is the most fun you can have with your clothes on."

Not tonight, Josephine. Napoleon Bonaparte did not, so far as we know, ever say the words that have become linked with him. The idea that he had better things to do than satisfy the Empress Josephine's famous appetite, or was not inclined or able to, must have grown up during the nineteenth century. There was a saying, attributed to Josephine, *"Bon-a-parte est Bon-à-rien"* ("Bonaparte is good for nothing").

The catch phrase probably arose through music-hall in Victorian times. A knockabout sketch filmed for the Pathé Library in c. 1932 has Lupino Lane as Napoleon and Beatrice Lillie as Josephine. After signing a document of divorce (which Napoleon crumples up), Josephine says, "When you are refreshed, come as usual to my apartment." Napoleon says, "Not tonight, Josephine," and she throws a custard pie in his face.

The phrase is featured in the film *I Cover the Waterfront* (1933).

On a scale of one to ten. Often used allusively, as in "she's a six," "a minus two," etc. In a West Coast party scene in the film *Annie Hall* (1977), a character says of a woman, "She's a ten," indicating that she is his ideal. This usage was further popularized by the film *10* (1979), in which the sexual allure or performance of the hero's girlfriends was so rated. Some people still use it. *The Naff Sex Guide* (1984) quoted an unidentified celebrity as having said, "On a scale of one to ten I'd give him a two, but that's only because I've never met a one." An ad in *The New York Times* (March 26, 1989) quoted Gary Franklin of KABC-TV as rating the film *Heathers* "A 10! Absolutely brilliant, a remarkable film."

Out of the closet (and into the streets). Slogan of the homosexual rights organization known as the Gay Liberation Front, c. 1969. The starting point was the term "closet homosexual" or "closet queen" for one who hid his sexual inclinations from others.

Seven-year itch, the. The urge to be unfaithful to a spouse after some years of marriage. The *OED2* provides examples of this phrase going back to the mid-nineteenth century, but without the specific matrimonial context. For example, the "seven-year itch" describes a rash from poison ivy that was believed to recur every year for a seven-year period. Then one has to recall that since biblical days, seven-year periods of lean or fat have had special significance. And there is also the army saying, "Cheer up—the first seven years are the worst!"

But the specific matrimonial use was not popularized until used as the title of George Axelrod's play (1952) and film (1955). "Itch" had long been used for the sexual urge, but as Axelrod commented on my *Quote . . . Unquote* program (BBC Radio, 1979), "There was a phrase which referred to a somewhat unpleasant disease, but nobody had used it in a sexual [I think he meant "matrimonial"] context before. I do believe I invented it in that sense."

Oddly, I can find no mention in any reference book of "itch" being used in connection with venereal diseases. Nonetheless, I was interested to come across the following remark in *W. C. Fields: His Follies and Fortunes* (Robert Lewis Taylor, published as early as 1950): "Bill exchanged women every seven years, as some people get rid of the itch."

Sex rears its ugly head. And how curious. Why? Because the penis rises? If so, then why ugly? A very odd usage, except that the construction "to raise/rear its ugly head" was probably used about other matters before sex. The image is presumably of a Loch Ness-type monster emerging from the deep.

The "sex" form has been current since at least 1930 when James R. Quirk used it in a *Photoplay* editorial about the film *Hell's Angels*. It is used both as an explanation for people's behavior (like *"cherchez la femme"*) and as a complaint about the intrusion of sex in books, TV programs, etc.

She should lie back and enjoy it. This is best described— as it is in Paul Scott's novel *The Jewel in the Crown* (1966)— as "that old, disreputable saying." Daphne Manners, upon whose "rape" the story hinges, adds, "I can't say, Auntie, that I lay back and enjoyed mine."

It is no more than a saying—a "mock-Confucianism" is how Partridge/*Slang* describes it, giving a date c. 1950— and one is unlikely to ever learn when, or from whom, it first arose.

A word of caution to anyone thinking of using it. Broadcaster Tex Antoine said in 1975, "With rape so predominant in the news lately, it is well to remember the words of Confucius: 'If rape is inevitable, lie back and enjoy it.'" ABC News suspended Antoine for this remark, then demoted him to working in the weather department and prohibited him from appearing on the air.

Straight out of Central Casting.   This would be a person who conforms to type, or to what you would expect. From the London *Observer* (March 19, 1939): "If you had asked Central Casting, or Equity, to provide an archetypal bigot, it's unlikely they could come up with someone as perfect as Jan van der Berg . . . owner of one of the better restaurants in Windhoek, the capital of Namibia."

Central Casting was set up in 1926 and maintained by all major Hollywood studios as a pool for film extras. David Niven, for example, claimed to have been listed on their books in the mid-1930s as "Anglo-Saxon Type No. 2008."

Tall, dark, and handsome.   This description of a romantic hero's attributes (most likely to be found in women's fiction) seems to have surfaced in the early 1900s. Flexner places it in the late 1920s as a Hollywood term referring to Rudolph Valentino (who was not particularly tall). Cesar Romero played the lead in a 1941 film, *Tall, Dark and Handsome*, which no doubt helped put the phrase into popular use. However, in a piece called "Loverboy of the Bourgeoisie" (1965), Tom Wolfe writes: "It was Cary Grant that Mae West was talking about when she launched the phrase 'tall, dark and handsome' in *She Done Him Wrong* (1933)."

They all look the same in the dark.   Contemptuous male view of women as objects. Ovid in his *Ars Amatoria* says much the same thing more diplomatically: "The dark makes every woman beautiful."

Was it good for you too?   What one is supposed to say to one's sexual partner after intercourse. (Compare DID THE EARTH MOVE FOR YOU?, this chapter) Indications that the phrase had "arrived" came when Bob Chieger so entitled a book of quotations about love and sex in 1983.

What's new, pussycat?   Of Warren Beatty, the film actor, Sheilah Graham wrote in *Scratch an Actor* (1969): "He uses the telephone as a weapon of seduction. He curls up with it, cuddles it, whispers into it, 'What's new, pussycat?' (He coined the phrase, and the picture was originally written for him.)"

The film of this title (and the Tom Jones song) came out in 1965. Perhaps Graham was right. Whatever the case, I would guess that the use of "pussycat" to describe someone, particularly a woman, as "attractive, amiable, submissive" (*OED2*) probably emanates from the U.S., if not precisely from Hollywood.

Would you be shocked if I put on something more comfortable?   "Do you mind if I put on something more comfortable?" and "Excuse me while I slip into something more comfortable" are just two of the misquotations of a famous film line. What Jean Harlow as Helen actually says to Ben Lyon as Monte in *Hell's Angels* (1930) is as above. It is, of course, a proposition, as she exchanges her fur wrap for a dressing gown.

You've made an old man very happy.   As though said by an old man to a woman for sexual favors granted, now a humorous way of expressing thanks for anything. Neatly inverted in the film *The Last Remake of Beau Geste* (1977). Terry-Thomas, as a prison governor, says to Ann-Margret, as a woman who has slept with him to secure an escape, "Delighted you came, my dear, and I'd like you to know that you made a happy man feel very old."

11

ONE FOOT
IN THE GRAVE

To have "one foot in the grave" has long meant to be near
death. The earliest citation in the OED2 is from Burton's
Anatomy of Melancholy (1621): "An old acherontic diz-
zard that hath one foot in his grave." In Gulliver's Travels
(1726) Swift uses the phrase in connection with the immor-
tal Struldbruggs of Laputa. Mencken quotes William
George Smith as tracing "One of his feet is already in the
grave" to 1566. Bartlett provides a translation of
Plutarch's Morals: Of the Training of Children that goes,
"An old doting fool, with one foot already in the grave."

Proof that the phrase was well-known by the eighteenth
century can be found in a punning inscription on the
grave of one Samuel Foote in Westminster Abbey, London.
Foote (1720–1777) was an actor and dramatist, famous for
his mimicry and for making Samuel Johnson laugh
against his will. He was buried by torchlight in an un-
marked grave with the inscription:

Here lies one Foote, whose death may thousands save,
For death has now one foot within the grave.

Now, here lie phrases for the dear departed:

Another page turned in the book of life.   The first funeral
I ever went to was a sparsely attended affair at a cremato-
rium. A cracked record of "The Lord Is My Shepherd" was
used to supplement our hymn-singing, and the minister
Uriah-Heeped his way through the service. When we went
home for the wake, one of the dear departed's contempo-
raries sighed deeply and declared to all and sundry, "Well,
that's another page turned in the book of life." As such, it is
one of the numerous clichés of bereavement, designed to
keep the awfulness of death at bay.

Compare what the English clergyman and diarist Francis Kilvert wrote on September 2, 1872: "Left Clyro for
ever. A chapter of life closed and a leaf in the Book of Life
turned over."

Boots on, to die with one's.   To die violently, or to be
hanged summarily (sometimes "to die in one's boots/
shoes"). *OED2* finds this by the eighteenth century, and in
the American West in 1873. It was firmly ensconced in the
language by the time of the 1941 Errol Flynn film *They
Died with Their Boots On*, about General Custer and his
death at Little Big Horn.

Now in a general way it refers to someone who dies "in
harness," going about his work like a soldier in the course
of duty.

"To die with one's boots *off*" suggests, of course, that
one dies in bed.

Gone, but not forgotten.   On tombstones, memorial notices, and such, and used as the title of a Victorian print
showing children around a grave. In the 1950s and 60s
there was an album of the BBC radio *Goon Show* with the
title "Goon . . . But Not Forgotten."

His death diminishes us all. In obituaries, possibly deriving originally from John Donne's *Devotions, XVII* (1624): "Any man's death diminishes me because I am involved in mankind, and therefore never send to know for whom the bell tolls; it tolls for thee."

Legend in one's own lifetime, a/living legend, a. Both of these phrases are now clichés of tribute. A possibility exists that the first person to whom both versions of the epithet were applied actually deserved them. Lytton Strachey in *Eminent Victorians* (1918) wrote of Florence Nightingale: "She was a legend in her lifetime, and she knew it. . . . Once or twice a year, perhaps, but nobody could be quite certain, in deadly secrecy, she went for a drive in the park. Unrecognised, the living legend flitted for a moment before the common gaze."

Turn/roll over in one's grave, to. The action of a dead person, as if appalled by something that has happened or been proposed. Mencken describes "It is enough to make _____ turn over in his grave" as an "English saying, not recorded before the nineteenth century." In *Pudd'nhead Wilson* (1894), Mark Twain has: "You has disgraced yo' birth. What would yo' pa think o' you? It's enough to make him turn in his grave." In about 1976, one of the idiocies attributed to President Gerald Ford was (of some political scandal) "If Abraham Lincoln was alive today, he'd be turning in his grave."

We shall not see his like again. Used in obituaries, this phrase alludes to Shakespeare, *Hamlet* (Act I, scene ii, line 187), where the prince says of his late father:

> He was a man, take him for all in all.
> I shall not look upon his like again.

In *Joyce Grenfell Requests the Pleasure* (1976), the actress recalled being phoned by United Press for a comment on the death of Ruth Draper, the monologist: "My diary records: 'I said we should not see her like again. She was a genius.' Without time to think, clichés take over and often, because that is why they have become clichés, they tell the truth."

12

IS IT BIGGER
THAN A BREADBOX?

Well, if it's a TV set, then it probably is! Televised on and off since 1950, the Goodson-Todman production What's My Line? *remains the archetypal TV panel game. Guessing the jobs of contestants and then donning masks to work out the identity of a visiting celebrity turned panelists into national figures. Trying to figure out the size of an article made by one contestant, Steve Allen formulated the classic inquiry, "Is it bigger than a breadbox?"*

Like the Hollywood film, the American TV series has strayed far beyond its native shores. Sold and shown all over the world, programs like What's My Line?, Dallas, *and* I Love Lucy *are a powerful but generally benign form of cultural colonialism. Wherever the English language is spoken, the phrases resound:*

All we want is the facts, ma'am. *Dragnet* was made between 1951 and 1958 and revived in 1967–69. It was

largely the creation of Jack Webb (1920–1982), who produced, directed, and starred in it. As Police Sergeant Joe
Friday he had a deadpan style that was much parodied.
The show first appeared on radio in 1949 and was said to
draw its stories from actual cases dealt with by the Los
Angeles police—hence the famous announcement: "Ladies and gentlemen, the story you are about to hear is true.
Only the names have been changed to protect the innocent."

The signature tune was almost a catch phrase in itself:
"Dum-de-dum-dum." Joe Friday had a staccato style of
questioning: "just the facts, ma'am," or "all we want is the
facts, ma'am." To add to the list of memorable phrases,
here is the opening from a typical TV episode: "Ladies and
gentlemen, the story you are about to see is true. Only the
names have been changed to protect the innocent. . . .
This is the city. Everything in it is one way or the other.
There's no middle ground—narrow alleys, broad high-
ways; mansions on the hill, shacks in the gulleys; people
who work for a living and people who steal. These are the
ones that cause me trouble. I'm a cop. It was Monday, April
17. We were working the day-watch on a forgery detail.
My partner: Frank Smith. The boss is Captain Welch. My
name's Friday . . ."

The phrase "all we want is the facts" is also a cliché when
importunate journalists are represented in sketches. In
"Long-Distance Divorce," a revue sketch from *Nine Sharp*
(1938), Herbert Farjeon put it in the mouth of a British
reporter interviewing a Hollywood star.

And awa-a-aay we go! On the *Jackie Gleason Show*
(1952–70), the rotund comic hosted variety acts and used
this phrase to lead into the first sketch. He had a special
pose to accompany it—head turned to face left, one leg
raised ready to shoot off in the same direction. Gleason's
other stock phrase was "How sweet it is!" and he popularized the word "labonza" for posterior, as in "a kick in the
labonza."

And now for something completely different . . .   From
Monty Python's Flying Circus and used as the title of the
comedy team's first film in 1971. Usually delivered by John
Cleese as a dinner-jacketed BBC radio announcer seated
before a microphone on a desk in some unlikely setting,
the phrase was taken from a slightly arch "link" much
loved by magazine-program hosts. These folks were thus
deprived of a very useful phrase.

And that's the way it is.   Walter Cronkite (b. 1916) retired
after nineteen years of anchoring the CBS-TV Evening
News—for most of which he had concluded with these
words. On the final occasion he said: "And that's the way it
is, Friday, March 6, 1981. Goodnight."

Beam me up, Scotty.   The TV science-fiction series *Star
Trek* (1966–69), though short-lived, nevertheless acquired
a considerable afterlife through countless repeats and the
activities of "Trekky" fans. It was the series whose spoken
introduction proposed "to boldly go where no man has
gone before!" (In one of the feature films that spun off from
the series—the 1988 one—the split infinitive remained,
but it became "where no *one* has gone before.")
    Capt. Kirk (William Shatner) would say, "Beam me up,
Scotty" to Lt. Commander "Scotty" Scott, the chief engineer—which meant that he should transpose body into
energy.

Book 'em, Danno!   From the series *Hawaii Five-O* (1968–
80). Upon making an arrest, Det. Steve McGarrett (Jack
Lord) would say to Det. "Danno" Williams (James MacArthur), "Book 'em, Danno!"—adding "Murder one" if the
crime required that charge.

Boy Wonder.   Batman and Robin are characters created
by Bob Kane and were featured in comic books for over
thirty years before being portrayed in a television series
(1966–68) and a movie (1990). Adding the prefix "Holy

_____" to exclamations was a hallmark of the program—
"Holy flypaper!" /"Holy cow!"/ "Holy schizophrenia!" ,
etc. Also used were "Quick thinking, Batman!"—a typi-
cally crawling remark from sidekick Robin—and "Boy
wonder!"—Batman's commendation in return.

(The subtitles "Pow! Biff! Thwack! Crunch! Rakkk!
Oooofff! and Bonk!" could also be said to be a kind of catch
phrase.)

Calling all cars, calling all cars!   From cops and robbers
films and TV series of the 1950s. What the police controller
says on the radio to patrolmen. For some reason the archetypal cop phrase of the period, and evocative. However,
the formula had obviously been known before this if the
British films *Calling All Stars* (1937), *Calling All Ma's*
(1937), and *Calling All Cars* (1954) are anything to go by.

Come on down!   In the TV consumer game *The Price Is
Right* (1957–), the host would appear to summon contestants from the studio audience by saying, "[Name], come
on down!"

Days of Our Lives.   The title of the long-running daytime soap opera could be alluding to more than one thing
—"the happiest days of your life," "the best years of our
lives," or "the best days of our lives."

"Days of our lives" does not occur in the Bible, though
there are any number of near-misses: "Labors all the days
of his life" (Ecclesiastes 8:15), etc.

Dead parrot.   Meaning something that is quite incapable
of resuscitation. This expression derives from the most famous of the *Monty Python's Flying Circus* sketches (first
shown in the U.K. in 1969, several years later in the U.S.),
in which a man who has just bought a parrot that turns out
to be dead registers a complaint with the pet-shop owner
in these words: "This parrot is no more. It's ceased to be.
It's expired. It's gone to meet its maker. This is a late

parrot. It's a stiff. Bereft of life it rests in peace. It would be pushing up the daisies if you hadn't nailed it to the perch. It's rung down the curtain and joined the choir invisible. It's an ex-parrot."

Devil made me do it!, the. Flip Wilson, host of a comedy variety hour (1970–74), became famous for saying this, wide-eyed, about any supposed misdemeanor.

Diff'rent Strokes. This was the title of a series (first aired in 1978) about a widowed millionaire (Conrad Bain) who adopts two orphaned black boys (Todd Bridges and the comic discovery Gary Coleman). The title came from an African-American slang expression, "Different strokes for different folks," meaning different people have different requirements.

Eat my shorts! The first new media hero of the 1990s is Bart, the skateboard-toting son of Homer and Marge Simpson. *The Simpsons* first hit television in short takes on Fox Network's the Tracy Ullman Show and then graduated to their own series. Bart's vocabulary is colorful, if not always comprehensible: "Yo, dude!"; "Aye, caramba!"; "Whoa, mama"; "Au contraire, mon frère"; and "Don't have a cow, man!" sound as if they've been plucked straight off the streets, but probably haven't—even if they've soon found their way there on a host of T-shirts, buttons, and bumper stickers. "Eat my shorts!" has become a threatening imperative; "I'm Bart Simpson—who the hell are you?" and "Underachiever and proud of it" have become curiously potent slogans.

Goodnight . . . and good luck. The eminent broadcaster Edward R. Murrow (1908–1965) used this farewell at the end of such programs as *See It Now* (1951–55) and *Person to Person* (1953–61).

Hello, good evening, and welcome!   A greeting known on both sides of the Atlantic because of David Frost (b. 1939), who commuted back and forth to host TV talk shows in London and New York. It may have been contrived to say three things where only one was needed, but it became an essential part of the Frost-impersonator's kit (not to mention the Frost self-impersonator's kit). He was certainly saying it by 1970 and was still staying it in 1983 when, with a small alteration, it became "Hello, good *morning*, and welcome!" for the debut of TV-am, the London breakfast-TV company.

Here's Johnny!   Said with a drawn-out, rising inflection on the first word, this has been Ed McMahon's introduction of Johnny Carson on NBC's *Tonight* show since 1961: "[*Drum roll*] And now . . . heeeeere's Johnny!" Jack Nicholson playing a psychopath chopped through a door with an ax and cried "Here's Johnny!" in the film *The Shining* (1981).

Hi-ho, Silver (away)!   "Who *was* that masked man? . . . A fiery horse with the speed of light, a cloud of dust, and a hearty 'Hi-ho, Silver!' The Lone Ranger! With his faithful Indian companion Tonto, the daring and resourceful masked rider of the plains led the fight for law and order in the early western United States. Nowhere in the pages of history can one find a greater champion of justice. Return with us now to those thrilling days of yesteryear. . . . From out of the past come the thundering hoofbeats of the great horse Silver. The Lone Ranger rides again!

" 'Come on, Silver! Let's go, big fellow! Hi-ho, Silver, away!' "

The above was more or less the introduction to the masked Lone Ranger and his horse, Silver, in the various TV, radio, and film accounts of their exploits—accompanied, of course, by Rossini's "William Tell Overture."

Groucho Marx used to say that George Seaton (the first Lone Ranger on radio, from 1933) invented the call "Hi-ho, Silver!" because he was unable to whistle for his horse. It seems that the phrase was minted by Seaton and not by Fran Striker, the chief scriptwriter in the early days. The Lone Ranger's Indian friend, Tonto, wrestled meanwhile with such lines as, "Him bad man, kemo sabe!" ("Kemos sabe"—whichever way you spell it—is supposed to mean "trusty scout" and was derived from the name of a boys' camp at Mullet Lake, Michigan, in 1911.)

I'se regusted!   When the long-running *Amos 'n' Andy* radio show of the 1930s and 40s was transferred to TV in 1951–53, African-American actors had to be found to play the characters originally portrayed by whites. But the catch phrases and stock phrases were carried over intact. "Holy mackerel, Andy! We's all got to stick together in dis heah thing. . . . Remember, we is brothers in that great fraternity, the Mystic Knights of the Sea"; "Check and double check"; and "Now ain't dat sump'n?"

Kiss my grits!   Polly Holliday, the man-hungry waitress from the South, had a wonderful catch phrase in the sitcom *Alice* (1976–80), which deserves to be better known. She went on to have her own series, *Flo.*

"Kookie (Lend Me Your Comb)."   During his time with the cop show *77 Sunset Strip* (which ran from 1958–63), Ed Byrnes as Kookie had a habit of constantly combing his hair. This was celebrated in the words of a hit record on which he appeared with Connie Stevens.

Mission Impossible.   The title of this TV series has achieved catch-phrase status—or, rather, the phrase has proved useful in other situations. The series was first broadcast from 1966 to 1972 and had to do with government agents and investigators in the Impossible Missions Force. From the *Washington Post* (January 3, 1984): "When Kissinger took the commission post, his associates warned that it was mission impossible. Even if the objective of achieving a national consensus on Central America is unattainable, as it probably is, however, Kissinger by no means will be an automatic loser."

Move 'em on, head 'em up. ("Head 'em up, move 'em on,/Move 'em on, head 'em up . . . Rawhide!") *Rawhide*, the Western series (1959–66), was notable for its Frankie Laine theme song over the credits.

Nanu, nanu. When Robin Williams played Mork, an alien from Ork, in *Mork and Mindy* (1978–81), his good-bye in Orkan caught on briefly.

Sixty-four (thousand) dollar question, the. "Ah, that's the sixty-four-dollar question, isn't it?" some people will exclaim, when surely they mean "sixty-four *thousand.*" Or do they? Put it down to inflation. Webster's Dictionary says that $64 *was* the highest award in a CBS radio quiz called *Take It or Leave It,* which ran from 1941–48 and in which the value of the prize doubled every time the contestant got a right answer (The progression was 1, 2, 4, 8, 16, 32, 64 —hence the title *Double Your Money* given to the first of the British TV versions). This is how the saying entered common parlance, meaning "that is the question that would solve all our problems if only we knew the answer to it."

In February 1989 I heard a weather forecaster being asked, "Is the mild weather going to continue?" She replied, "That's the sixty-four-million-dollar question." So inflation is still rampant.

Smarter than the average bear, (Booboo). Said of himself by Yogi Bear to his sidekick, Booboo, in the Yogi Bear cartoon TV series (1958–). The character was voiced by Charles "Daws" Butler. At his death in May 1988, it was suggested that he might have coined the phrase as well.

Sock it to me! An enormous hit from its inception in 1967, *Rowan and Martin's Laugh-In* lasted until 1973 and was briefly revived, without Rowan and Martin—and with little success—in 1977. The original was a brightly colored, fast-moving series of sketches and gags with a wide range of stock characters, linked together by the relaxed charm of Dan Rowan (1922–1987) and Dick Martin (b. 1923).

For a while the whole of America was ringing to the program's catch phrases. A quintessential late 1960s sound was announcer Gary Owens, with hand cupped to ear, intoning, "This is beautiful downtown Burbank"—an ironic compliment to the area of Los Angeles where NBC-TV's studios are located and where *Laugh-In* was recorded. The most famous of these phrases was "Sock it to me!" spoken by the English actress Judy Carne (b. 1939), who became known as the Sock-It-to-Me Girl. She would appear and chant the phrase until—ever unsuspecting—something dreadful happened to her. She would be drenched with a bucket of water, fall through a trap door, get blown up, or find herself shot from a cannon.

The phrase "to sock it to someone" originally meant to put something bluntly (and was used as such by Mark Twain). African-American jazz musicians gave it a sexual meaning, as in "I'd like to sock it to *her*" (by the 1920s).

The precise way in which this old phrase came to be adopted by *Laugh-In* was described to me by Judy Carne in 1980: "George Schlatter, the producer, had had great success in America with a show starring Ernie Kovacs in the 1950s. The wife on that show used to get a pie in the face every week and got enormous sympathy mail as a result. So George wanted a spot where an actress would have *horrendous* things done to her each week—a sort of 'Perils of Pauline' thing—and then find a catch phrase to fit it."

In the summer of 1967 Aretha Franklin had a hit record with "Respect," which featured a chorus repeating "Sock it to me" quite rapidly in the background. The previous year there had been a record called "Sock It to 'Em, J. B." by Rex Garvin with Mighty Craven, and in February 1967 an LP entitled "Sock It to Me, Baby" had come from Mitch Ryder and the Detroit Wheels. But Aretha Franklin's record was where the *Laugh-In* catch phrase came from. "George came up with the idea of making it literal. I said, 'Well it should be Cockney.' He said, 'How far are you prepared to go?' And I said, 'I'll do anything for a laugh. If I'm safe, I don't mind what you do to me.'

"It all happened very fast. . . . In about three weeks we were No. 1 with fifty million people watching. The sayings caught on at exactly the same time the show did. . . . It had a dirty connotation and it was also very clean and was great for the kids. That's why I think that it took off the way it did—because it appealed to everyone at one level or another."

On being known as the Sock-It-to-Me Girl: "It got in the way for a while. You have to go through a period of living a tag like that down, and proving that you are not just a saying. The main thing is not to identify with it, not to sit about worrying that people think of you as a saying. But better they think of you as a saying than not at all."

Among the guests on the show who spoke the line were John Wayne, Mae West, Jack Lemmon, Jimmy Durante, Marcel Marceau (even), and Richard Nixon. The latter, running for the U.S. presidency, said it on the show broadcast on September 16, 1968. He pronounced it in a perplexed manner: "Sock it to *me*?" And, lo, they finally did.

The next most famous phrase from the show was probably "Very interesting . . . but stupid!" (or "but it stinks," or some other variant). This was spoken in a thick accent by Arte Johnson as a bespectacled German soldier wearing a helmet and peering through a potted plant.

The third notable phrase was "You bet your sweet bippy!"— usually spoken by Dick Martin.

Other phrases from the show included:

Here come de judge!   The old vaudeville phrase had
a revival when Dewey "Pigmeat" Markham, a vaudeville veteran, was brought back to take part in a series
of blackout sketches to which the build-up was the
chant, "Here comes de judge!"

> *Judge:* Have you ever been up before me?
> *Defendant:* I don't know—what time do you
> get up?

In July 1968, Pigmeat and an American vocalist called
Shorty Long both had records of a song called "Here
Come(s) the Judge" on the U.S. and U.K. charts.

Is that a chicken joke?   Asked by Jo Ann Worley (presumably alluding to the age-old joke: *Q*. Why did the
chicken cross the road? *A*.To get to the other side/For
some foul reason, etc).

Is this the party to whom I am speaking?   Lily Tomlin
as Ernestine, the insufferably rude, snobbish switch-
board operator.

Look that up in your Funk and Wagnalls!   Referring
to the dictionary.

Say goodnight, Dick/goodnight, Dick!   Rowan and
Martin's concluding exchange was a straight lift from
the old George Burns and Gracie Allen sign-off on *The
Burns and Allen Show:*

> *Burns:* Say goodnight, Gracie.
> *Allen:* Goodnight, Gracie!

Flying Fickle Finger of Fate Award, the.   This was
the name of the prize in a mock talent-contest seg-
ment of the show ("Who knows when the Fickle Finger of Fate may beckon *you* to stardom?"). According
to Partridge/*Slang*, "fucked by the Fickle Finger of
Fate" was a Canadian armed forces' expression in the
1930s.

Ten-four! In the cop series *Highway Patrol* (1955–59), Chief Dan Matthews (Broderick Crawford) was always bellowing this into his radio. It signifies agreement and conforms to the "ten-code" of radio communication used by police, especially from the 1960s onward.

thirtysomething. There is nothing new about giving someone's age as "twenty something" or "thirty something" when you don't know the exact figure, but the TV series (shown from 1987) popularized the usage. Initially the series was about a suburban married couple who gave up two incomes to have a baby and how they dealt with "old friends who feel neglected" and wondered how to "retain the magic that brought them together." From the *Washington Post* (March 13, 1990): "MEN AND WOMEN AT MIDLIFE—LOOKING FOR ADULT LOVE IN THE '90s: Judy is a successful and attractive businesswoman toward the far end of her thirtysomething decade. Yet she feels frustrated, alone and angry about her failed relationships with men."

Who loves ya, baby? Telly Savalas, as the lollipop-sucking New York police lieutenant in the TV series *Kojak* (1973–77), created a vogue for this phrase. Inevitably, there was also a song with the title, performed by Savalas (1975).

Who shot J. R.? The hero/villain J. R. Ewing (played by Larry Hagman) of the top-rated soap opera *Dallas* was shot in the cliff-hanging final episode of the program's 1979–80 season. For reasons not entirely clear, the question of who had inflicted this far from mortal wound caused a sensation in the U.S. and U.K. Consequently, the first episode of the next season attracted 53.3 percent of the American viewing audience, the highest-ever rating. All those who had posed the question, or sported bumper stickers declaring "I hate J. R.," discovered that the guilty party was a jilted lover.

Will the real _____ please stand up?   In *To Tell the Truth*, devised by Goodson-Todman Productions and shown from 1956–66, a panel had to decide which of three contestants, all claiming to be a certain person, was telling the truth. After the panelists had interrogated the challenger and the impostors, they had to declare which person they thought was the real one. Emcee Bud Collyer would then say, "Will the real _____ please stand up!" and he or she did so.

In March 1984 Elizabeth Taylor, the actress, was quoted as saying, "I'm still trying to find the real Elizabeth Taylor and make her stand up."

You've got big dreams . . . ("You want fame. Well, fame costs, and right here's where you start paying.") A spin-off from the feature film about students at the High School of Performing Arts in New York, the TV series *Fame* (from 1982) began each episode with dance teacher Lydia Grant (Debbie Allen) giving this warning.

13

TO COIN
A PHRASE

"There is no bigger peril either to thinking or to education than the popular phrase," wrote Frank Binder in Dialectic (1932). Logan Pearsall Smith, however, provided the perfect defense in an essay on English Idioms (1923): "Idiom is held in little esteem by schoolmasters and old-fashioned grammarians, but good writers love it. . . . It may be regarded as the sister of poetry, for like poetry it retranslates our concepts into living experiences, and breathes that atmosphere of animal sensation which sustains the poet in his flights."

To "coin" a phrase means to invent one or to give one "currency." But in the twentieth century the expression "to coin a phrase" has become an ironic way of excusing a cliché or banal statement.

And so to some popular phrases of a general nature:

Alive and well and living in _____. It probably began in a perfectly natural way—"What's happened to old so-and-so?" "Oh, he's alive and well and living in Chicago," etc. In the preface to *His Last Bow* (1917), Conan Doyle wrote: "The Friends of Mr. Sherlock Holmes will be glad to learn that he is still alive and well . . ."

The phrase was given a tremendous fillip when the Belgian-born songwriter and singer Jacques Brel (1929–1978) was made the subject of an off-Broadway musical show entitled *Jacques Brel Is Alive and Well and Living in Paris* (1968–72). Quite why Brel should have merited the "Where are they now?" treatment I have never been quite sure.

But the format caught on. It was used as part of religious sloganeering—"God is not dead . . . He's alive and well and living in your heart"—and in jokes: "Walter Lippman —God is not dead. He is alive and appearing twice a week in the *Washington Post*" (cited by Art Buchwald c. 1970); "God is not dead—but alive and well and working on a much less ambitious project" (quoted in 1979); "Jesus Christ is alive and well and signing copies of the Bible at Macy's" (quoted in 1980).

A film in 1975 was lumbered with the title *Sheila Devine Is Dead and Living in New York.*

All dressed up and nowhere to go. According to the *OED2* this phrase started life in a song by G. Whiting (1912), "When You're All Dressed Up and Have No Place to Go." But Lowe's *Directory of Popular Music* (ASCAP, 4th ed.) ascribes it to Silvio Hein and Benjamin Burt. Cole Porter wrote a parody in 1914 concluding with the words '. . . and don't know Huerto Go.' But the song appears to have been chiefly popularized by the American comedian Raymond Hitchcock in *The Beauty Shop* (New York, 1914) and *My Manhattan* (London, 1915). The words gained further emphasis when they were used by William Allen White to describe the Progressive Party following Theodore Roosevelt's decision to retire from presidential competition in 1916. He said they were "all dressed up with nowhere to go."

All the world and his wife. A popular way of saying "everybody," though in decline since the feminism of the 1970s. The *ODQ* cites Christopher Anstey's use of the phrase in *The New Bath Guide* (1766):

> You may go to Carlisle's, and to Almack's too;
> And I'll give you my head if you find such a host,
> For coffee, tea, chocolate, butter, and toast:
> How he welcomes at once all the world and his wife,
> And how civil to folk he ne'er saw in his life.

But the phrase was clearly an established one by 1738 when Swift included it in *Polite Conversation:* "Who were the Company?—Why; there was all the World and his Wife.'

There is an equivalent French expression: "All the world and his father." Also, a variant of the basic English is "Everyone and his/her mother."

Am I right, or am I right? Brooking no debate. From the world of business. It is in the script of the film *Shampoo* (U.S., 1975). Compare what Mae West asks in *I'm No Angel* (1933): "Is that elegant, or is that elegant?"

And thereby hangs a tale. This storytelling device, still very much in use, indicates that some tasty tidbit is about to be revealed. It occurs a number of times in Shakespeare. In *As You Like It* (Act II, scene vii, line 28) Jaques, reporting the words of a motley fool (Touchstone), says:

> And so, from hour to hour, we ripe and ripe,
> And then, from hour to hour, we rot and rot,
> And thereby hangs a tale.

Other examples occur in *The Merry Wives of Windsor* (I, iv, 143) and *The Taming of the Shrew* (IV, i, 50). In *Othello* (III, i, 8), the Clown says, "O, thereby hangs a tail," emphasizing the innuendo that may or may not be present in the other examples.

Animal, vegetable, or mineral.   Not a quotation from any-one in particular, so far as I can tell; merely a way of describing three types of matter. And yet why does the phrase trip off the tongue so? Why not "animal, *mineral,* vegetable"? Or *"vegetable,* animal, mineral"? Perhaps be-cause these variants are harder to say, although in W. S. Gilbert's lyrics for *The Pirates of Penzance* (1879), Major-General Stanley does manage to sing:

> But still in matters vegetable, animal, and mineral,
> I am the very model of a modern Major-General.

Animal, Vegetable and Mineral was the title of a long-running archaeological quiz show on British television in the 1950s in which eminent university dons had to identify ancient artifacts by looking at them. The trio of words was also evoked in the long-running radio series *Twenty Questions.* Originally on the Mutual Radio Network in the U.S. in 1946, it was created by Fred Van De Venter and family —who transferred with the show to NBC-TV from 1949 to 1955. The program ran on BBC radio from 1947 to 1976 (though I'm not sure it was ever tried out on British TV). Panelists simply had to guess the identity of a "mystery object" by asking a maximum of twenty questions. A fourth category—"abstract"—was added in time.

The key to the matter is that the original American show was based on the old parlor game of "Animal, Vegetable, or Mineral," which seems to have been known on both sides of the Atlantic in the nineteenth century. In *Charles Dickens: His Tragedy and Triumph* by Edgar Johnson, we find (1839–41): "Dickens was brilliant in routing everybody at 'Animal, Vegetable, or Mineral,' although he himself failed to guess a vegetable object mentioned in 'mythological history' and belonging to a queen, and was chagrined to have it identified as the tarts made by the Queen of Hearts."

In the same book, in a chapter on the period 1858–65, we also read: "[Dickens] was swift and intuitive in 'Twenty Questions.' . . .   On one occasion, he failed to guess 'The powder in the Gunpowder Plot,' although he succeeded in reaching Guy Fawkes."

Presumably, then, the game was known by both names, though Dickens also refers to a version of it as "Yes and No" in *A Christmas Carol* (1843). "Twenty Questions" is referred to as such in a letter from Hannah Moore as early as 1786.

As busy as a one-armed paperhanger with the itch. Mencken listed this in 1942 as an "American saying," and most of these colorful comparisons are also American in origin. Here are a few more:

> As useless as a chocolate kettle (of a U.K. football team, quoted on BBC Radio *Quote . . . Unquote* 1986).
> As scarce as rocking-horse manure (an example from Australia).
> As lonely as a country dunny (ditto).
> As mad as a gumtree full of galahs (ditto).
> As inconspicuous as Liberace at a wharfies' picnic (ditto).
> As easy as juggling with soot.
> As jumpy as a one-legged cat in a sandbox.
> As much chance as a fart in a windstorm.
> As likely as a snowstorm in Karachi.

Beat Generation, the. On April 4, 1988, the London *Guardian* announced in an obituary: "Although a novelist, poet and lecturer at many universities, John Clellon Holmes was chiefly known for giving the Beat Generation its name. The phrase first appeared in his 1952 novel *Go.*" The headline to the piece (by W. J. Weatherby) was "The Naming of a Generation."

This came as news to those of us who had always believed that Jack Kerouac (1922–1969) was not only the presiding genius of that phenomenon of the fifties but had also named it. Indeed, in his book *The Origins of the Beat*

Generation, Kerouac admitted to borrowing the phrase from a broken-down drug addict called Herbert Huncke.

Turning to Randy Nelson's *The Almanac of American Letters* (1981), we may discover a description of the moment of coinage. He reports Kerouac as saying, "John Clellon Holmes . . . and I were sitting around trying to think up the meaning of the Lost Generation and the subsequent existentialism and I said, 'You know, this is really a beat generation,' and he leapt up and said, 'That's it, that's right.'" Holmes actually attributed the phrase directly to Kerouac in *The New York Times Magazine* of November 16, 1952.

When I put these versions to William J. Weatherby in New York, he replied, "I based my comment on what Holmes told me close to the end of his life. It's possible his memory was shadowed by then or he had oversimplified the past, but the majority view seems to be he fathered the phrase or at least it emerged in a conversation in which he was involved. I don't believe Kerouac himself thought it up or even cared much for it."

Beautiful people, the.   Coinage of this term is credited in *Current Biography* (1978) to the fashion journalist Diana Vreeland (c. 1903–1989). Whether she deserves this or not is open to question, although she does seem to have helped launch the similar term "Swinging London."

The earliest *OED2* citation with capital letters for each word is from 1966. The *OED2* refers it primarily to "'flower people,' hippies," though I would prefer the 1981 Australian *Macquarie Dictionary*'s less narrow "fashionable social set of wealthy, well-groomed, usually young people." The Lennon and McCartney song "Baby, You're a Rich Man" (released in July 1967) contains the line "How does it feel to be one of the beautiful people?"

William Saroyan's play *The Beautiful People* had been performed long before all this, in 1941, and Oscar Wilde in a letter to Harold Boulton (December 1879) wrote: "I could have introduced you to some very beautiful people.

Mrs. Langtry and Lady Lonsdale and a lot of clever beings who were at tea with me."

Bee's knees, to be the.   There has always been fascination with bees' knees. From the eighteenth century comes the expression "As big as a bee's knee," and from the nineteenth, "As weak as a bee's knee." But the bee whose knees became celebrated in U.S. slang from the 1920s was a very different kettle of fish . . . *OED2* has it in 1923.

To say that something was the "bee's knees" was to convey that it was the best around. I am sure that the particular part of the bee's anatomy singled out was chiefly important because of the rhyme. One of the most basic aspects of coining popular expressions lies in rhyme, alliteration, and assonance.

Hence, at around the same time, we find "the kipper's knickers." We also encounter "the cat's whiskers" (perhaps because of the importance of these in tuning wireless crystal sets in the 1920s), "the cat's pajamas" (still new enough to be daring), "the cat's meow/eyebrows/ankles/ tonsils/ adenoids/galoshes/cufflinks/roller skates."

Not to mention "the snake's hips," "the clam's garter," "the eel's ankle," "the elephant's instep," "the flea's eyebrows," "the canary's tusks," "the tiger's spots," "the leopard's stripes," "the sardine's whiskers," "the pig's wings"— "and just about any combination of animal, fish, or fowl with a part of the body or clothing that was inappropriate for it" (Flexner).

Big Apple, the.   "The Big Apple," a nickname for New York City, seems to have arisen in the 1930s and is still used to promote the city. But why? Take your pick: The Spanish word for a block of houses between two streets is *manzana,* which is also the word for apple; in the mid-1930s there was a Harlem nightclub called "The Big Apple," which was a mecca for jazz musicians; there was also a jitterbugging dance from the swing era c.1936 that took its name from the nightclub; "big apple" was racetrack argot, and New York City had a good reputation in this field.

Safire plumps for the jazz version, recalling a 1944 jive "handbook" defining "apple" as "the earth, the universe, this planet. Any place that's large. A big Northern city." Hence you called New York City the Big Apple if you considered it to be the center of the universe. It was, if you like, a place full of opportunity and ripe for plucking.

Blah-blah-blah. "Blah" and "blah-blah," signifying empty talk, airy mouthings, have been around (originally in the U.S.) since the end of World War I. More recently the tripartite version has become marginally more common to denote words omitted or as another way of saying "and so on." Ira Gershwin wrote a song called "Blah, Blah, Blah" for a show called *Delicious* (1931); it contains such lines as "Blah, blah, blah, blah moon . . . Blah, blah, blah, blah croon." From *Chez Nous,* the play (1974) by Peter Nichols: *"Burt* [a journalist]: You wouldn't object to that angle for the piece? Here's what he says: The Family bla-bla-bla, here's how he lives . . ."

From the *Washington Post* (January 22, 1989): "Saul Kelner, 19 . . . was the first person in line to see the President. He arrived at the White House . . . 11 1/2 hours before the open house was to begin. 'We didn't sleep,' he said. 'What we did, we circulated a list to ensure our places on line. "We the people, blah, blah, blah," and we all signed it.' "

"Bush referred to the diplomatic language [after a NATO summit conference in Bonn] in casual slang as 'blah, blah' " (*Washington Post,* May 31, 1989)—which caused foreign journalists problems in covering the President—"After all, how do you translate 'blah, blah' into Italian?"

Blow one's own trumpet, to. To boast of one's own achievements. This is sometimes said to have originated with the statue of Fame on the parapet of Wilton House,

near Salisbury. The figure—positioned after a fire in 1647
—originally held a trumpet in each hand.

This is pushing it a bit. Why does one need a precise
origin for such an obvious phrase? Brewer states that the
"allusion is to heralds, who used to announce with a flourish of trumpets the knights who entered a list."

By hook or by crook. "By hook or by crook I'll be last in
this book" is the cliché you append to the final page of an
autograph book when asked to contribute a little something more than your signature. But why "hook" and
"crook," apart from the rhyme? The *OED2* finds a couple
of references in the works of John Wycliffe around 1380
but states firmly that, while there are many theories, there
is no firm evidence for the origin of the phrase.

In fact, the only theory of any substance is the one about
peasants in feudal times being allowed to take for firewood
only those tree branches that they could pull down "by
hook or by crook." "Crook" here meaning the hooked staff
carried by shepherds (and also, symbolically, by bishops).

Brewer quotes the *Bodmin Register* (1525): "Dynmure
wood was ever open and common to the . . . inhabitants
of Bodmin . . . to bear away upon their backs a burden of
lop, crop, hook, crook, and bag wood." Neil Ewart in *Everyday Phrases* (1983), without giving a source, claims a
precise origin in the granting of a right to collect wood in
this way to a certain Purkiss, charcoal burner in the New
Forest, at the time of William Rufus's death in 1100.

Can dish it out but can't take it, (s)he. Said of people who
can't take the sort of criticism they dispense to others. A
reader's letter to *Time* (January 4, 1988) remarked of co-
medienne Joan Rivers's action in suing a magazine for
misquoting her about her late husband: "For years she has
made big money at the expense of others with her caustic
remarks. Obviously Rivers can dish it out but can't take it
in."

In the film *49th Parallel* (1941), Raymond Massey as a

Canadian soldier plays with the phrase when he says to a Nazi, "When things go wrong, we can take it. We can dish it out, too."

Cock and bull story, a. A long, rambling, unbelievable story. The phrase is used notably in Laurence Sterne's *Tristram Shandy* (1760–67). The last words of the novel are: "L—d! said my mother, what is all this story about?—A cock and a bull, said Yorick—And one of the best of its kind, I ever heard."

Other suggested origins for the phrase include old fables in general that have talking animals, going right back to Aesop—confirmed perhaps by the equivalent French phrase *"coq à l'âne"* (literally "cock to donkey"). Someone who hated having to listen to such fables was probably the first to dub them as such. Samuel Fisher's 1660 story about cock and a bull being transformed into a single animal, which people may have thought pretty improbable, is another possibility. The Cock and Bull public houses, which are but a few doors apart in Stony Stratford, Buckinghamshire, have also been suggested as the place of origin; generally confused tales told first in one pub, the Cock, were then retold in another, the Bull.

The *OED2*'s earliest citation in this precise form is from the Philadelphia *Gazette of the United States* (1795): "a long cock-and-bull story about the Columbianum [a proposed national college]."

Come hell and/or high water. This phrase, meaning come what may, is mentioned in Partridge/*Slang* as a cliché, but as phrases go it is curiously lacking in citations. The *OED2* finds no examples earlier than this century. And I have to admit defeat too. *Come Hell or High Water* was used as the title of a book by yachtswoman Clare Francis in 1977, which she followed in 1978 with *Come Wind or Weather. Hell and High Water* was the title of a film (1954).

Graeme Donald in London *Today* (April 26, 1986) linked

it to punishments meted out to witches in the Middle Ages: "Lesser transgressions only warranted the miscreant being obliged to stand in boiling water, the depth of which was directly proportional to the crime. Hence the expression 'From Hell and high water, may the good Lord deliver us.'

This seems rather fanciful. Was he thinking of the so-called Thieves' Litany—"From Hull, Hell and Halifax, good Lord deliver us" (because the gibbet was much used in these Yorkshire towns in the sixteenth and seventeenth centuries)?

Crazy like a fox. Meaning "apparently crazy but with far more method than madness" (Partridge/*Catch Phrases*). Craziness is hardly a quality one associates with foxes, so the expression was perhaps formed in parallel with the older (and more understandable) "cunning as a fox."

But foxes always seem to get into expressions like these. Interviewing the actress Judy Carne in 1980, I asked about Goldie Hawn, her one-time colleague on *Laugh-In*. Carne said, "She's not a dizzy blonde. She's about as *dumb* as a fox. She's incredibly bright."

Crazy Like a Fox was the title of a U.S. TV series about a "sloppy old private eye" and his "smart lawyer son" (from 1984). Before that, it was used as the title of a book by S. J. Perelman (1945).

Dead as a doornail, as. In the Middle Ages the doornail was the knob on which the knocker struck: "As this is frequently knocked on the head, it cannot be supposed to have much life in it" (Brewer). The phrase occurs as early as 1350, then in 1362 in Langland's *Piers Plowman* ("And dead as a doornail"). Shakespeare uses it a couple of times, in the usual form and, as in *The Second Part of King Henry IV* (Act V, scene iii, line 126):

Falstaff: What, is the old King dead?
Pistol: As nail in door.

Dickens uses the phrase in *A Christmas Carol*: "Old Marley was as dead as a doornail."

Dirty work at the crossroads. A Hollywood idiom, but not quite a cliché, that means despicable, suspicious behavior in any situation. The earliest citation I have found is from the film *Flying Down to Rio* (1933), but P. G. Wodehouse has it in *Man Upstairs* (1914). Brewer suggests that it may have something to do with the old custom of burying people at the crossroads.

Do not pass "Go." A London *Sunday Mirror* editorial (May 3, 1981) stated: "The laws of contempt are the ones under which editors and other media folk can be sent straight to jail without passing Go." A businessman said to a woman who had paid for her husband to be beaten up (report of trial, *The Times* (London) November 30, 1982), "If the police find out you are paying, you will go to jail, directly to jail, you will not pass 'go' or collect £200."

These two citations are testimony to the enduring use of Monopoly phraseology. Monopoly is the name of a board game invented by an unemployed salesman, Charles Darrow, in 1929, the year of the Wall Street crash, and is based on fantasies of buying up real estate in Atlantic City. Players begin on the square marked "Go," may in due course come back to that square to "collect salary as you pass," land on the "Go to jail" square, or draw a "Chance" card with the penalty:

GO TO JAIL
MOVE DIRECTLY TO JAIL
DO NOT PASS GO

Don't go near the water. That is to say, "be careful." Mencken quotes "author unidentified":

> Mother, may I go out to swim?
> Yes, my darling daughter;

> Hang your clothes on a hickory limb,
> But/And don't go near the water.

Don't Go Near the Water was the title of a film (1957)
about U.S. sailors on a South Pacific island, based on a
William Brinkley novel. "Yes, My Darling Daughter" was a
popular song of 1941—the Andrews Sisters recorded it—
and there was also a play with the title in the late 1930s,
subsequently filmed (1939). *No, My Darling Daughter* was
the title of a British film comedy in 1961. I take it (from
"hickory limb") that the rhyme is of American origin.

Don't spit—remember the Johnstown flood. This admonition against spitting is a turn-of-the-century Americanism. The Johnstown flood of May 31, 1889, entered folklore
when a dam burst near Johnstown, Pennsylvania, and
2,200 people died. A silent film, *The Johnstown Flood,* was
made in the U.S. in 1926. Partridge/*Catch Phrases* finds
that notices bearing this joke were exhibited in bars before
Prohibition started in 1919.

William Allen White's comment on the defeat of Alfred
Landon in the 1936 U.S. presidential election was: "It was
not an election the country had just undergone, but a
political Johnstown flood." Mencken lists it as an "American proverb."

Don't teach your grandmother to suck eggs. Meaning
don't try to tell anyone things that, given the person's age
and experience, he/she might be expected to know anyway. According to Partridge/*Slang,* variations of this very
old expression include advice against instructing grandmothers to "grope ducks," "grope a goose," "sup sour
milk," "spin," and "roast eggs." In 1738 Swift's *Polite Conversation* has "Go teach your grannam to suck eggs."
OED2 has a 1707 example.

It has been suggested that, in olden days, sucking eggs
would have been a particularly important thing for a

grandmother to be able to do because, having no teeth, it would be all she was capable of.

Dragged kicking and screaming into the twentieth century.   For a well-known phrase, this is curiously little documented. The only example I have found in this precise form comes from an article by Kenneth Tynan written in 1959 and collected in *Curtains* (1961): "A change, slight but unmistakable, has taken place; the English theatre has been dragged, as Adlai Stevenson once said of the Republican Party, kicking and screaming into the twentieth century." From the *Washington Post* (December 19, 1988): "Still, Jones and Hawke, prodded by other corporate-minded partners, have dragged Arnold & Porter—sometimes kicking and screaming—into a 21st century mode of thinking, which they believe will position the firm to compete with firms that already have more than 1,000 lawyers." Also from the *Post* (January 8, 1990): " 'Ireland had to be dragged kicking and screaming into the 20th century from the 19th—and now it's being dragged back again,' said Christine Donaghy, chief executive of the Irish Family Planning Association."

Dressed up to the nines.   Or very smartly dressed. This may have come to us via a pronunciation shift. If you were to say dressed up "to then eyne" in Old English, that would mean "dressed up to the eyes" (*eyne* being the old plural of eye). The snag with this is that no examples of the phrase being used occur before the eighteenth century.

Other suggested origins include: (from the *Longman Dictionary of English Idioms*, 1989) that the phrase refers to the setting of a standard with ten as the highest point one can reach and nine as very nearly the best; (from Neil Ewart, *Everyday Phrases*, 1983) that it has to do with setting oneself up to match the Nine Muses of classical mythology; (from Partridge/*Slang*) that it has to do with the mystic number nine; that as the 99th Regiment of Foot was

renowned for smartness of dress, anyone well turned out
was "dressed up [to equal] the nines."

The origin remains a bit of a mystery.

Drop a clanger, to.   To say or do something socially em-
barrassing. *OED2* 's first citation is from 1958, but according to a photograph caption in the London *Sunday Times
Magazine* (January 30, 1983), "The nerveless men who
worked on the construction of New York's Woolworth
Building in 1912 had nightmares of dropping a girder, or
'clanger' in the phrase they gave to the language." Curiously, Partridge/*Slang* calls a "clanger" in this phrase a
synonym for "testicle," but derives it from the inoffensive
"drop a brick."

Due to circumstances beyond our control.   Cliché of apol-
ogy. The first Duke of Wellington used the phrase "Circumstances over which I have no control" in an 1839
letter. Charles Dickens had Mr. Micawber talk of "circumstances beyond my individual control" in *David Cop-
perfield* (1849–50). The broadcaster Fred W. Friendly entitled a critical survey of American TV *Due to
Circumstances Beyond Our Control* (1967), presumably
from the TV announcer's "We regret we are unable to
proceed with the scheduled program, due to circumstances beyond our control."

Dukes/dooks up, to put one's.   Describing a summit between Soviet and American leaders, *Time* (October 20,
1986) stated: "Reagan and Gorbachev both came to office
not with their hands outstretched but with their dukes
up." If "dukes" means "fists," why so?

One theory is that because the first Duke of Wellington
had such a large nose, a "duke" became a synonym for one.
Then, so this theory goes, a man's fist became a "duke
buster." In time this was shortened, fists became simply
"dukes," and at some stage in the nineteenth century the

phrase crossed the Atlantic to enter into popular American use.

Morris prefers another theory, that the use derives from Cockney rhyming slang: "Duke of York's" = "forks" = "fingers" (standing for the whole hand or fist). Though it is an involved explanation, I agree with it.

OED2 has the expression by 1874. Winston Churchill neatly played on the phrase in a public speech about House of Lords reform on September 4, 1909: "In the absence of any commanding voice, the Tory party have had to put up their 'dooks.' " A report of the speech adds, "Great laughter and a voice: 'What about your grandfather?' "—Churchill's grandfather was the Duke of Marlborough.

Few vouchers short of a pop-up toaster, a. A phrase used to describe mental shortcomings, or "a deficiency in the marbles department." I first noticed this one being used around May 1987. Another version is "Not quite enough coupons for the coffee percolator and matching set of cups." More venerable idioms for the same thing would include: "rowing with one oar in the water"; "not playing with a full deck"; "one brick/a few bricks short of a load"; "two sandwiches short of a picnic"; "the elevator doesn't go to the top floor"; or "the light's on, but no one's in."

Moving a shade to one side, I can but print my favorite description of a TV producer who was not at his best after lunch. Said his assistant, apologetically, "He transmits, but he doesn't receive."

God's own country. There can be few countries that have not elected to call themselves this. It is certainly not exclusive.

Of the United States: The *OED2* provides an example from 1865 and tags the phrase as being of U.S. origin. Flexner says that during the Civil War the shorter "God's country" was the Union troops' term for the North, "especially when battling heat, humidity, and mosquitoes in the

South. Not until the 1880s did the term mean any section
of the country one loved or the open spaces of the West."
A 1937 U.S. film had the title *God's Country and the
Woman.*

Of Australia: Dr. Richard Arthur (1865–1932), a state
politician and President of the Immigration League of Aus-
tralasia, was quoted in *Australia Today* (November 1,
1911) as saying, "This Australia is 'God's Own Country' for
the brave." The *Dictionary of Australian Quotations*
(1984) notes that at the time, "Australia was frequently
referred to as 'God's Own Country,' the phrase drawing
satirical comments from the foreign unenlightened."

Of South Africa/Ireland: I have heard both these countries so dubbed informally (in the 1970s), with varying
degrees of appropriateness and irony.

I have also heard Yorkshiremen describe their homeland
as "God's own *county.*" "Yorkshire's natural reluctance to
play second fiddle to London has faced some difficulty in
the matter of house prices. . . . God's own county is at the
centre of things yet again"—*Guardian,* January 23, 1989.

Compare the expression "God's acre," which means a
cemetery or churchyard and is a borrowing from the German—although Longfellow called it "an ancient Saxon
phrase" (Brewer).

Happiest days of your life, the. The traditional platitude
intoned by the old duffer who speaks at graduations is that
his listeners will agree that schooldays are "the happiest
days of your life." It was used as the title of a famous play
by John Dighton (produced in London in 1948, filmed in
1950). However, the schoolchildren in that work may have
had special cause to believe the catch phrase, as the plot
hinges on wartime confusion in which a boys' school and a
girls' school are lodged under the same roof.

The Best Years of Our Lives is the title of a film (1946)
about what happens to a group of ex-servicemen when
they return from the war —having "given the best years of

their lives" to their country. "The best days of our lives" is an expression also used in this kind of context.

Have gun will travel.   Best known as the title of a Western TV series (1957–64), this led to a format phrase with many variations. Originally the phrase might have been on the calling card of a hired gun—e.g. "Have gun, will travel. . . . Wire Paladin, San Francisco." Later it turned up in many ways—as joke slogans ("Have pill, will"; "Have wife, must travel") and even as the U.K. title of another TV series (1981), *Have Girls, Will Travel* (known as *The American Girls* in the U.S.).

He can't fart and chew gum at the same time.   Or, "he's stupid." This is the correct version—advanced on the authority of John Kenneth Galbraith, no less—of what President Lyndon Johnson once said about Gerald Ford. It's rather more colorful than "he can't *walk* and chew gum at the same time," the version usually quoted when Ford became President in 1974. Like much of Johnson's earthy speech, it was probably a Texan expression rather than of his own invention.

Hole in the head, to need something like a.   Meaning to need something not at all. Leo Rosten in *Hooray for Yiddish* (1982) describes this phrase as "accepted from Alaska to the Hebrides" and states that it comes directly from the Yiddish *lock in kop:* "It was propelled into our vernacular by the play *A Hole in the Head* by Arnold Schulman and more forcibly impressed upon mass consciousness by the Frank Sinatra movie (1959)." J. D. Salinger in *The Catcher in the Rye* (1951) has: "The Disciples . . . were about as much use to Him as a hole in the head."

Homer nods, even.   Even the greatest, best, and wisest of us can't be perfect all the time, and can make mistakes. Mencken has "Even Homer sometimes nods" as an English proverb derived from Horace, *De Arte Poetica*, c. 8

B.C. ("I am indignant when worthy Homer nods"), and familiar since the seventeenth century.

If it's _____, this must be _____. *If It's Tuesday, This Must Be Belgium* was the title of a 1969 film about a group of American tourists rushing around Europe. It popularized a format phrase that people could use when they were in the midst of some hectic activity, while also reflecting on the confused state of tourists superficially "doing" the sights without knowing where they are.

If you can't beat 'em, join 'em. A familiar proverb, probably American in origin in the alternative form, "If you can't lick 'em, join 'em." The earliest citation in the *CODP* is from Quentin Reynolds, the American writer, in 1941. Mencken had it in his dictionary, however, by 1942.

Safire calls it "a frequent bit of advice, origin obscure, given in areas dominated by one (political) party. . . . The phrase, akin to the Scottish proverb 'Better bend than break,' carries no connotation of surrender; it is used to indicate that the way to take over the opposition's strength is to adopt their positions and platform."

The Oxford Dictionary of Current Idiomatic English (1985) takes in a broader view of the phrase's use: "If a rival faction, political party, business firm, foreign power, etc., continues to be more successful than one's own, it is better to go over to their side and get what advantages one can from the alliance."

Illegitimi non carborundum. This made-up Latin phrase—supposed to mean "Don't let the bastards grind you down"—was U.S. General "Vinegar Joe" Stilwell's motto during World War II, though it is not suggested he devised it. According to Partridge/*Catch Phrases,* the phrase finds its origins in British army intelligence very early on in the same war. "Carborundum" is the trade name of a very hard substance composed of silicon carbide, used in grinding.

The same meaning is also conveyed by the phrase *"nil carborundum . . ."* (as in the title of a play by Henry Livings, 1962) —a pun upon the genuine Latin *nil desperandum* ("never say die," literally, "there is nought to be despaired of").

Perhaps because it is a made-up one, the phrase takes many forms, e.g.: *"nil illegitimis . . ."*; *"nil bastardo illegitimi . . ."*; *"nil bastardo carborundum . . ."* When the Rt. Rev. David Jenkins, the Bishop of Durham, was unwise enough to make use of the phrase at a private meeting in March 1985, a cloth-eared journalist reported him as having said, *"Nil desperandum illegitimi . . ."*

I love it but it doesn't love me. People say this when refusing something offered to them—usually food or drink. And they have been using it for many a year. Swift lists it in *Polite Conversation:*

> *Lady Smart:* Madam, do you love bohea tea?
> *Lady Answerall:* Why, madam, I must confess I do love it; but it does not love me . . .

_____ is the name of the game. An overused phrase from the mid-1960s, meaning "_____ is what it's really about." Partridge/*Catch Phrases* finds an example in 1961. National Security Adviser McGeorge Bundy, talking about foreign policy goals in Europe in 1966, said, "Settlement is the name of the game." In time almost everything was "the name of the game," following the title of a 1966 TV movie called *Fame Is the Name of the Game.* Then followed several years of TV's *The Name of the Game* (1968–71). The expression was replaced for a while by "_____ is where it's at."

Is there life after _____? Presumably derived from the age-old question, "Is there life after death?" There seems no end to the variations on this theme. *Is There Sex After*

Marriage? was the title of a film (1973); *Is There Life After Housework?*, a book by Don A. Aslett (1981).

It seemed like a good idea at the time.   Partridge/*Catch Phrases* has this limp excuse for something that has gone awry as dating back to the 1950s. But Leslie Halliwell found it in a 1931 film called *The Last Flight.* It is the story of a group of American airmen who remain in Europe after World War I. One of them is gored to death when he leaps into the arena during a bullfight. Journalists outside the hospital ask his friend why the man should have done such a thing. The friend (played by Richard Barthelmess) replies, "Because it seemed like a good idea at the time."

Just one of those things.   Something inexplicable or inevitable. The *OED2* finds this first in John O'Hara's book *Appointment in Samarra* (1934) and in the following year as the title of the Cole Porter song, which undoubtedly ensured its enduring place in the language. Five years earlier, however, Porter had used the title for a completely different song that, though published, was dropped from the show it was supposed to be in.

Keep up with the Joneses, to.   To strive not to be outdone by one's neighbors. Yes, but why the Joneses in particular? A straightforward answer. "Keeping Up with the Joneses" was the title of a comic strip by Arthur R. "Pop" Momand that appeared in the New York *Globe* from 1913 to 1931.

It is said that Momand had at first intended to call his strip "Keeping Up with the Smiths," but refrained because his own neighbors were actually of that name and some of the exploits he wished to report had been acted out by them in real life.

_____**land.**   As in "radioland," "listenerland," "viewerland," this is a suffix construction originating in the U.S. "Hi there, all you folks out there in radioland!" a presenter might well have said in the 1930s or 40s. Since 1955 Disneyland has proliferated with its "Adventureland," "Frontierland," and "Tomorrowland." From *Spy* magazine (February 1989): "And from the *Spy* mailroom floor: The Unsoliciteds out in Returnenvelopeland continue to ply us with free verse and promises of loose fiction."

Leave no stone unturned, to. Meaning to search for something with complete thoroughness. It was used by President Johnson in 1963 when announcing the terms of the Warren Commission's investigation of President Kennedy's assassination. An example from an anonymously published attack on dice-playing, c. 1550: "He will refuse no labor nor leave no stone unturned, to pick up a penny."

The actress Diana Rigg neatly twisted the phrase for her book of bad theatrical reviews—*No Turn Unstoned* (1982).

Let's get down to the (real) nitty-gritty. Or "let's get down to the real basics of a problem or situation" (like getting down to brass tacks). Sheilah Graham, the Hollywood columnist, in her book *Scratch an Actor* (1969), says of Steve McQueen: "Without a formal education—Steve left school when he was fifteen—he has invented his own vocabulary to express what he means. . . . His 'Let's get down to the nitty-gritty' has gone into the American language."

All she meant, I feel, is that McQueen popularized the term, for it is generally held to be an African-American phrase and was talked about before the film star came on the scene. It seems to have had a particular vogue among Black Power campaigners c. 1963, and the first *OED2* citation is from that year. In 1963 Shirley Ellis recorded a song "The Nitty Gritty" to launch a new dance (like "The Locomotion" before it). The opening line of the record is "Now let's get down to the real nitty-gritty."

Stuart Berg Flexner (*Listening to America*, 1982) comments: "It may have originally referred to the gritlike nits or small lice that are hard to get out of one's hair or scalp or to a Black English term for the anus."

Life of Reilly/ Riley, to live the. Idiom that means to have a high old time, wallow in luxury, live it up, without much effort—have an easy life. *The Life of Riley* was used as the title of a TV series with Jackie Gleason (1949–50), but I have not come across an earlier citation. Partridge/ *Catch Phrases* guesses c. 1935 and suggests an Anglo-Irish origin—but, surely, it is not necessary to assume that. In 1919 there was a song by Harry Pease with the title "My Name Is Kelly," which went, "Faith and my name is Kelly, Michael Kelly,/ But I'm living the life of Reilly just the same." But that seems to be using an established phrase— for the origins of which the hunt continues.

Morris thinks the name was "O'Reilly" and that the association arose from a U.S. vaudeville song from the 1880s about such a character—though it doesn't appear to incorporate the line as we know it. Bartlett, however, quotes from the chorus of an 1882 song with the title "Is That Mr. Reilly" and adds that this is the "assumed origin of 'the life of Riley.'"

Like a fairy-tale (princess). The urge to say that everything in sight was "like a fairy tale" was, of course, rampant at the nuptials of the Prince of Wales and Lady Diana Spencer in July 1981. Tom Fleming, the BBC-TV commentator, said the bride was "like a fairy-tale princess." Even Robert Runcie, Archbishop of Canterbury, began his address at St Paul's: "Here is the stuff of which fairy tales are made."

"It was just like a fairy tale" is also a cliché put into the mouths of unsuspecting members of the public by popular journalists when they are trying to describe some rather pleasant thing that has happened to them. As Iona and Peter Opie point out, however, in *The Classic Fairy Tales* (1974), this is a very partial way of looking at such matters: "When the wonderful happens, when a holiday abroad is a splendid success or an unlikely romance ends happily, we commonly exclaim it was 'just like a fairy tale,' overlooking that most events in fairy tales are remarkable for their unpleasantness, and that in some of the tales there is no happy ending, not even the hero or heroine escaping with their life."

Like a red rag to a bull. Meaning obviously provocative. Christy Brown in *Down All the Days* (1970) has: "Sure they [breasts] only get you into trouble, woman dear. . . . Showing them off to a man is like waving a red cloth at a bull." There is no example before 1873, but John Lyly in *Euphues and His England* (1580) has: "He that cometh before [a bull] will not wear . . . red," based on the belief that bulls are aggravated by the color. In fact, they are color blind. If they do react, it is probably the movement of a bright-colored cloth that causes the animal to charge.

Charles Dickens in *Bleak House* (Chapter 43, 1853) seems to allude to the saying in: "You know my old opinion of him. . . . An amiable bull, who is determined to make every colour scarlet."

Like rats deserting/leaving a sinking ship. This phrase, which means "hurriedly, desperately," comes from the English proverb to the effect that "rats desert/forsake/leave a falling house/sinking ship." *ODP* finds an example of the "house" version in 1579 and of the "ship" (in Shakespeare) in 1611. Brewer adds: "It was an old superstition that rats deserted a ship before she set out on a voyage that was to end in her loss."

"Rat," meaning "a politician who deserts his party," was used by the first Earl of Malmesbury in 1792 (*OED2*). In the U.S. it made its first appearance in the saying "Like a rat deserting a sinking ship" around 1800, and was alluded to by Thomas Jefferson in an 1812 letter: "I think the old hulk [England] in which you are is near her wreck, and that, like a prudent rat, you should escape in time."

Many good jokes have grown from this usage. In Malcolm Muggeridge's diary for February 14, 1948 (published 1981), he notes: "Remark of Churchill's was quoted to me about the Liberal candidature of Air Vice-Marshal Bennett in Croydon. 'It was the first time,' Churchill said, 'that he had heard of a rat actually swimming out to join a sinking ship.' "

In his diary for January 26, 1941, John Colville noted that Churchill had reflected on the difficulty of "crossing the floor" (changing parties) in the House of Commons: "He had done it and he knew. Indeed he had re-done it, which everybody said was impossible. They had said you could rat but you couldn't re-rat."

Moment of truth, the.   A turning point or other significant moment. Originally the phrase comes from *"El momento de la verdad"* in Spanish bullfighting—the final sword thrust that kills the animal. Compare *The Moment of Truth* (*Il Momento della Verità*), the title of a 1964 Italian/Spanish film with a bullfighting theme. In *I, Claud* (1967), Claud Cockburn said of European intellectuals who had fought in the Spanish Civil War: "They proclaimed, however briefly, that a moment comes when your actions have to bear some kind of relation to your words. This is what is called the Moment of Truth."

My name is mud.   An exclamation acknowledging that one has made a mistake and is held in low esteem. It so happens that when John Wilkes Booth, the actor who assassinated President Lincoln in 1865, was escaping from the theater in which he had committed the deed, he fell and broke his leg. A country doctor named Dr. Samuel Mudd tended Booth's wound without realizing the circumstances under which it had been received. When he did realize, he informed the authorities, was charged with being a coconspirator, and was sentenced to life imprisonment.

Mudd was pardoned by Andrew Johnson, Lincoln's successor, after he had helped stop an outbreak of fever at the prison in which he was incarcerated. A hundred years later Mudd's descendants were still trying to clear his name.

But how do we come by the expression that someone's

name "is mud"? Is it not sufficient that we are comparing it to the dark, murky substance?

As Morris points out, "mud," in the sense of scandalous and defamatory charges, goes back to a time well before the Civil War. There had been an expression, "the mud press," to describe mudslinging newspapers before 1846. "So it seems most likely that the expression was well-established before Dr. Mudd met his unhappy fate."

OED2 has an 1823 citation for "And his name is mud!" as an ejaculation at the end of a silly oration (from "Jon Bee," *Slang*). Also, by then a "mud" was a name for a stupid fellow (from *A Dictionary of the Turf*). Which seems to be conclusive.

No more chance than (or as much chance as) a snowball/snowflake in Hell/Hades.   Sometimes abbreviated to "a snowball's chance." Meaning absolutely no chance at all. Mencken had this listed as an "American saying" by 1943; *American Speech* had found it by 1931. It was well-established by the time of Kurt Vonnegut's *Sirens of Titan* (1962): "The Army of Mars didn't have the chance of a snowball in hell." Partridge/*Catch Phrases* thinks it may date from the turn of the century.

Off one's trolley, to be.   This means "to be mad." *DOAS* finds it by 1909 and calls it "probably the oldest of the 'off [one's] _____' = crazy terms." Not quite true. "Off one's head" and "rocker" are a little older.

An entertaining but probably coincidental derivation of the phrase comes from the days of the Acoustic Recording Machine (c. 1910). The best effects were obtained not by the use of a volume control but by physically adjusting the distance between the singer and the machine according to the noise the singer was making. A trolley was employed to effect this. If a singer flounced off from the arrangement, she was said to be "off her trolley." Well, it's a thought.

Only in America . . . !   Used as the title of a British documentary TV series in 1980, this exclamation means "Only in America is this possible." Leo Rosten in *Hooray for Yiddish!* (1982) wrote: "Not a week passed during my boyhood (or two weeks, since then) without my hearing this exclamation. It is the immigrants' testament, an affirmation of the opportunities imbedded in that Promised Land . . . America. Scarcely a new shop, new product, a new journal or school or fad could appear without ecstatic *Only in America!*s."

Over the top.   Exaggerated in manner of performance, "too much." The expression "to go over the top" originated in the trenches of World War I. It was used to describe the method of charging over the parapet and out of the trenches on the attack. In a curious transition, the phrase was later adopted for use by show-business people when describing a performance that has gone beyond the bounds of restraint, and is sometimes abbreviated "O.T.T."

Rags-to-riches.   Usually in publishers' blurbs, a type of novel is inevitably dubbed a "rags-to-riches saga." Or the phrase is used to describe actual people who have risen from nothing to wealth. Taken from the story of Cinderella, of course. An early citation: In 1947 R. de Toledano wrote in *The Frontiers of Jazz:* "[Benny] Goodman was the first real rags-to-riches success in the swing-jazz field."

Real McCoy, the.   The real thing, the genuine article. Inevitably, many attempts at establishing which particular Mr. McCoy gave his name to the language in this way have been made.

The answer usually given is that it was "Kid" McCoy, a U.S. welterweight boxing champion in the late 1890s. When challenged by a man in a bar to prove he was who he said he was, McCoy flattened him. When the man came around he declared that this was indeed the "real" McCoy.

As Tom Burnam notes in *More Misinformation* (1980), "Kid" McCoy promoted this story about himself.

However, Messrs. G. Mackay, the Scottish whiskey distillers, were promoting their product as "the real *Mackay*" in 1870, as though alluding to an established expression. This could have derived from the Mackays of Reay in Sutherland claiming to be the principal branch of the Mackay clan. Robert Louis Stevenson used this version in an 1883 letter.

The association with booze endured. During Prohibition it was common to say that first-rate hooch was "the real McCoy" or simply "the McCoy."

Morris suggests that, as boxers used to take the names of famous predecessors, "Kid" McCoy may have had to bill himself as "Kid 'The Real' McCoy" to distinguish himself from his imitators. This seems a bit elaborate.

There are a number of other candidates for the original: a cattle baron (Joseph McCoy of Abilene, Texas); an Irishman, a character in an Irish ballad; and a Prohibition rumrunner (Bill McCoy)—not to mention "the real Macao" used to denote uncut heroin from Macao. Which, of all these, is the real "real McCoy" is anybody's guess.

Right stuff, the. Tom Wolfe helped repopularize the phrase "the right stuff" when he chose it as the title of a book (1979, filmed 1983). He used it to describe the qualities needed by test pilots and would-be astronauts in the early years of the U.S. space program.

Much earlier, however, the "right sort of stuff" had been applied to qualities of manly virtue, of good officer material, and even of good cannon fodder. Partridge/*Slang* has an example from the 1880s. In this sense the phrase was used by Ian Hay as the title of a novel—"some episodes in the career of a North Briton"—in 1908. It has also been used as an expression for alcohol.

School of hard knocks, the. Experience, hardship, considered as an educative force. The *OED2* calls this "U.S.

slang" and finds it in 1912. *The Complete Naff Guide* (1983) has it as a "naff boast": "But then, of course, I left university without a degree. I like to think I have a First from the School of Hard Knocks."

Receiving an honorary doctorate in the humanities from the University of Nevada in May 1976, Frank Sinatra said, "I am a graduate of the school of hard knocks." On losing his job as chairman of Mecca (producers of the Miss World competition) in October 1978, Eric Morley said, "I went to the College of Hard Knocks, and last week I got my doctorate." At least he didn't say he had attended "the university of life." Partridge/*Slang* prefers "the university of hard knocks" and dates it c. 1910. Lord Baden-Powell wrote a book called *Lessons from the 'Varsity of Life* (1933).

Sixes and sevens, to be at. To be confused; in an unresolved situation. The usual origin given for this expression (by, for example, Neil Ewart in *Everyday Phrases*, 1983) is that in the days when the medieval guilds of London took pride in their order of precedence, the Merchant Taylors and the Skinners could not agree on who should be sixth and who seventh. After an intervention by the Lord Mayor, they agreed to take it in turns—as they do to this day.

Morris, on the other hand, supports the theory that it dates from a dice game (as mentioned by Chaucer in one of his poems) in which the dice bore marks up to seven, if not further: "Only a confused or disorganized person would roll for this point" (i.e., a "six and seven"). This is the origin supported by the *OED2*.

I note that Shakespeare's only use of the phrase occurs in *King Richard II* (Act II, scene ii, line 121): "All is uneven,/ And everything is left at six and seven"—though it strikes me that in *Pericles* (IV, vi, 80) he may be making a punning allusion to it when (in a sexual context) Lysimachus says, "Did you go to 't [copulate] so young? Were you a gamester at five or at seven?"

Some of my best friends are _____. Originally ending
with "Jews/Jewish" but has come to be applied to any
oppressed minority. A self-conscious (and occasionally
jokey) disclaimer of prejudice. In a May 1946 letter, Somerset Maugham replied to charges that he was anti-Semitic
and said, "God knows I have never been that; some of my
best friends in England and America are Jews. . . ."

So, clearly, at that date the phrase could be used without
irony. However, the line may—according to one source—
have been rejected as a cartoon caption by *The New Yorker*
prior to World War II and presumably dates, in any case,
from the Nazi persecution of the Jews from the 1930s on.

In the (Jewish) Marx Brothers' film *Monkey Business*
(1931) there is the line, "Some of my best friends are
housewives." The Russian prime minister, Alexei Kosygin,
was apparently unaware of the phrase's near-cliché status
in 1971 when he said, "There is no anti-Semitism in Russia.
Some of my best friends are Jews."

Somebody up there likes me. I have been unable to find
an earlier use of this phrase, meaning that one is favored in
heaven, than as the title of a 1956 film written by Ernest
Lehman. It starred Paul Newman and was based on the life
of the World Middleweight Boxing Champion of 1947–48,
Rocky Graziano (d. 1990) (not to be confused with Rocky
Marciano). I believe Graziano's autobiography had the
same title. There was a title song from the film; also, a song
in 1957 was called "Somebody Up There Digs Me."

Soufflé rise twice, you can't make a. Meaning that it is
pointless to try and make something happen again if it is
unrepeatable. Alice Roosevelt Longworth supposedly said
it of Governor Thomas E. Dewey's nomination as the Republican challenger in 1948 (Dewey had previously stood
against F. D. Roosevelt in 1944).

Paul McCartney has more than once used the phrase to
discount the possibility of a Beatles reunion.

Stuffed shirt, a.   Obituary writers seem to have an urge to
credit the recently deceased with the coining of phrases,
even where the facts do not really support it. Patrick Brogan, writing of Clare Boothe Luce in the London *Independent* (October 12, 1987), stated: "She wrote a series of
articles poking fun at the rich and pompous, coining for
them the descriptive phrase 'stuffed shirts,' a title she used
for her first book."

That book was published in 1933, but the *OED2* has an
example of the phrase dating from 1913 (when Luce was a
mere ten), which makes it clear that by then it was already
current usage for a pompous person: "He characterized
Frank Shabata by a Bohemian expression which is the
equivalent of stuffed shirt," from Willa S. Cather's *O, Pio-
neers!* So, though Mrs. Luce may have repopularized the
phrase, she certainly didn't coin it.

Tender loving care.   Understandably, this is a phrase that
appears irresistible to songwriters:

As "T.L.C.": There is a song by Lehman, Lebowsky, and
C. Parker dating from 1960 (and translated as 'Tender
Loving *and* Care"). Also with this title there is a Motown
song by Jones, Sawer, and Jerome (1971); an instrumental
by R. L. Martin and Norman Harris (1975); and a song by
the Average White Band.

As "Tender Lovin' Care": There is a song written by
Brooks and Stillman (1966), and one written and performed by Ronnie Dyson (1983).

As "Tender Loving Care": There is a song written by
Mercer, Bright, and Wilson and recorded in 1966 by
Nancy Wilson. It was also used as the title of an album
by her.

The *OED2* recognizes the phrase as a colloquialism de-
noting "especially solicitous care such as is given by
nurses," and cites the *Listener* (May 12, 1977): "It is in a
nurse's nature and in her tradition to give the sick what is
well called 'TLC,' 'tender loving care,' some constant little
service to the sick."

The earliest use of the phrase, in this sense, that I have come across occurs in the final chapter, "TLC Treatment," of Ian Fleming's *Goldfinger* (1959). James Bond says to Pussy Galore, "All you need is a course of TLC." "What's TLC," she asks. "Short for Tender Loving Care Treatment," Bond replies. "It's what they write on most papers when a waif gets brought in to a children's clinic."

Well, there's no phrase like a good phrase. In Shakespeare's *The Second Part of King Henry VI* (Act III, scene ii, line 278) we read:

Commons (Within) [i.e., a rabble offstage]: An answer from the King, or we will all break in!
King: Go, Salisbury, and tell them all from me
I thank them for their tender loving care . . .

That's what _____ is all about. This appears most often in sports. The basic notion is that "winning is what it's all about" (and never mind all that nonsense of the Olympic motto). Often ascribed to Vince Lombardi, coach and general manager of the Green Bay Packers pro-football team from 1959, in the form "Winning isn't everything, it's the only thing," it was nevertheless said by John Wayne as a football coach in the 1953 movie *Trouble Along the Way*. President Nixon's notorious Committee to Re-Elect the President in 1972 had as its motto: "Winning in politics isn't everything; it's the only thing."

Wanna buy a duck? Joe Penner, a Hungarian-American, rocketed to fame on radio in 1934 with rapid-fire one-liners and a number of catch phrases, including "Wanna buy a duck?" and "You naaasty man!" He carried a real duck, called Goo Goo, in a basket. Almost as rapidly, his fame declined, but the duck phrase is still remembered.

When the world was young. A wistful expression not only of "long ago" but also of a time more innocent than the present. It may derive ultimately from this verse in the

Bible: "For the world has lost his youth, and the times begin to wax old" (2 Esdras 14:10).

I have found "When the World Was Young" used as the title of a painting (1891) by Sir E. J. Poynter PRA, which shows three young girls in a classical setting relaxing by a pool. It was also used by Johnny Mercer as the title of his very popular version of a French song known as *"Le Chevalier de Paris"* or *"Ah! Les Pommiers Doux"* (c. 1951).

Compare the lines "When all the world is young, lad,/ And all the trees are green/ . . . Young blood must have its course, lad,/ And every dog his day," from "Young and Old" in *The Water Babies* (1863) by Charles Kingsley.

_____, **where are you now?** An ironic plea to someone long-since departed when one finds present circumstances as bad as when the person was around. For example, one might have said during the Reagan Irangate scandal, "Richard Nixon, where are you now?"

As such, it is a truncation of "_____, where are you now that your country needs you?" or "Come back, _____, all is forgiven," which, once upon a time, might have been said about a warrior who had retired to his farm. It appeared ironically in the graffito "Lee Harvey Oswald, where are you now that your country needs you?" during the presidencies of both Lyndon Johnson and Richard Nixon.

Where were you when the lights went out? The 1968 film *Where Were You When the Lights Went Out?* was inspired by the blackout of 1965 when the electricity supply failed and, it was popularly believed, the birth rate shot up nine months later. The phrase echoes an old music-hall song and perhaps also the American nonsense rhyme "Where was Moses when the light went out?/ Down in the cellar eating sauerkraut." This last appears to have developed from the "almost proverbial" riddle (as the Opies call it in *The Lore and Language of Schoolchildren*, 1959):

Q. Where was Moses when the light went out?
A. In the dark.

The Opies find this in *The Riddler's Oracle,* c. 1821.

With one bound/spring, he/Jack was free.   Said now of anyone who escapes from a tricky situation or tight corner. I presume this comes from either cartoon strips, subtitles to silent films, or boys' adventure serials of the early twentieth century. The hero would frequently escape from seemingly impossible situations, usually after he had been condemned to them in a "cliff-hanger".

The phrase underlines the preposterousness of the adventures in which such lines can be "spoken." Author Barbara Newman, writing from Washington, D.C., to the London *Observer* (October 29, 1989), says of TV correspondent and former Beirut hostage Charles Glass: "His motivation is to keep alive the fiction that he miraculously escaped from his Hizbollah capturers, offering a Ramboesque picture of himself amounting to 'and with one spring Jack was free.' "

Writing on the wall, the.   Any hint, sign, or portent, often doom-laden. The idea—though not the precise phrase—comes from the Bible (Daniel, 5) where King Belshazzar is informed of the forthcoming destruction of the Babylonian Empire through the appearance of a man's hand writing on a wall.

In a BBC broadcast to resistance workers in Europe (July 31, 1941), "Colonel Britton" (Douglas Ritchie) talked of the "V for Victory" sign that was being chalked up in occupied countries: "All over Europe the V sign is seen by the Germans and to the Germans and the Quislings it is indeed the writing on the wall. . . ."

14

THAT'S SHOW BIZ!

This exclamation, like "That's life!," is now used to cover disappointment at bad luck or over the failure of anything, and is no longer limited to actual show business. At times it is used to mean "There you are, it's just unpredictable." The phrase was established by the 1960s and probably dates from the 1930s, sometimes in the form "That's show biz for you!" The similar-sounding "That's Entertainment" was used (by Howard Dietz) as the title of a song in The Band Wagon *(1953) and then as the title of a film (1974).*

More phrases from the world of entertainment:

Anyone for tennis? This perkily expressed inquiry from a character entering through French windows and carrying a tennis racquet has become established as typical of the "teacup" theater of the 1920s and 1930s (also in the forms "Who's for tennis?" and "Tennis, anyone?"). A clear example of it being used has proved elusive, however, although there are many near-misses. The opening line of Part II of

Strindberg's *Dance of Death* (1901) is (in translation): "Why don't you come and play tennis?" A *very* near miss occurs in the first act of Shaw's *Misalliance* (1910), in which a character asks, "Anybody on for a game of tennis?" One informant assures me that the line was used in one of the shows presented by Edward Laurillard and George Grossmith—which must have been in the years 1914–21. Another states that Gladys Cooper said it in the musical *The Dollar Princess* (1909), but tangible evidence is lacking. Teddie in Somerset Maugham's *The Circle* (1921) always seems on the verge of saying it, but only manages, "I say, what about this tennis?" Myra in Noël Coward's *Hay Fever* (1925) says, "What a pity it's raining, we might have had some tennis." Another informant assured me I could find it in Terence Rattigan's *French Without Tears* (1936)—which sounded a very promising source —but it does not occur in the printed text.

Perhaps it was just another of those phrases that was never actually said in the form popularly remembered? Unfortunately, a terrible wild-goose chase was launched by Jonah Ruddy and Jonathan Hill in their book *Bogey: The Man, The Actor, The Legend* (1965). Describing Humphrey Bogart's early career as a stage actor (c. 1921), they said, "In those early Broadway days he didn't play menace parts. 'I always made my entrance carrying a tennis racquet, baseball bat, or golf club. I was the athletic type, with hair slicked back and wrapped in a blazer. The only line I didn't say was, "Give me the ball, coach, I'll take it through." Yes, sir, I was Joe College or Joe Country Club all the time.'

"It was hard to imagine him as the originator of that famous theatrical line—'Tennis anyone?'—but he was."

This extract clearly shows that the authors were adding their own gloss to what Bogart had said. Bartlett (1968) joined in and said it was his "sole line in his first play." But Bogart (who died in 1957) had already denied ever having said it (quoted in Goodman, *Bogey: The Good-Bad Boy*, and in an ABC-TV film of 1974 using old film of him doing so). Alistair Cooke in *Six Men* (1977) is more cautious: "It is said he appeared in an ascot and blue blazer and tossed off the invitation 'Tennis, anyone?' "—and adds that Bogart probably did not coin the phrase. Another possibility is that Bogart uttered the line in his first major *film* role—*A Devil with Women* (1930).

In British show business it has been suggested that Leon Quatermaine, a leading man of the 1920s and 30s who was at one time married to Fay Compton, was the first man to say it. Alan Melville, the playwright and revue artist, said (1983), "I know who *claimed* to have said it in a play first: Freddy Lonsdale. But he was such a delightful liar he probably invented the invention. Years ago, just after the war, down in the South of France, he maintained that he'd first put it in a play—when quizzed, he couldn't remember which one—and was quite miffed that it had gone into general circulation without due acknowledgement being made to him as the creator." Alas, Frances Donaldson, Lonsdale's daughter, told me in 1983 that she was pretty sure he hadn't coined the phrase—or even used it, as "it's not his style."

In the form *Anyone for Tennis?* the phrase was used by J. B. Priestley as the title of a 1968 television play, and in 1981 it was converted into *Anyone for Denis?* by John Wells as the title of a London West End farce making fun of Prime Minister Margaret Thatcher's husband.

Break a leg! A traditional theatrical greeting before a performance, especially a first night. Supposedly it's bad luck to wish anyone "good luck" directly.

Partridge/*Slang* has "to break a leg" as "to give birth to a bastard," dating from the seventeenth century, but that is probably unconnected. As also is the fact that John Wilkes Booth, an actor, broke his leg after assassinating President Lincoln in a theater.

Morris passes on a suggestion that it is based on a German good-luck expression, *Hals-und-Beinbruch* (May you break your neck and your leg—literally, neck-and-bone-break). Perhaps this entered theatrical speech (like several other expressions) via Yiddish?

Theatrical superstition is understandable in a profession so dependent on luck. However, the euphemism "The Scottish play," invariably used for Shakespeare's *Macbeth,* is based on a well-documented history of bad luck associated with productions of the play. Merely to utter the name of the play would thus be to invoke misfortune.

Cat on a Hot Tin Roof.   Title of Tennessee Williams's play (1955), in which the "cat" is Maggie, Brick's wife, "whose frayed vivacity derives from the fact that she is sexually ignored by her husband" (wrote Kenneth Tynan). From the American expression "As nervous as a cat on a hot tin roof," which derives from the English expression "Like a cat on hot bricks," meaning ill-at-ease, jumpy.

Clap hands, here comes Charley.   This apparently nonsensical catch phrase, popular at one time, appears to derive from its use in the signature tune of Charlie Kunz (1896–1958). Born in America, Kunz became a feathery-fingered, insistently rhythmic pianist popular on British radio in the 1930s and 40s.

The song went, "Clap hands, here comes Charley . . . here comes Charley now." With lyrics by Billy Rose and Ballard MacDonald and music by Joseph Meyer, it was recorded in the U.S. in 1925. According to *The Book of Sex Lists,* the song was written "in honor of a local chorine, first-named Charline, who had given many of the music publishers' contact men [song pluggers] cases of gonorrhea —a venereal disease commonly known as 'the clap.' "

According to Partridge/*Slang,* "to do a clap hands Charlie" was 1940s RAF slang for flying an aircraft in such a way as to make the wings appear to meet overhead.

"Day in the Life, A."   The most-remembered track from the 1967 Beatles album *Sgt. Pepper's Lonely Hearts Club Band* presumably takes its name from a type of magazine article and film documentary that depicts twenty-four hours in the life of a person or organization. In 1962 a novel by Aleksandr Solzhenitsyn was published in English as *One Day in the Life of Ivan Denisovich* (film, U.K., 1971).

John Lennon and Paul McCartney's use of the phrase for the description of incidents in the life of a drug-taker may have had something to do with the title of the play *A Day in the Death of Joe Egg* by Peter Nichols (1967; film, UK, 1971).

Don't call us, we'll call you. What directors say to auditionees, the implication being that "we" will never actually get around to calling "you." Now more widely applied to anyone unwelcome asking a favor. The *OED2* finds no example before 1969 (from the *Listener*): "Jelly Roll Morton . . . played his compositions to the Harlem team, eyebrows were raised no further than the pejorative 'don't ring *us*' level." Also used in this situation: "We'll let you know" (which was the title of an audition sketch on a Peter Sellers record album in 1959).

Don't worry, be happy. Bobby McFerrin's song with this title became George Bush's unofficial campaign theme in the presidential election of 1988 and won the Grammy Award for the year's best song. "The landlord says the rent is late, he might have to litigate, but don't worry, be happy," sang McFerrin, in a song that became a minor national anthem, reflecting a feeling in the U.S. at the time. McFerrin also wrote a book entitled "Don't Worry, Be Happy."

The Times of London (March 8, 1989) noted: "The song has spawned a whole 'happy' industry and re-launched the Smiley faces that emerged in the late 1960s. . . . Bloomingdales, the Manhattan department store, now features a 'Don't worry, be happy shop.' "

Fiddler on the roof, a.   This expression became known to a wide audience as a result of the musical *Fiddler on the Roof*, first produced on Broadway in 1964 and filmed in 1971, with a book by Joseph Stein and lyrics by Sheldon Harnick. The story of Tevye, a Jewish milkman in pre-Revolutionary Russia, who cheerfully survives family and political problems before emigrating to America, was based on Sholom Aleichem's stories collected under the title *Tevye and His Daughters*.

I can only assume that the title is used allusively to describe the easygoing nature of the hero. The title song of the musical is not very helpful. It merely asks the question, why is the fiddler playing up on the roof all day and in all weathers? It concludes, "It might not mean a thing/ But then again it might!" The expression would seem to signify "an opportunist, one who takes life easy, one who does what he pleases, a happy-go-lucky person."

"Fiddling on the roof," however, is one of the proverbial expressions portrayed (literally) in the painting known as "The Proverbs" by David Teniers the Younger (1610–1690), which hangs in Belvoir Castle, England. In the key to these Flemish proverbs, "fiddling on the roof" is compared to "eat, drink, and be merry." I am not sure at what date the English key was provided, but it is odd that the saying does not seem to have taken hold in the language, though there is the nautical expression "Fiddler's Green," defined in *OED2* as "a sailor's elysium, in which wine, women and song figure prominently." From the nineteenth century citations given, it appears that nonsailors also aspired to it. There is also the English proverb, "In the house of the fiddler, all fiddle."

In Marc Chagall's painting "The Dead Man" (1908), he shows—literally—a fiddler on a roof. Chagall often drew on Russian folktales in his work, and the character also turns up in his painting "The Fiddler" (1912–13). Werner Haftmann in his book on the artist calls the fiddler on the roof "representative of the artist; a solitary individual, isolated by the strangeness and mystery of his art . . . a metaphorical figure who can be identified with . . . Chagall himself." One source tells me that the writers of the musical were definitely thinking of this second picture when they came to settle on their title.

A further attempt at explanation can be found in *Gänzel's Book of the Musical Theatre* (1988), where Tevye is described as "the epitome of the Jewish people of Anatevka who each scratch out a living, as the fiddler scratches out his tune, while perilously perched on the edge of existence as represented by the unsafe roof."

Fifth Beatle, the.   Meaning someone who has missed out on success. The original "fifth Beatle" was Brian Epstein (1934–1967), the group's manager. He was so dubbed in 1964, much to his annoyance, by Murray the K, the American disc jockey. Others merited the title more—Stu Sutcliffe, an early member of the group who was eased out and died before fame struck; Pete Best, who was replaced as drummer by Ringo Starr; Neil Aspinall, road manager, aide, and friend; and George Martin, the group's arranger and record producer.

When I was discussing this phrase on a radio call-in program in 1989, a listener suggested that the fifth Beatle was the Volkswagen Beetle that figures on the sleeve of the group's "Abbey Road" album!

The phrase is sometimes applied to other people who miss out on the success of something they have once been a part of.

Funny thing happened (to me) on the way to the theater tonight . . . , a.   The uninspired preliminary to telling a joke, and dating presumably from music-hall/vaudeville days. Compare the title of the comedy musical *A Funny Thing Happened on the Way to the Forum* (filmed 1966) set in ancient Rome and based on Plautus (but the phrase can't be *quite* as old as that, surely!).

Great White Way, the. Nickname for Broadway—because of the intense brightness of the illumination. From the title of a novel (1901) by Albert Bigelow Paine (1861–1937). For a while Broadway was also known as "the Gay White Way," though for understandable reasons this is no longer so.

Here we are again!   Perhaps the oldest catch phrase that can be attached to a particular performer. Joseph Grimaldi (1779–1837) used it as Joey the Clown in pantomime, and it has subsequently been used by almost all clowns on entering the circus ring or theater stage . . . for example, by Harry Paine in the 1870s and 1880s. He would turn a somersault on entering and declare, "Here we are again."

It'll be all right on the night.   Theatrical saying dating from the late nineteenth century, at least. Curiously, when it has to be invoked, things quite often *are* better on the subsequent night. In the same way, a disastrous dress rehearsal is said to betoken a successful first night. The phrase was used as the title of a song by Alan Melville and Ivor Novello in the musical *Gay's the Word* (1950).

It's a-one for the money, a-two for the show.   (". . . a-three to get ready, now go, cat, go!") The start to the Carl Perkins song "Blue Suede Shoes" (immortalized by Elvis Presley in 1956), is often used by children at the start of a race. A version used in Britain and dating from 1888 is "One for the money, two for the show, three to make ready, and four to go." Another version, from 1853, is "One to make ready, and two to prepare; good luck to the rider, and away goes the mare."

It's only rock 'n' roll.   "It doesn't matter; the importance should not be exaggerated." The title of a Mick Jagger and Keith Richard composition of 1974 has entered the language to a certain extent. From *Zigzag* magazine (August 5, 1977): "Y'see I write about punk and you just want to read about something that'll scare your mum, I'm sure that elsewhere someone will let ya know it IS only rock 'n' roll." In a 1983 London *Sunday Express* interview, lyric-writer Tim Rice was quoted as saying, "It would be nice if [the musical *Blondel*] is a success but I won't be upset if it isn't. It is only rock 'n' roll after all and it doesn't really matter a hoot."

It went from failure to classic without ever passing through success.   Mostly arts or show-biz use. Origin unknown. For example, George Axelrod, writer of the film *The Manchurian Candidate,* said it to *Time* magazine (March 21, 1988). The film was a flop when first launched in 1962, languished in a vault for twenty-five years, and then became something of a cult hit.

Magical mystery tour, a.   Name given to a winding journey, caused by a driver who doesn't know where he is going. A "mystery tour" is a journey undertaken in a bus from a holiday resort to a destination unknown to the passengers (and known as such, I should think, from the 1920s onward). The "magical" derives from the Beatles' title for a largely unsuccessful attempt at making their own film in 1967. In *Next Horizon* (1973), Chris Bonington wrote: "Climbing with Tom Patey was a kind of Magical Mystery Tour, in which no one, except perhaps himself, knew what was coming next." From the London *Daily Express* (April 12, 1989): "On and on went the city bus driver's magical mystery tour. Passengers point out their way home—and get a lift to the door."

Man for All Seasons, A.   Robert Bolt's title for his 1960 play about Sir Thomas More (filmed 1967) has provided a popular phrase for an accomplished, adaptable, appealing person, as well as a format phrase verging on the cliché, whereby almost anything can be described as "a _____ for all seasons." From Laurence Olivier, *On Acting* (1986): "[Ralph Richardson] was warm and what the public might call ordinary and, therefore, quite exceptional. That was his ability, that was his talent; he really was a man for all seasons."

Robert Bolt found his play title in a description of More (1478–1535) by a contemporary, Robert Whittington: "More is a man of angel's wit and singular learning; I know not his fellow. For where is the man of that gentleness, lowliness and affability? And as time requireth, a man of marvelous mirth and pastimes; and sometimes of as sad a gravity: as who say a man for all seasons."

Whittington (c. 1480–c. 1530) wrote the passage for schoolboys to put into Latin in his book *Vulgaria* (c. 1521). It translates a comment on More by Erasmus—who wrote in his preface to *In Praise of Folly* (1509) that More was *"omnium horarum hominem."*

My Fair Lady. I suppose it was understandable that when Lerner and Loewe wished to make a musical out of Shaw's *Pygmalion* they should want a new title. After all, not even Shaw's Preface (only his Afterword) alludes to the relevance of the Greek legend to his story of a Covent flowergirl who was raised up and taught to "speak proper" just like a Mayfair lady.

Lerner and Loewe turned, it seems, to the refrain of the nursery rhyme (first recorded in the eighteenth century):

> London Bridge is broken down,
> Broken down, broken down,
> London Bridge is broken down,
> My fair lady.

It has also been suggested that they were drawn to the title because "my fair lady" is how a Cockney flowerseller would pronounce the phrase "Mayfair lady." The working title for the show when Rex Harrison first became involved was *Lady Liza*.

Oh! Calcutta! Kenneth Tynan's sexually explicit stage revue, first presented on Broadway in 1969, took its title from a curious piece of wordplay. It is the equivalent of the French *"Oh, quel cul t'as,"* meàning—broadly speaking— "Oh, what a lovely butt you've got." French *cul* is derived from the Latin *culus* ("buttocks"), but according to the context, it may be applied to the female vagina or male anus.

Shakespeare in *The Second Part of King Henry VI* (Act IV, scene vii, line 30) calls the Dauphin of France "Monsieur Basimecu" because of his fawning manners—i.e., *"Bus mine cue/baise mon cul/* kiss my backside."

In her *Life of Kenneth Tynan* (1987) Kathleen Tynan states that she was writing an article on the surrealist painter Clovis Trouille, one of whose works was a naked odalisque lying on her side to reveal a spherical backside. The title was "Oh! Calcutta! Calcutta!" "I suggested to Ken that he call his erotic revue *Oh! Calcutta!* . . . I did not know at the time that it had the further advantage of being a French pun."

A professor of French who is an authority on puns suggests that this one may date from the *belle époque*.

On with the motley!   An ironic use of the Clown's cry— *"Vesti la giubba"*— from Leoncavallo's opera *I Pagliacci* (1892). The Clown has to "carry on with the show" in spite of his broken heart. Today it is said jokingly by anyone who is having to proceed with something in spite of difficulties —though Laurence Olivier used the phrase in its original sense when describing a sudden return dash from Ceylon during a crisis in his marriage to Vivien Leigh: "I got myself on to a plane . . . and was in Paris on the Saturday afternoon. I went straight on home the next day as I had music sessions for *The Beggar's Opera* from the Monday; and so, on with the motley" (*Confessions of an Actor,* 1982).

"Giubba," in Italian, simply means "jacket" (in the sense of costume). "The motley" is the old English word for an actor or clown's clothes, originally the many-colored coat

worn by a jester or fool (as mentioned several times in Shakespeare's *As You Like It*).

Queen for a Day.   This phrase, when used for a woman who is given a special treat, derives from the title of a radio program that ran for ten years in the 1940s. According to an informant, "Being a queen for a day didn't mean they gave you a country; you only got your wish, that's what. No one complained." Adapted as a daytime TV show, it was a big hit from 1955–64, but *Halliwell's Television Companion* calls it "the nadir of American TV."

I note that when Radio Luxembourg adopted the format in 1955 (introduced by Richard Attenborough, sponsored by Phensic), they changed the title to *Princess for a Day.* Was this because the wishes fulfilled were more modest, the participants younger, or had the word "queen" become too tainted by that time?

Rhubarb, rhubarb!   Actors mumble this in crowd scenes to give the impression of speech, as a background noise, without actually producing coherent sentences. I suppose some unwise actors might think they could actually get away with saying "rhubarb," but the idea is to repeat a word that, uttered by various voices, adds together to sound like the noise a crowd makes. I am not sure that this custom dates from much before this century, but it is a well-known concept now, as demonstrated by the use of the verb "to rhubarb," meaning to talk nonsense.

Another phrase said to have been repeated by actors in this situation is "My fiddle, my fiddle, my fiddle," and I am assured there is a phrase used by Russian actors meaning, literally, "I speak and I don't speak."

One wonders whether the adoption of the word "rhubarb" in the English version has anything to do with its slang use to denote the male (and occasionally female) genitals. Or could there have been some rhyming slang phrase, i.e., rhubarb (tart) = fart (akin to raspberry tart =

fart)? The rhyming slang books I have consulted do not support me in this, however.

See you later, alligator.   Note how a phrase develops: According to Flexner, the simple "See you later" as a form of farewell entered American speech in the 1870s. By the 1930s it had some "jive use" as "See you later, alligator." To this was added the response, "In a while, crocodile."

This exchange became known to a wider public through the song "See You Later, Alligator," sung by Bill Haley and his Comets in the film *Rock Around the Clock* (1956), which recorded the origins of rock 'n' roll. Princess Margaret and her set became keen users. There was even a sudden vogue for keeping pet alligators in New York.

The next stage was for the front and back of the phrase to be dropped off, leaving the simple "Later" as a way to say good-bye.

Send in the clowns.   The tradition that the "show must go on" grew out of the circus. Whatever mishap occurred, the band was told to go on playing and the cry went up to "send in the clowns"—for the simple reason that panic had to be avoided, the audience's attention had to be diverted, and the livelihood of everybody in the circus depended on not having to give the audience its money back. So, like "Send in the clowns," "The show must go on" seems primarily a circus phrase, though no one seems able to turn up a written reference much before 1930.

In 1950 "The show must go on" is spoken in the film *All About Eve,* and in the same decade, Noël Coward wrote a song that posed the question, "*Why* Must the Show Go On?"

Stephen Sondheim used "Send in the Clowns" as the title of a song in *A Little Night Music,* 1974.

_____ Superstar.   The suffix "_____ Superstar" became fashionable following the success of the musical *Jesus Christ Superstar* (1970). Tim Rice, its lyricist, tells me that he and the composer, Andrew Lloyd Webber, settled on the title after seeing a 1960s Las Vegas billing for "Tom Jones—Superstar."

The show-biz use of the term "superstar," although very much a 1960s thing (it was also used by Andy Warhol), has been traced back to 1925. In Warwick Deeping's *Sorrell & Son:* "You wouldn't expect a couple of cinema super-stars to be running away from publicity."

Who do I have to fuck to get out of this _____? Presumably from show biz. Having (as legend would have it) had to fuck to get cast in a show or picture, the speaker is wondering how the process can be reversed—because the show is turning out to be no good. Bob Chieger in *Was It Good For You, Too?* ascribes to "Shirley Wood, talent coordinator for NBC's *The Tonight Show* in the 1960s," the quote: "Who do you have to fuck to get *out* of show business?" The line "Listen, who do I have to fuck to get *off* this picture?" occurs in Terry Southern's *Blue Movie* (1970). Steve Bach in *Final Cut* (1985) ascribes "Who do I fuck to get off this picture?" simply to "Anonymous Hollywood starlet (circa 1930)."

Who's Afraid of Virginia Woolf? The title of the play (1962, film 1966) was found by Edward Albee as a piece of graffiti. It echoes, of course, the song "Who's Afraid of the Big Bad Wolf" by Churchill and Ronell in the Walt Disney film (1933) *Three Little Pigs.* Virginia Woolf, the British novelist and writer, is evoked because one of the characters is a professor of English literature.

You're famous when they can spell your name in Karachi. A modern show-biz proverb that deserves to be more widely known. It is quoted by Steve Aronson in *Hype* (1983).

Yowsir, yowsir, yowsir. The 1969 film *They Shoot Horses Don't They?* (from Horace McCoy's 1935 novel—the title using what I presume was an old Western expression for exhaustion) portrayed a dance marathon contest of the Depression years. Appropriately, it highlighted the "yow-sir, yowsir" cry (meaning "yes, sir") originated in the 1930s by the orchestra leader and entertainer Ben Bernie.

15

READ MY LIPS

*Politicians are always being quoted—even when they have
nothing to say. By the second half of the century little a
president or prime minister said went unrecorded. Relent-
less monitoring by the media exposed every kind of remark, both intentional and unintentional. Richard Nixon
was not the only president who added to the process by
having his private conversations recorded.*

*Although popularized by George Bush in his acceptance
speech for the Republican nomination on August 19, 1988,
"Read my lips" was not a new phrase. Bush wanted to
emphasize his pledge not to raise taxes, whatever pressure
Congress applied, so what he said was, "I'll say no, and
they'll push, and I'll say no, and they'll push again, and
I'll say to them, 'Read my lips, no new taxes.'" The promise
lasted until mid-1990. The phrase is rooted in 1970s rock
music (although there is a song with the title copyrighted
by Joe Greene in 1957). The British actor/singer Tim Curry
used the phrase as the title of an album of songs in 1978.
Curry said he took it from an Italian-American recording*

engineer who used it to mean, "Listen and listen very hard, because I want you to hear what I've got to say." Several lyricists in the 1980s used the phrase for song titles. A Chicago Bears coach was nicknamed Mike (Read My Lips) Ditka. There has also been a thoroughbred racehorse so named.

The phraseology of politics:

Agonizing reappraisal. Political term for the process of reconsideration, possibly before a decision is made to take a U-turn. The modern use stems from a speech that Secretary of State John Foster Dulles made to the National Press Club in Washington, in December 1953: "When I was in Paris last week, I said that . . . the United States would have to undertake an agonizing reappraisal of basic foreign policy in relation to Europe."

All the way with LBJ. A classic example of the simple rhyme slogan, this was employed (together with "USA for LBJ") by Lyndon B. Johnson in the 1964 presidential election that gave him a landslide victory over the Republican challenger, Barry M. Goldwater, in the year following the Kennedy assassination. However, "All the way with LBJ" had first been used when Johnson was seeking the presidential nomination that eventually went to John F. Kennedy in 1960. "All through the fall and winter of 1959 and 1960," wrote Theodore H. White in *The Making of the President 1964,* "the noisemakers of the Johnson campaign . . . chanted 'All the way with LBJ' across the South and Far West, instantly identifiable by their Texan garb, their ten-gallon hats (and, said their enemies, by the cow-flap on their boots.)"

America cannot stand pat. "To stand pat," meaning to keep a fixed position or belief or to stand fast, may come originally from poker, in which you can decline to exchange the cards you are dealt. A "pat hand" is one that is exactly suited to your purpose. In the 1960 presidential election John F. Kennedy pointed to the old slogan "Stand pat with McKinley" as an example of Republican reaction. So Richard Nixon countered with "America cannot stand pat"—until it was politely pointed out to him that he was married to a woman with that name. "America cannot stand still" was rapidly substituted.

Are you now or have you ever been . . . ? Stock phrase of McCarthyism, the pursuit and public ostracism of suspected communist sympathizers at the time of the Korean War in the early 1950s. Senator Joseph McCarthy (1908–1957) instigated the "witch hunts" that led to the blacklisting of people, notably in the movie business. Those appearing at hearings of the House of Representatives Committee on UnAmerican Activities (1947–c. 1957) were customarily challenged with the question, "Are you now or have you ever been a member of the Communist Party?" It was a particular favorite with J. Parnell Thomas. Counsel Richard Arens (1913–1969) would sometimes take things a stage further and thunder, "Are you now or have you ever been a member of a godless conspiracy controlled by a foreign power?"—one of those questions, as in Latin, that anticipates the answer "no."

In the U.K. there has been a radio/stage play by Eric Bentley (1978) with the title *Are You Now Or Have You Ever Been?*

Ban the bomb. One of the simplest and best-known alliterative slogans, current from 1953. The Campaign for Nuclear Disarmament—whose semiofficial slogan it became —was not publicly launched until February 1958.

Better red than dead. Slogan used by nuclear disarmers. Bertrand Russell wrote in 1958: "If no alternative remains except communist domination or the extinction of the human race, the former alternative is the lesser of two evils." The counter cry, "Better dead than red," may also have had some currency.

(In the 1964 film *Love with a Proper Stranger*, Steve
McQueen proposed to Natalie Wood with a picket sign
stating, "Better Wed Than Dead.")

Black is beautiful.   The Rev. Dr. Martin Luther King, Jr.,
launched a poster campaign based on these words in 1967,
but Stokely Carmichael had used the phrase at a Memphis
civil rights rally in 1966. Compare this from the Song of
Solomon 1:5: "I am black, but comely."

Black power.   Slogan encompassing just about anything
that people want it to mean, from simple pride in the black
race to a threat of violence. Adam Clayton Powell, Jr., the
Harlem congressman, said in a baccalaureate address at
Howard University in May 1966: "To demand these God-
given rights is to seek black power—what I call audacious
power—the power to build black institutions of splendid
achievement."

On June 6 the same year, James Meredith, the first black
American to integrate the University of Mississippi (in
1962), was shot and wounded during a civil rights march.
Stokely Carmichael, heading the Student Nonviolent Co-
ordinating Committee, continued the march, during
which his contingent first used the phrase as a shout. Carmichael used it in a speech at Greenwood, Mississippi, the
same month. It was also adopted as a slogan by the Congress for Racial Equality. However, the notion was not
new in the 1960s.

Langston Hughes had written in *Simple Takes a Wife*
(1953): "Negro blood is so powerful—because just *one* drop
of black blood makes a colored man—*one* drop—you are a
Negro! . . . Black is powerful."

Blood, sweat, and tears.   In his classic speech to the House
of Commons on May 13, 1940, upon becoming prime minister, Winston Churchill said, "I would say to the House, as
I said to those who have joined this Government: I have
nothing to offer but blood, toil, tears and sweat."

Ever since then people seem to have had difficulty in getting the order of his words right. The natural inclination is to put "blood, sweat, and tears" together—as did Byron in 1823 with "blood, sweat and tear-wrung millions," and as did the Canadian-American rock group Blood Sweat and Tears in the late 1960s and 70s. Much earlier, however, there had been yet another combination of the words in John Donne's *An Anatomy of the World* (1611): " 'Tis in vain to do so or to mollify it with thy tears or sweat or blood."

Churchill seemed consciously to avoid these configurations, however. In 1931 he had written of the czarist armies: "Their sweat, their tears, their blood bedewed the endless plain." Having launched his version of the phrase in 1940, he referred to it five more times during the course of the war.

But, right from the word go, people misremembered his precise order: Joan Wyndham in *Love Lessons—A Wartime Diary* (1985) concludes her entry for May 13, 1940, with, "Later we listened to a very stirring speech by Churchill about 'blood, toil, sweat and tears.' " (I have a slight suspicion that this diary may have been "improved" somewhat in the editing, but not, obviously, to the point of imposing accuracy.)

BOMFOG. Idiom for a pompous, meaningless generality. When Governor Nelson Rockefeller (1908–1979) was competing against Barry Goldwater for the Republican nomination in 1964, reporters latched on to a favorite saying of the candidate—"the brotherhood of man under the fatherhood of God"—and rendered it with the acronym "BOMFOG." In fact, according to Safire they had been beaten to it by Hy Sheffer, a stenotypist on the Governor's staff who had found the abbreviation convenient for the previous five or six years. The words come from a much-quoted saying of John D. Rockefeller (1874–1960): "These are the principles upon which alone a new world recognizing the brotherhood of man and the fatherhood of God can be established. . . ."

Later "BOMFOG" was used by feminists to denote language that reflected patrician attitudes and thus demeaned women. The phrases "brotherhood of man" and "fatherhood of God" do not appear to have been known before the nineteenth century.

Buck stops here, the.   President Truman had a sign on his desk bearing these words, indicating that the Oval Office was where the passing of the buck had to cease. It appears to be a saying of his own invention. "Passing the buck" is a poker player's expression. It refers to a marker that can be passed on by someone who does not wish to deal. Later Jimmy Carter restored Truman's motto to the Oval Office.

When President Nixon published his memoirs (1978), people opposed to its sale went around wearing buttons that said, "The book stops here."

Burn, baby, burn!   An African-American extremists' incitement slogan that arose from the August 1965 riots in the Watts district of Los Angeles, when thirty-four people were killed and entire blocks burned. (The 1974 hit song by Hudson and Ford with this title had, rather, a quite separate sexual connotation.)

Burn your bra!   A feminist slogan, c. 1970, encouraging women to destroy an item of apparel quite clearly designed by a male chauvinist and likely to make a woman more of a sex object. The analogy is with the burning of draft cards as a protest against the Vietnam War.

Business as usual.   The standard declaration when a shop has suffered some misfortune like a fire or is undergoing alterations. However, during World War I the phrase was adopted in a more general sense. H. E. Morgan (later Sir Herbert Morgan), an advertising man working for W. H. Smith and Sons, promoted this slogan, which had quite a vogue until it was proved to be manifestly untrue and hopelessly inappropriate. Morgan was an advertising consultant to H. Gordon Selfridge, the American-born store owner, who also became associated with the slogan. On August 26, 1914, Selfridge said, " 'Business as usual' must be the order of the day." In a Guildhall speech on November 9 of that year, Winston Churchill said, "The maxim of the British people is 'Business as usual.' "

Cross of gold. One of the most notable examples of American oratory is William Jennings Bryan's speech to the Democratic Convention in July 1896. It contained an impassioned attack on supporters of the gold standard. "You shall not press down upon the brow of labor this crown of thorns. You shall not crucify mankind upon a cross of gold."

Bryan (1860–1925) had said virtually the same in a speech to the House of Representatives on December 22, 1894. He won the nomination and fought the presidential election against William J. McKinley, who supported the gold standard. Bryan lost.

Cut off at the pass, to. One of the milder sayings that emerged from the transcripts of the Watergate tapes (published as *The White House Transcripts,* 1974) was "to cut something/someone off at the pass." This was a recycled phrase from old-time Western films where the cry would be uttered, meaning "to intercept, ambush," when one group planned to stop another group from moving forward. As said by President Nixon it simply meant "We will use certain tactics to stop them." The phrase occurred in a crucial exchange in the White House Oval Office on March 21, 1973, between the President and John Dean. It concerned the Special Counsel's fears that he could be sent to jail for his part in the cover-up of the Watergate robbery:

P: You are a lawyer, you were a counsel. . . . What would you go to jail for?

D: The obstruction of justice.
P: The obstruction of justice?
D: That is the only one that bothers me.
P: Well, I don't know. I think that one . . . I feel it could be cut off at the pass, maybe, the obstruction of justice.

Deep Throat. A person within an organization who supplies information anonymously about wrongdoing by his colleagues. From the nickname given to the source within the Nixon White House who fed *Washington Post* journalists Carl Bernstein and Bob Woodward information that helped in their Watergate investigations (1972–74). It has been suggested that "Deep Throat" never existed but was a cover for unjustified suppositions. However, the reporters explained:

> Woodward had promised he would never identify him or his position to anyone. . . . In newspaper terminology, this meant the discussions were on "deep background." . . . Woodward explained the arrangement to managing editor Howard Simons one day. He had taken to calling the source "my friend," but Simons dubbed him Deep Throat, the title of a celebrated pornographic movie. The name stuck.

> *All the President's Men* (1974)

Indeed, *Deep Throat* was the most notorious porno movie of the early seventies. It concerned a woman, played by Linda Lovelace, whose clitoris was located in the back of her throat. It is said that the film grossed in excess of $600 million.

Evil empire. Toward the end of his presidency Ronald Reagan took a much more accommodating attitude toward the Soviet Union than had ever been predicted of the arch-anti-Soviet. Earlier, in a speech to the National Association of Evangelicals at Orlando, Florida, on March 8, 1983, Reagan had said, "In your discussions of the nuclear freeze proposals, I urge you to beware the temptation of pride—the temptation blithely to declare yourselves above it all and label both sides equally at fault, to ignore the facts of history and the aggressive impulses of an *evil empire . . .*"

The reason for this startling turn of phrase was made later the same month when he first propounded his "Star Wars" proposal as part of a campaign to win support for his defense budget and arms-control project. The proposal, better known by its initials, SDI (for Strategic Defense Initiative), was to extend the nuclear battleground into space.

The President did not use the term "Star Wars," but it was an inevitable tag to be applied by the media, given his own fondness for adapting lines from the movies. The film *Star Wars* and the sequel *The Empire Strikes Back* had been released in 1977 and 1980, respectively.

As for his view of the Soviet Union, it remained constant until the final shift. In 1964 he had said it was "the most evil enemy mankind has ever known in his long climb from the swamp to the stars." During his visit to Moscow in June 1988, President Reagan was asked about his "evil empire" phrase. He replied, "I was talking about another time, another era."

Flower power.   A hippy slogan—formed, no doubt, in emulation of BLACK POWER (this chapter), to describe the beliefs of the so-called Flower Children. Flowers were used as a love and peace symbol when the phrase came into use c. 1967.

Four more years.   This is the standard cry in presidential elections, where the incumbent seeks, or is being urged to seek, a further term. His supporters chanted it of Richard Nixon in 1972, and look what happened. Several times Ronald Reagan's supporters interrupted his remarks with it when he was accepting the GOP presidential nomination in Dallas, Texas, on August 23, 1984. Their prayer was answered.

Freedom now!   In the early 1960s there was an African-American litany that went:

> Q. What do you want?
> A. Freedom!
> Q. Let me hear it again—what do you want?
> A. Freedom!
> Q. When do you want it?
> A. Now!

This format may have arisen from a petition delivered to Governor George Wallace of Alabama in March 1965. On this occasion Martin Luther King, Jr., and other civil rights leaders led some three thousand people in a fifty-mile march from Selma to Montgomery. The petition began: "We have come to you, the Governor of Alabama, to declare that we must have our *freedom now*. We must have the right to vote; we must have equal protection of the law, and an end to police brutality."

Free the _____.   This all-purpose slogan came into its own in the 1960s—often in conjunction with a place and number. Hence: "Free the Chicago 7" (charged with creating disorder during the Democratic Convention in 1968), "Free the Wilmington 10," and so on. Dignifying protesters with a group name incorporating place and number began with the "Hollywood 10" (protesters against McCarthyite investigations) in 1947.

The form has become a cliché of sloganeering now. Various joke slogans from the late 1970s demanded: "Free the Beethoven 9/the Heinz 57/the Indianapolis 500/the Grecian 2000."

From Log Cabin to White House.   This was the title of a biography (1881) of President James Garfield, written by the Rev. William Thayer. Earlier presidents Henry Harri-

son and Abraham Lincoln had used the log cabin as a prop
in their campaigns. Subsequently all presidential aspirants
have sought a humble "log cabin" substitute to help them
on their way.

Give 'em hell, Harry.   At the beginning of his 1948 campaign for reelection, President Harry S Truman told his
running mate, Alben Berkeley, "I'm going to fight hard.
I'm going to give them hell." "Give 'em hell, Harry" became a battle cry, and later "Give 'em hell" became a
widely used expression of encouragement.

Haves and the have-nots, the.   A way of distinguishing
between the advantaged and disadvantaged of society.
Safire points to Sancho Panza's saying in *Don Quixote,*
"There are only two families in the world, the Haves and
the Have-Nots" (Spanish *el tener* and *el no tener*). Edward
Bulwer-Lytton in *Athens,* 1836, wrote: "The division . . .
of the Rich and the Poor—the havenots and the haves."

Heartbeat away from the presidency, a.   The traditional
description of the position of the vice president and a
warning to voters to consider carefully their choice for the
office. Adlai Stevenson began an attack on Richard Nixon
in 1952 with, "The Republican vice-presidential candidate, who asks you to place him a heartbeat from the
presidency . . ."
   Jules Witcover titled a book on Vice President Spiro
Agnew's forced resignation *A Heartbeat Away.* The phrase
was revived when George Bush selected Dan Quayle as his
running mate in 1988.

Hearts and minds.   (Of the South Vietnamese people.)
Description of what had to be won over in the Vietnam
War by the U.S. government. John Pilger, writing on August 23, 1967 (quoted in *The Faber Book of Reportage,*
1987): "When Sergeant Melvin Murrell and his company
of United States Marines drop by helicopter into the vil-

lage of Tuylon, west of Danang, with orders to sell 'the
basic liberties as outlined on page 233 of the Pacification
Program Handbook' and at the same time win the hearts
and minds of the people (see same handbook, page 86
under WHAM) they see no one: not a child or a chicken."

The origins of the phrase go back to Theodore
Roosevelt's day, when Douglas MacArthur, as a young
aide, asked Roosevelt (in 1906) to what he attributed his
popularity. The President replied, "[My ability] to put into
words what is in their hearts and minds but not in their
mouths."

Safire also points out that, in 1954, Earl Warren ruled in
the case of *Brown* v. *Board of Education of Topeka:* "To
separate [Black children] from others of similar age and
qualifications solely because of their race generates a feeling of inferiority as to their status in the community that
may affect their hearts and minds in a way unlikely ever to
be undone."

The blessing in the Holy Communion service of the
Prayer Book is: "The peace of God, which passeth all un-
derstanding, keep your hearts and minds in the knowledge
and love of God, and of his Son Jesus Christ Our Lord."
This is drawn from the Epistle of Paul the Apostle to the
Philippians 4:7.

How'm I doing? Ed Koch (b. 1924), mayor of New York
City from 1977–89, helped balance the books after the city
went through a period of bankruptcy. He did this by drasti-
cally cutting services. His catch phrase during this period
was "How'm I doing?" He would call it out as he ranged
around New York. "You're doing fine, Ed," the people
were supposed to shout back. An old song with the title
was disinterred in due course. Unfortunately for him,
Koch's achievements in the city did not carry him forward
to the state governorship as he had hoped, and finally
everything turned sour on him.

A 1979 cartoon in *The New Yorker* showed a woman
answering the phone and saying to her husband, "It's Ed

Koch. He wants to know how he's doin'." A booklet of Koch's wit and wisdom used the phrase as its title and included: "You know how I always ask everybody how am I doing? Well, today I asked myself and the answer was 'Terrific.' "

Ich bin ein Berliner. On June 26, 1963, President John F. Kennedy paid a visit to West Berlin and gave an address to a large and enthusiastic crowd outside the city hall. He had rejected state department drafts for his speech and found something better of his own to say: "Two thousand years ago the proudest boast was *'Civis Romanus sum.'* ["I am a Roman citizen"—from Cicero's oration against Verres, c. 60 B.C.] Today, in the world of freedom, the proudest boast is *Ich bin ein Berliner."* According to Ben Bradlee (*Conversations with Kennedy,* 1975), Kennedy spent "the better part of an hour with Frederick Vreeland and his wife" learning how to pronounce this phrase. He concluded, "All free men, wherever they may live, are citizens of Berlin, and, therefore, as a free man, I take pride in the words *'Ich bin ein Berliner.'* "

Stirring words, and it is only slightly detracting to know that the President need only have said *"Ich bin Berliner"* to convey the meaning "I am a Berliner." It could be argued that the *"ein"* adds drama because he is saying not "I was born and bred in Berlin" or "I live in Berlin" but "I am one of you." But by saying what he did he drew attention to the fact that in Germany *"ein Berliner"* is a doughnut.

In July 1978, when President Jimmy Carter was due to go to West Germany and wanted to come up with a slogan equally ringing, one of his aides (allegedly Gerald Rafshoon) impishly suggested he should go instead to Frankfurt and say . . .

I do not choose to run. Having been President since 1923, Calvin Coolidge said to newsmen in 1927, "I do not choose to run for President in 1928." Actually "Silent Cal" didn't *say* this, he handed the newsmen slips of paper with the words on them. The unusual wording of the announcement captured people's fancy, and the phrase was remembered. In New York in 1928, a silly song about a recalcitrant wristwatch was recorded. It was performed by Six Jumping Jacks with Tom Stacks (vocal) . . . and was called "I Do Not Choose to Run."

If it looks like a duck, walks like a duck, and quacks like a duck, it's a duck.   Usually ascribed to Walter Reuther, the American labor leader during the McCarthy witch hunts of the 1950s. He came up with it as a test of whether someone was a communist: "If it walks like a duck, and quacks like a duck, then it just may be a duck."

Later it was applied elsewhere—usually in politics: "Mr. Richard Darman, the new budget director, explained the other day what 'no new taxes' means. He will apply the duck test. 'If it looks like a duck, walks like a duck and quacks like a duck, it's a duck' "—London *Guardian*, January 25, 1989.

If you can't stand the heat, get out of the kitchen.   In 1960 former President Harry S Truman said, "Some men can make decisions and some cannot. Some men fret and delay under criticism. I used to have a saying that applies here, and I note that some people have picked it up."

When Truman announced that he would not run for President again, *Time* (April 28, 1952) had him give a "down-to-earth reason for his retirement, quoting a favorite expression of his military jester Major General Harry Vaughan," namely, "If you can't stand the heat, get out of the kitchen."

The attribution is usually given to Truman himself, but it may not be what he said at all. "Down-to-earth" is not quite how I would describe this remark, whereas "If you can't stand the stink, get out of the shithouse" would be. I have only hearsay evidence for this, but given Truman's reputation for salty expressions, it is not improbable.

Bartlett quotes Philip D. Lagerquist of the Harry S Truman Library as saying, "President Truman has used variations of the aphorism . . . for many years, both orally and in his writings" (1966). Note the "variations."

I have seen the future and it works. Lincoln Steffens (1866–1936) was a muckraking journalist who paid a visit to the newly formed Soviet Union as part of William C. Bullitt's U.S. diplomatic mission of 1919. As did a number of the first visitors to the new Soviet system, he returned with an optimistic view: "I have seen the future, and it works." In his *Autobiography* (1931) he phrases it a little differently: " 'So you've been over into Russia?' said Bernard Baruch, and I answered very literally, 'I have been over into the future, and it works.' " Bullitt said Steffens had been rehearsing the formula even before arriving in the USSR. Later he tended to use the shorter, more popular form himself.

I like Ike. These words began appearing on buttons in 1947 as the World War II U.S. general, Dwight David Eisenhower, began to be spoken of as a possible presidential nominee (initially as a Democrat). By 1950 Irving Berlin was including one of his least memorable songs, "They Like Ike," in *Call Me Madam*, and fifteen thousand people at a rally in Madison Square Garden were urging Eisenhower to return from a military post in Paris and run as a Republican in 1952, with the chant "We like Ike." It worked. The three sharp monosyllables and the effectiveness of the repeated *I* sound in "I like Ike" made it an enduring slogan throughout the 1950s.

I'm as mad as hell and I'm not going to take it anymore. Peter Finch played a TV pundit-cum-evangelist in the film *Network* in 1976. He exhorted his viewers, "All I know is that first you've got to get mad . . . I want you to get up right now and go to the window, open it and stick your head out and yell, I'm as mad as hell, and I'm not going to take it anymore!"

In 1978 Howard Jarvis (1902–1986), the social activist and author of California's Proposition 13—the one that cut taxes—campaigned with the slogan, "I'm mad as hell and I'm not taking any more." Fifty-seven percent voted to reduce their property taxes. Jarvis entitled his book *I'm Mad as Hell* and credited Paddy Chayevsky, the screenwriter, with the coinage: "For me, the words 'I'm mad as hell' are more than a national saying, more than the title of this book; they express exactly how I feel and exactly how I felt about . . . countless victims of exorbitant taxes."

In your heart you know I'm/he's right. This was Barry Goldwater's much-parodied slogan when he attempted to unseat President Lyndon Johnson in the 1964 U.S. presidential election. Comebacks included: "In your gut, you know he's nuts" and "You know in your heart he's right— far right."

It'll play in Peoria. In about 1968, during the Nixon election campaign, John Ehrlichman is credited with having devised a yardstick for judging whether policies would appeal to voters in Middle America. They had to be judged on whether they would "play in Peoria." He later told William Safire, "Onomatopoeia was the only reason for Peoria, I suppose. And it . . . exemplified a place, far removed from the media centers of the coasts where the national verdict is cast." Peoria is in Illinois and was earlier the hometown of one of Sgt. Bilko's merry men in the 1950s TV series—so good for a laugh even then, though less so in recent years.

I've got his pecker in my pocket. Meaning "he is under obligation to me," this was one of Lyndon Johnson's earthy phrases from his time as Senate majority leader in Washington. "Pecker" means "penis" in North America— though this should not inhibit people from using the old

British expression "Keep your pecker up," where the word has been derived from "peck" meaning appetite. In other words, this phrase is merely a way of wishing someone good health, though *OED2* has "pecker" meaning "courage, resolution" in 1855.

Jimmy who? This was the question posed when James Earl Carter (b. 1924) came from nowhere to challenge President Ford in 1976. His official campaign slogan, used as the title of a campaign book and song, was "Why not the best?" This stemmed from an interview Carter had had with Admiral Hyman Rickover when applying to join the nuclear submarine program in 1948. "Did you do your best [at the Naval Academy]?" Rickover asked him. "No, sir, I didn't *always* do my best," replied Carter. Rickover stared at him for a moment and then asked, "Why not?"

Just and lasting settlement, a. Cliché of politics, and usually with regard to the Middle East. However, it does come with the Abraham Lincoln seal of approval. He talked of a "just and lasting peace" in his second inaugural address, referring to the end of the Civil War.

Kiss of death/life, the. "Kiss of death" derives from the kiss of betrayal given by Judas to Christ, which foreshadowed the latter's death. In the Mafia, too, a kiss from the boss is an indication that your time is up (compare the title of the gangster film *Kiss of Death*, 1947). Safire defines the political use of the phrase as "unwelcome support from an unpopular source, occasionally engineered by the opposition." He suggests that Governor Al Smith popularized the phrase in 1926 when he called William Randolph Hearst's support for Smith's opponent, Ogden Mills, "the kiss of death."

"Kiss of life" as the name of a method of mouth-to-mouth artificial respiration was current by the beginning of the 1960s.

Last hurrah, a/the. This is an aging politician's last outing and takes its name from a novel by Edwin O'Connor (1918–1968). Published in 1956, the book tells of the last campaign of a Boston-Irish politician (played in the 1958 film by Spencer Tracy).

Let's get America moving again. A recurring theme in election slogans is that of promising to move forward after a period of inertia. John F. Kennedy used this one in 1960 —Walt Rostow is credited with suggesting it (sometimes it was "Let's get this country moving again"). It is a short step from these to Ronald Reagan's "Let's make America great again" in 1980. All of them are interchangeable slogans that could apply to any politician, party, or country.

Light at the end of the tunnel. The *OED2* 's earliest citation is from 1922, but in a nonpolitical context. In June 1983 the diarist of *The Times* (U.K.) tried to find the first British Conservative politician to have spotted this phenomenon. Stanley Baldwin in 1929 was the first, it seems, and Neville Chamberlain spotted it again at a lord mayor's banquet in 1937.

As for Winston Churchill—John Colville, his private secretary, seems to quote a French source in his diary for June 13, 1940 ("Some gleam of light at the far end of the tunnel"); quotes Paul Reynaud, the French prime minister on June 16 ("The ray of light at the end of the tunnel"); and himself uses it on May 31, 1952, "I think it is more that he [Churchill] cannot see the light at the end of the tunnel." But I have been unable to locate the source of Churchill's reported use of the cliché on May 3, 1941.

The old expression was later dusted off and invoked with regard to the Vietnam War. In 1967 New Year's Eve invitations to the American Embassy in Saigon bore the legend: "Come and see the light at the end of the tunnel." President Kennedy had alluded to the expression at a press conference on December 12, 1962: "We don't see the end of the tunnel, but I must say I don't think it is darker than it was a year ago, and in some ways lighter."

Somewhere about this time a joke was added: "If we see the light at the end of the tunnel, it's the light of the oncoming train." Though not original to him, the line appears in Robert Lowell's poem "Day by Day" (1977). In 1988 a graffito in Dublin read: "Because of the present economic situation, the light at the end of the tunnel will be switched off at weekends."

Make love, not war. A "peacenik" and "flower power" sentiment from the mid-1960s onward. It was not just applied to the Vietnam War but was used to express the attitude of a whole generation of protest. It was written up (in English) at the University of Nanterre during the French student revolution of 1968.

In the 1970 and 80s it was still current as part of a well-known bumper-sticker joke: "Make love not war—see driver for details."

Man from _____, the. There has been an intermittent tendency to describe American presidents as if they were shadowy characters from Westerns. Thus Harry Truman was dubbed "The Man from Missouri," Dwight Eisenhower "The Man from Abilene," and Jimmy Carter "The Man from Plains." None of this was very convincing and the craze was best left to the cinema, from whence we have had *The Man from Bitter Ridge/Colorado/Dakota/ Del Rio/Laramie/the Alamo/Wyoming*. Not to mention the non-Western *Man of La Mancha*, TV's *The Man from U.N.C.L.E.*, and any number of "The Man Who _____"s and "A Man Called _____"s.

Mr. Clean. "The Secretary of State, James Baker, always regarded as Mr. Clean among several highly placed roguish officials in Ronald Reagan's administration . . ." (London *Independent*, February 15, 1989). Originally the name of a household cleanser, this is a fairly generally applied nickname. Others to whom it has been applied are: Pat Boone (b. 1934), the pop singer and actor noted for his clean image and habits (he would never agree to kiss in films); John Lindsay (b. 1921), mayor of New York (1965–73); Elliot Richardson (b. 1920), attorney general who resigned in 1973 rather than agree to the restrictions President Nixon was then placing on investigations into the Watergate affair.

My friends . . .   Cliché of politics. Politicians are probably presuming a lot when they use this phrase. The first American to do so—noticeably, at any rate—was Franklin D. Roosevelt, who acquired the salutation in 1910 from Richard Connell, who was running for Congress at the same time. But Abraham Lincoln had used this form of address on occasion.

During a party political broadcast on June 4, 1945, Winston Churchill said, "My friends, I must tell you that a Socialist policy is abhorrent to the British idea of freedom." On February 7, 1952, he began a radio tribute: "My friends, when the death of the King was announced to us yesterday morning . . ."

Night of the long knives, a/the.   *"Die Nacht der Langen Messer"*—the Night of the Long Knives—occurred the weekend of June 29–July 2, 1934 in Nazi Germany. The phrase has passed into common use to mean any kind of surprise purge in which no actual blood is spilled. For example, it was applied to Prime Minister Harold Macmillan's wholesale reorganization of his cabinet in Britain (1962).

On the original "night of the long knives," Hitler, with the help of Himmler's black-shirted SS, liquidated the leadership of the brown-shirted SA. The latter undisciplined storm troopers had helped Hitler gain power but were now getting in the way of his dealings with the German army. Some eighty-three were murdered on the pretext that they were plotting another revolution.

"It was no secret that this time the revolution would have to be bloody," Hitler explained to the Reichstag on July 13. "When we spoke of it, we called it 'The Night of the Long Knives.' . . . In every time and place, rebels have been killed. . . . I ordered the leaders of the guilty shot. I also ordered the abscesses caused by our internal and external poisons cauterized until the living flesh was burned." It seems that in using the phrase Hitler was quoting from an early Nazi marching song.

No more Mr. Nice Guy. "Mr. Nice Guy" is a nickname applied to "straight" figures (especially politicians) who may possibly be following someone who is palpably not "nice" (Gerald Ford after Richard Nixon, for example). They then sometimes feel the need to throw off some of their virtuous image, as presidential challenger Senator Ed Muskie did in 1972 when his aides declared, "No more Mr. Nice Guy." In the mid-1950s a joke had been current about Hitler agreeing to make a comeback with the words, "But this time—no more Mr. Nice Guy." In 1973 Alice Cooper had a song titled "No More Mr. Nice Guy" on the charts.

No such thing as a free lunch, there is. This old expression meaning "There's no getting something for nothing" dates back to the mid-nineteenth century. Flexner puts an 1840s date on the supply of "free lunch"—even if no more than thirst-arousing snacks like pretzels—in saloon bars. This was not free, strictly speaking, because you had to buy beer to obtain it.

The notion was given a new lease on life in the 1970s by the economist Milton Friedman. Indeed, the saying was sometimes ascribed to him by virtue of the fact that he published a book with the title and wrote articles and gave lectures incorporating the phrase. When Margaret Thatcher and Ronald Reagan attempted to embrace, up to a point, Friedman's monetarist thinking, the phrase was trotted out by their acolytes (in Thatcher's case, according to press reports, specific instructions were given for ministers to drop it into their speeches).

In July 1989 Representative Richard Gephardt, commenting on the announcement of a new American goal in space, said, "We don't have the economic strength we need to make it a reality. . . . There is no such thing as a free launch."

No surrender!   In 1689, the year after the Catholic King James II was replaced with the Protestant William of Orange, forces still loyal to James maintained a siege against the citizens of Derry in Ulster. The siege was raised after a month or two. "No surrender!" was the Protestant slogan, and "Long live Ulster. No surrender" is still a Loyalist slogan. Another version is, "No popery, no surrender." *No Surrender* was the title of a 1985 film written by Alan Bleasdale about warring Protestant and Roman Catholic factions in Liverpool.

One step forward, two steps back.   In 1904 Lenin wrote a book about "the crisis within our party" under this title. I regularly used to interview an expert on Portugal (in the early 1970s), who invariably made use of this phrase to describe the Caetano regime and its moves, such as they were, toward any form of liberalization. Variations occur, of course: "Alternatively, try retro-dressing. It's here again. One step forward, thirty years back. The Fifties look is determined to make a comeback . . ." (*Cosmopolitan,* February 1987).

Power to the people.   Shouted with clenched fist raised, this was a slogan of the Black Panther movement and publicized as such by its leader, Bobby Seale, in Oakland, California, in July 1969. Also used by other dissident groups, as illustrated by Eldridge Cleaver: "We say 'All power to the people'—Black Power for Black People, White Power for White People, Brown Power for Brown

People, Red Power for Red People, and X Power for any group we've left out."

It was this somewhat generalized view of "People Power" that John Lennon appeared to promote in the 1971 song "Power to the People (Right On!)" "All Power to the Soviets" was a cry of the Bolsheviks during the Russian Revolution of 1917.

Remember the _____! This has been a common theme of sloganeering, particularly enabling wars to begin or continue by keeping alive a cause of anger. Perhaps the first was "Remember the River Raisin!", a war cry of Kentucky soldiers dating from the War of 1812. In the Raisin River massacre, seven hundred Kentuckians, badly wounded trying to capture Detroit, were scalped and butchered by Indians who were allies of the British.

Then came "Remember the Alamo!" after the siege of 1836, and "Remember Goliad!" from the same Texan conflict. "Remember the *Maine*!" helped turn the sinking of the battleship *Maine* in Havana harbor (1898) into an excuse for the Spanish-American War (as well as for the contemporary graffito: "Remember the Maine/ To hell with Spain/ Don't forget to pull the chain").

"Remember the *Lusitania*!" followed the sinking of another ship (in 1915). "Remember Belgium!" was originally a recruiting slogan of World War I. It eventually emerged with ironic emphasis amid the mud of Ypres, encouraging the rejoinder, "As if I'm ever likely to forget the bloody lace!"

"Remember Pearl Harbor!" followed from the 1941 incident, and "Remember the *Pueblo*!" commemorated the capture of the USS *Pueblo* by North Korea in 1968.

Shining city on a hill, a. Ronald Reagan often used the image of a shining city on a hill to describe America as a land of security and success. He used the phrase particularly during his bid for reelection as President in 1984. At the Democratic Convention, New York Governor Mario

Cuomo remarked that a shining city might be what Reagan saw "from the veranda of his ranch," but he failed to see despair in the slums. "There is despair, Mr. President, in the faces that you don't see, in the places that you don't visit in your shining city. . . . This nation is more a tale of two cities than it is just a shining city on a hill."

Earlier, in a 1969 speech, Reagan had acknowledged his source by quoting Governor Winthrop of the Massachussetts Bay Colony, who told new settlers in 1630, "We shall be as a city upon a hill, the eyes of all people are upon us." It was meant as a warning as much as a promise. He didn't use the word "shining." If anything, the image is biblical. Matthew 5:14 has "A city that is set on a hill cannot be hid. . . . Let your light so shine before men that they may see your good works"; the "holy hill" of Zion is a "sunny mountain" according to one etymology; New Jerusalem was the jeweled city lit by the glory of God, in Revelation.

Smoke-filled room, a. Suite 408-409-410 (previously Rooms 804–5) of the Blackstone Hotel in Chicago was the original "smoke-filled room" in which Warren Harding was selected as the Republican presidential candidate in June 1920. The image conjured up by this phrase is of cigar-smoking political bosses coming to a decision after much horse-trading.

Although he denied saying it, the phrase seems to have come out of a prediction by Harding's chief supporter, Harry Daugherty (1860–1941). He foresaw that the convention would not be able to decide between the two obvious candidates, and that a group of senators, "bleary-eyed for lack of sleep," would have to "sit down about two o'clock in the morning around a table in a smoke-filled room in some hotel and decide the nomination." This was precisely what happened and Harding duly emerged as the candidate.

Smoking gun. Incriminating evidence, as though a person holding a smoking gun could be assumed to have committed an offense with it (as in one of Conan Doyle's Sherlock Holmes stories, "The 'Gloria Scott'," 1894: "Then we rushed on into the captain's cabin . . . and there he lay . . . while the chaplain stood with a smoking pistol in his hand"). The term was popularized during Watergate when Representative Barber B. Conable, Jr. said that a tape of President Nixon's conversation with H. R. Haldeman, his chief of staff, on June 23, 1972, "looked like a smoking gun." It contained discussion of how the FBI's investigation of the Watergate burglary might be limited.

Speak softly and carry a big stick.   Speaking at the Minnesota State Fair in September 1901, President Theodore Roosevelt gave strength to the idea of backing negotiations with threats of military force when he said, "There is a homely adage which runs, 'Speak softly and carry a big stick; you will go far.' If the American nation will speak softly and yet build up and keep at a pitch of the highest training a thoroughly efficient navy, the Monroe Doctrine will go far."

The "homely adage" is said to have started life as a West African proverb.

Special relationship, the.   This term is used most often about relationships between countries—the earliest *OED2* citation is for one between Britain and Galicia in 1929— but it particularly refers to the relationship between Britain and the United States, who have historical ties and share a common language. The notion was principally promoted by Winston Churchill in his attempts to draw the U.S. into the 1939–45 war, though whether he used the phrase prior to 1941 I do not know. In the House of Commons on November 7, 1945, Churchill said, "We should not abandon our special relationship with the United States and Canada about the atomic bomb." In his 1946 "Iron Curtain" speech at Fulton, Missouri, he asked, "Would a special relationship between the United States and the

British Commonwealth be inconsistent with our overriding loyalties to the World Organization? [i.e., the UN]."

Spirit of _____, the.   Cliché of politics. Like "the message of _____," this is a highly versatile phrase. "The Spirit of '76" came into use following the American Revolution in the eighteenth century. Later, President Eisenhower was very fond of the format, several times speaking of "the Spirit of Geneva" in 1955 and "the Spirit of Camp David" in 1959.

Teflon-coated presidency, the.   Phrase coined for Ronald Reagan's presidency, in a speech to the House of Representatives by Patricia Schroeder in August 1983. Because, she said, no hint of scandal, no trace of failure, ever stuck to Reagan.

There ain't gonna be no war.   As British foreign secretary to Anthony Eden, Harold Macmillan attended a four-power summit conference in Geneva, where the chief topic for discussion was German reunification. Nothing much was achieved, but the "Geneva spirit" was optimistic and on his return to London he breezily told a press conference on July 24, 1955, "There ain't gonna be no war." Why this conscious Americanism?

One rather good suggestion was that he was alluding to Mark Twain's *Tom Sawyer Abroad* (1894): "There's plenty of boys that will come hankering . . . when you've got an apple . . . but when they've got one . . . they . . . say thank you 'most to death, but there ain't a-going to be no core." This situation may also have appeared as a *Punch* cartoon c. 1908.

But the phrase is almost certainly a direct quote from the c. 1910 music-hall song that was sung in a raucous Cockney accent by a certain Mr. Pélissier (1879–1913), who had a show called "Pélissier's Follies" during the reign of King Edward VII:

There ain't going to be no waar
So long as we've a king like Good King Edward.
'E won't 'ave it, 'cos 'e 'ates that sort of fing.
Muvvers, don't worry,
Not wiv a king like Good King Edward.
Peace wiv honour is 'is motter [*snort*]—
Gawd save the King!

Although Macmillan was born the year *Tom Sawyer Abroad* was published, it is presumably to this song of his youth that he was referring. And yet why did he say "gonna"? Cockney pronunciation maybe, but some time before December 1941 an American called Frankl did write a song called, precisely, "There Ain't Gonna Be No War," which had a brief vogue. Sir David Hunt confirmed in 1988 that it was the Pélissier song that Macmillan had in mind. In fact, Hunt sang it to him on one occasion.

There you go again.   In a TV debate with President Carter in 1980, the Republican challenger, Ronald Reagan, laughed off Carter's charge that he would dismantle federal health support for the elderly, saying, "There you go again!" The phrase stuck with the voters and became a campaign refrain.

Thousand points of light, a.   Coined for George Bush by speech-writer Peggy Noonan during the 1988 presidential election campaign, this phrase was much used by him on the campaign trail and in his acceptance speech for the Republican nomination ("I will keep America moving forward, always forward—for a better America, for an endless enduring dream and a thousand points of light"). On the eve of his inauguration in January 1989, a crowd of forty thousand people in Washington switched on pen flashlights (handed out beforehand) to dramatize the phrase.

But what did it mean? It was said to symbolize individual endeavor, voluntary charity efforts, across the country. In June 1989 President Bush announced details for his

"Points of Light Program," costing $25 million, to en-
courage a voluntary crusade to fight poverty, drugs, and
homelessness. But even Mr. Bush never seemed too sure.
On one occasion he called it "One thousand points of life."
Herblock, the cartoonist, drew a drunk at a bar pledging
his vote to Bush because he had promised "One thousand
pints of Lite."

Perhaps it was supposed to echo Shakespeare, *The Merchant of Venice* (Act V, scene 1, line 90): "How far that
little candle throws his beams!/ So shines a good deed in a
naughty world." Light often comes in thousands: "It was
but for an instant that I seemed to struggle with a thousand
mill-weirs and a thousand flashes of light" (Charles Dickens, *Great Expectations*, 1860–61).

Today _____, tomorrow _____. A foreign-language slogan occasionally impinges upon English speech. Such a
construction capable of innumerable variations is "Today
_____, tomorrow the world!" The concept can be
glimpsed in embryo in the slogan for the National Socialist
Press in Germany of the early 1930s: *"Heute Presse der
Nationalsozialisten, Morgen Presse der Nation"* ("Today
the press of the Nazis, tomorrow the nation's press"). This
reaches its final form in *"Heute gehört uns Deutschland—
morgen die ganze Welt"* ("Today Germany belongs to us—
tomorrow the whole world"). Although John Colville in
The Fringes of Power states that by September 3, 1939,
Hitler "had already . . . proclaimed that 'Today Germany is ours; tomorrow the whole world,'" I have not
found an example of Hitler actually saying it. However, in
Mein Kampf (1925) he said, "If the German people, in
their historic development, had possessed tribal unity like
other nations, the German Reich today would be the master of the entire world."

The phrase seems to have come from the chorus of a
song in the Hitler Youth "songbook" :

> *Wir werden weiter marschieren*
> *Wenn alles in Scherben fällt*
> *Denn heute gehört uns Deutschland*
> *Und morgen die ganze Welt.*

This may be roughly translated as:

> We shall keep marching on
> Even if everything breaks into fragments,
> For today Germany belongs to us
> And tomorrow the whole world.

Another version replaces the second line with *"Wenn Scheiße vom Himmel fällt"* ("When shit from Heaven falls"). Sir David Hunt recalls hearing the song in 1933 or possibly 1934.

By the outbreak of World War II it was sufficiently well-known, as dramatist John Osborne recalled in *A Better Class of Person* (1981), for an English school magazine to be declaring: "Now soon it will be our turn to take a hand in the destinies of Empire. Today, scholars; tomorrow, the Empire." In the 1941 British film *Forty-Ninth Parallel*, Eric Portman as a German U-boat commander gets to say, "Today, Europe . . . tomorrow, the whole world!"

So common is the construction now that a New York graffito (reported in 1974) stated: "Today Hollywood, tomorrow the world"; and one from El Salvador (March 1982) ran: *"Ayer Nicaragua, hoy El Salvador, mañana Guatemala!"* ("Yesterday Nicaragua, today El Salvador, tomorrow Guatemala!).

Tomorrow belongs to me/us. Has this ever been used as a political slogan, either as "Tomorrow belongs to me" or "to us"? British Labour Party leader Harold Wilson, in his final broadcast before the 1964 general election, said, "If the past belongs to the Tories, the future belongs to us—all of us." At a Young Conservatives rally before the 1983 general election, Margaret Thatcher asked, "Could Labour have organized a rally like this? In the old days perhaps, but not now. For they are the party of yesterday. Tomorrow is ours."

What one can say is that in the musical *Cabaret* (1968, filmed 1972), Fred Ebb (words) and John Kander (music) wrote a convincing pastiche of a Hitler Youth song:

O Fatherland, Fatherland, show us the sign your
  children have waited to see,
The morning will come when the world is mine,
  tomorrow belongs to me.

The idea seems definitely to have been current in Nazi Germany. A popular song, *"Jawohl, mein Herr"*, featured in the 1943 episode of the German film chronicle *Heimat* (1984), includes the line, "For from today, the world belongs to us."

The nearest the slogan appears to have been actually used by (an admittedly right-wing) youth organization is referred to in this report from the *Guardian* (October 30, 1987): "Contra leader Adolfo Calero . . . was entertained to dinner on Wednesday by Oxford University's Freedom Society, a clutch of hoorays. . . . A coach-load of diners . . . got 'hog-whimpering' drunk . . . and songs like 'Tomorrow Belongs To Us' and 'Miner, Cross that Picket Line' were sung on the return coach trip."

It is perhaps an obvious slogan for a young people's political organization. I have a note of something once said by the French memoirist Saint-Simon: "The future belongs to us. In order to do things one must be enthusiastic."

Too little, too late. Professor Allan Nevins wrote in an article in *Current History* (May 1935): "The former allies had blundered in the past by offering Germany too little and offering even that too late, until finally Nazi Germany had become a menace to all mankind." That was where the phrase began. On March 13, 1940, the former British Prime Minister David Lloyd George said in the House of Commons, "It is the old trouble—too late. Too late with Czechoslovakia, too late with Poland, certainly too late

with Finland. It is always too late, or too little, or both."
From there the phrase passed into more general use,
though usually political.

Twist slowly, slowly in the wind, (to allow someone to).
From the *Guardian* (January 28, 1989): "The foreign press
observed with admiration the way President Bush stressed
in words that he was not ditching the beleaguered Mikhail
Gorbachev by playing his China card, while making it
clear he was doing exactly that, and leaving the Soviet
leader to twist a little longer in the wind."

Richard Nixon's henchmen may have acted wrongly
and, for much of the time, spoken sleazily. However, some
of their political phrases have lingered on. John D. Ehrlichman (b. 1925), Nixon's assistant for domestic affairs until he
was forced to resign over Watergate in 1973, came up with
one saying that caught people's imagination. In a telephone conversation with John Dean (counsel to the President) on March 7/8, 1973, he was speaking about Patrick
Gray (acting director of the FBI). Gray's nomination to
take over the FBI post had been withdrawn by Nixon
during judiciary committee hearings—though Gray had
not been told of this. Ehrlichman said, "I think we ought to
let him hang there. Let him twist slowly, slowly in the
wind."

We shall not be moved.   Shout or chant of defiance, according to Bartlett originally from an African-American
spiritual (echoing more than one psalm): "Just like a tree
that's standing by the water/We shall not be moved."
Later widely taken up as a song of the civil rights and labor
movements, from the 1960s.

We shall overcome.   This phrase is to be found in a song
that became a civil rights anthem of the early 1960s. It
originated in pre-Civil War times, was adapted as a Baptist
hymn called "I'll Overcome Some Day" (c. 1900) by C.
Albert Hindley, and first became famous when sung by

African-American workers on a picket line in Charleston, South Carolina, in 1946. Pete Seeger and others added verses including:

> Oh, deep in my heart, I do believe that
> We shall overcome someday.

In the Spanish Civil War, there was a Republican chant *¡Venceremos!,* which means the same.

Where do we find such men? On the fortieth anniversary of the D-Day landings, President Reagan visited Europe and made a speech in which he eulogized those who had taken part in the event. "Where do we find such men?" he asked.

On a previous occasion he had said, "Many years ago in one of the four wars in my lifetime, an admiral stood on the bridge of a carrier watching the planes take off and out into the darkness bent on a night combat mission and then found himself asking, with no one there to answer—just himself to hear his own voice—'Where do we find such men?' "

But the very first time he had used the line he had made the origin clear and said that it was fiction. The story comes from James Michener's novel *The Bridges at Toko-Ri,* later filmed (1954) with William Holden, who asks, "Where do we get such men?" Over the years fiction became fact for Reagan. Perhaps he could not or was unwilling to distinguish between the two.

On another occasion he told a meeting of the Congressional Medal of Honor Society about an aircraft gunner who couldn't leave his post as his plane was crashing. He is told by his commanding officer that he has won a "Congressional Medal of Honor, posthumously awarded." No such incident happened in real life, though it did in the film *Wing and a Prayer* (1944).

In 1985 Michael Rogin, a professor of political science at Berkeley, explored similar borrowings of film lines in Reagan's speeches in a presentation entitled "Ronald Reagan:

The Movie." Among the examples he found, both credited and uncredited, were these:

During the New Hampshire primary of 1980 Reagan won a dispute over who should speak in a debate by declaring "I am paying for this microphone, Mr. Green!" Never mind that the man's name was actually "Breen." The line in the form "Don't you shut me off, I'm paying for this broadcast" was delivered by Spencer Tracy in the film *State of the Union* (1948).

In *Mr. Deeds Goes to Town*, Gary Cooper extolled man's responsibility to help his fellow man thus: "From what I can see, no matter what system of government we have, there will always be leaders and always be followers. It's like the road out in front of my house. It's on a steep hill. And every day I watch the cars climbing up. Some go lickety-split up that hill on high—some have to shift into second—and some sputter and shake and slip back to the bottom again. Same cars—same gasoline —yet some make it and some don't. And I say the fellas who can make the hill on high should stop once in a while and help those who can't." Reagan quoted the speech verbatim in selling his welfare voluntarism program, though he *did* credit the source.

Reagan credited the film *Rambo: First Blood, Part Two* (1985) when he said, "In the spirit of Rambo, let me tell you we're going to win this time." (John Rambo, a hunk who goes back to Vietnam to free POWs, asks in the film: "Do we get to win this time?")

He used his own line from the film *King's Row* ("Where's the rest of me?"—he'd just had his legs amputated) as the title of an early autobiography. He used *Star Wars* the movie to promote "Star Wars" the weapons system: "It isn't about fear, it's about hope, and in that struggle, if you'll pardon my stealing a film line, 'The force is with us.'" (See MAY THE FORCE BE WITH YOU, Chapter 9.)

Win this one for the Gipper.   On the campaign trail it was never possible to forget Ronald Reagan's Hollywood career. This slogan was a reference to George Gipp, a part he had played in *Knute Rockne—All-American* (1940). Gipp was a real-life football star who died young. At halftime in a 1928 Army game, Rockne, the team coach, recalled something Gipp had said to him: "Rock, someday when things look real tough for Notre Dame, ask the boys to go out there and win one for me."

Reagan used the slogan countless times. Perhaps one of the last was at a campaign rally for Vice President George Bush in San Diego, California on November 7, 1988. His peroration included these words: "So, now we come to the end of this last campaign. . . . And I hope that someday your children and grandchildren will tell of the time that a certain President came to town at the end of a long journey and asked their parents and grandparents to join him in setting America on the course to the new millennium. . . . So, if I could ask you just one last time. Tomorrow, when mountains greet the dawn, would you go out there and win one for the Gipper? Thank you, and God bless you all."

You ain't seen nothin' yet!   President Ronald Reagan appropriated this catch phrase as a kind of slogan in his successful 1984 bid for reelection. He used it repeatedly during the campaign and on November 7 in his victory speech.

Partridge/*Catch Phrases* has a combined entry for "You ain't seen nothin' yet" and "You ain't heard nothin' yet," in which "seen" is described as the commoner of the two versions. Both are dated from the 1920s. One could add that Bachman-Turner Overdrive, the Canadian pop group, had a hit with a song called "You Ain't Seen Nothin' Yet" in 1974.

As for "heard," it seems that when Al Jolson exclaimed "You ain't heard nothin' yet!" in the first full-length talking picture, *The Jazz Singer* (1927), he wasn't just ad-libbing as is usually supposed. He was promoting the title of one of his songs. He had recorded "You Ain't Heard Nothing Yet," written by Gus Kahn and Buddy de Sylva, in 1919.

You can run but you can't hide.   In the wake of the hijacking of a TWA airliner to Beirut in the summer of 1985, President Reagan issued a number of warnings to international terrorists. In October he said that America had "sent a message to terrorists everywhere. The message: 'You can run, but you can't hide.'"

He was alluding to an utterance by the boxer Joe Louis, who said of an opponent in a World Heavyweight Championship fight in June 1946, "He can run, but he can't hide." The opponent was Billy Conn—who was a fast mover—and Louis won the fight by a knockout.

LAST WORD

What passes for culture in my head is really a bunch of commercials.

—Kurt Vonnegut